Cambridge Middle East Studies 23

D0191594

Cambridge Middle East Studies has been established to publish books on the nineteenth- and twentieth-century Middle East and North Africa. The aim of the series is to provide new and original interpretations of aspects of Middle Eastern societies and their histories. To achieve disciplinary diversity, books will be solicited from authors writing in a wide range of fields including history, sociology, anthropology, political science and political economy. The emphasis will be on producing books offering an original approach along theoretical and empirical lines. The series is intended for students and academics, but the more accessible and wide-ranging studies will also appeal to the interested general reader.

A list of books in the series can be found after the index.

Citizens Abroad

Emigration and the State in the Middle East and North Africa

Laurie A. Brand

CAMBRIDGE UNIVERSITY PRESS

CAMBRIDGE UNIVERSITY PRESS
Cambridge, New York, Melbourne, Madrid, Cape Town, Singapore, São Paulo, Delhi

Cambridge University Press
The Edinburgh Building, Cambridge CB2 8RU, UK

Published in the United States of America by Cambridge University Press, New York

www.cambridge.org
Information on this title: www.cambridge.org/9780521858052

First published 2006
This digitally printed version 2008

A catalogue record for this publication is available from the British Library

ISBN 978-0-521-85805-2 hardback
ISBN 978-0-521-10091-5 paperback

Citizens Abroad

Despite the fact that the majority of emigration today originates in the global south, most research has focused on the receiving states of Europe and North America, while very little attention has been paid to the policies of the sending states toward emigration or toward their nationals abroad. Taking the country cases of Morocco, Tunisia, Lebanon and Jordan, this work explores the relationship between the government of the sending states, the outmovement of their citizens and the communities of expatriates that have developed. By focusing on the evolution of government institutions charged with various aspects of expatriate affairs, this work breaks new ground in explaining the changing nature of the relationship between expatriates and their home state. Far from suggesting that the state is waning in importance, the conclusions indicate that this relationship provides evidence both of state resilience and of new trends in the practice of sovereignty.

LAURIE A. BRAND is Professor of International Relations at the University of Southern California. She is also the author of *Palestinians in the Arab World* (1988), *Jordan's Inter-Arab Relations* (1994), and *Women, the State and Political Liberalization* (1998).

For Fayez

Contents

Tables

Preface

It was during a quiet Saturday afternoon in Los Angeles that a program on Arab-American television triggered my initial interest in the state and emigration. This particular day, the program featured an interview with Talal Arslan, the Lebanese Minister of Expatriates. Listening to the interview, I realized that I had not been aware that a ministry devoted to nationals abroad existed, in Lebanon or elsewhere in the Arab world. In the weeks that followed, I learned that in fact a number of Arab (and other) countries had similar institutions, but that little research had been done on them, and the idea for this research was born.

The subsequent development of the project, however, was far from what I had initially envisaged. First, heavy administrative duties as a center director, then the tremendous demands on my time placed by the aftermath of September 11 meant halting progress at best. By the time a sabbatical finally enabled me to focus fully on the research abroad, war drums had begun beating inside the Beltway. In spring 2003, the period I had set aside for the major drafting of the book, Washington launched its invasion of Iraq and, living in Beirut at the time, my attention turned from book writing to war protesting.

Since the invasion, there have been many times when the intellectual call of this project sadly paled in comparison with the need to devote time to speaking out against the Bush administration's domestic and foreign policy record. Indeed, there were times when doing anything other than standing against the evil of empire seemed not only pointless, but wrong. Nonetheless, I persevered in fits and starts, and have finally brought the project to fruition. It is for the reader to decide whether my time would have been better spent on more or less activism.

As I have noted in previous works that required extensive, multi-country fieldwork, my debts are many and my gratitude deep. First, for financial and fellowship support of this project I would like to thank: the School of International Relations at the University of Southern California for support for research in Jordan, summer 1999; the American Institute for Maghrebi Studies for a short-term grant for research in Morocco in summer 2000; the University of Southern California for sabbatical year support, 2002–3; Fulbright, for a seven-month research grant for Morocco, Tunisia and Lebanon, summer–winter 2002; and the Council of American Overseas Research Centers for fellowship support for research in Jordan and Lebanon, spring–summer, 2003.

Yet, it is really people who make the project. My ability to make effective use of the financial support I have received was greatly enhanced by the advice and assistance I received from many, many friends and colleagues.

For support during my stays in Morocco my thanks go to: Alain Rousillon, formerly of the Centre Jacques Berque, Rabat; Dawud Casewitt and Saadia Miski of the Moroccan American Commission on Educational and Cultural Exchange; Professors Driss Ben Ali and Abdelkrim Belguendouz from Mohammed V University, for assistance with contacts and sources; the staff at the archives of the Ministry of Communications; Nasser Amiyar, for research help in Tangiers; Fatema Bellaoui, for years of friendship; and last, but perhaps most important of all, to Lamia Radi and Jamal al-Ouariachi-Miguel for their boundless hospitality and support both personally and professionally.

For help during my work in Tunisia, I am grateful to: Jeanne Mrad, Andrea Flores Khalil, Riad Saadaoui and Najoua Saadaoui, from the Centre d'Etudes Magrebines à Tunis (CEMAT), for research assistance and advice; Oussama Romdhani and Bushra Malki of the Tunisian Agency for External Communication, for invaluable assistance in setting up interviews; and colleagues at the Institut de Recherche sur le Maghreb Contemporain (IRMC), Tunis, for fruitful discussions and use of library facilities.

In Lebanon, my deep thanks to: Professor Farid al-Khazen, chair of the Department of Political Studies and Public Policy at the American University of Beirut (AUB), for assistance with affiliation, logistics and research contacts; Professors Huda Zurayk, Marwan Khawaja and their colleagues at the Faculty of Public Health at AUB, for offering office space to someone whose connection with public health was tentative at best, and for personal support during the awful days of the Iraq war; Professors Sami Ofeish and Sabah Ghandour of Balamand University for logistical assistance as well as wonderful advice and friendship all along the way; Elias Khoury, for assistance in gaining access to the archives at Al-Nahar, and to the staff at the archives; Professors Hassan Krayyem and Nizar Hamzeh, of AUB, for valuable suggestions, advice and assistance in learning my way around Lebanon; to Dr. Salim Nasr, director of the Lebanese Center for Policy Studies, for wide-ranging help with sources and contacts; Professor Lina Choueri, whose friendship and support were true blessings; and to all the members of "Americans Against the War," our group of committed anti-war activists who gave me hope and energy to keep going in what seemed the ugliest of times.

In Jordan, thanks go to Dr. Mustafa Hamarneh, Director of the Center for Strategic Studies, Jordan University, and to his wonderful staff for assistance, advice and friendship; to Zein Soufan for research assistance; and to Dr. Amal Sabbagh, Hania Jarallah and Ahmed Soufan for years of friendship and support for this and other research projects.

I am also deeply indebted to two anonymous readers for Cambridge University Press who provided literally pages of detailed and useful critiques and suggestions, which forced me to rethink and substantially reshape significant aspects of this work; and to my editor, Marigold Acland, for her patient and understanding shepherding of the last stages of revisions and production. Finally, for comments on individual chapters at various stages in the writing, thanks go to Hayward Alker, Jean-Pierre Cassarino, Fayez Hammad, Farid al-Khazen, Hassan Krayyem, Sami Ofeish, Salim Nasr, Mark Tessler, Greg White and Geoff Wiseman.

The last several years of often vicious attempts to intimidate members of the academy, particularly the Middle East Studies community, have been both disturbing and angering. In the context of a country led by an administration that has brought us Guantánamo, Abu Ghraib and Falluja, I have continued to wonder whether endeavors such as writing this book serve a larger purpose. In the end, I have come to the conclusion that no matter how grim the circumstances, engaging in honest scholarship, whatever the topic, stands as a protest against those who seek to curb the polyphony of the academy. Moreover, ideally, our scholarly endeavors should also energize us and inform our work for change outside the university. Thus, in the current political climate in the United States, my research and writing, along with my teaching and my efforts in the realm of public education, constitute my modest contribution to the voice of the larger community saying "no" to the trampling of free speech, "no" to violations of civil and human rights, and "no" to occupation and pre-emptive war.

LAURIE A. BRAND
Los Angeles, February 2005

Acronyms

AAE	– Amicales des Algériens en Europe
API	– l'Agence de Promotion des Investissements
BP	– Banque Populaire
CFCM	– Conseil Français du Culte Musulman
CME	– Communauté marocaine à l'étranger
CTE	– Communauté tunisienne à l'étranger
EC	– European Community
EEC	– European Economic Community
EU	– European Union
FFFLN	– Fédération de France du Front de Libération Nationale
FHII	– Fondation Hassan II pour les marocains résidant à l'étranger
FIS	– Front Islamique du Salut
GDP	– gross domestic product
IMF	– International Monetary Fund
IPC	– Investment Promotion Corporation
JBA	– Jordanian Businessmen's Association
JD	– Jordanian dinar
JE	– Jordanian Expatriate
LE	– Lebanese Expatriate
ME	– Ministry of Expatriates
MENA	– Middle East North Africa
MFA	– Ministry of Foreign Affairs and Cooperation
MFAE	– Ministry of Foreign Affairs and Expatriates
MMCA	– Ministry of the Moroccan Community Abroad
MRE	– Marocain résidant à l'étranger
MTI	– Mouvement de la Tendance Islamique
NGO	– non-governmental organization
OFPE	– Office de la Formation Professionnelle et de l'Emploi
ONI	– Office National d'Immigration

OPETTE	– Office de la Promotion de l'Emploi et des Travailleurs Tunisiens à l'Étranger
OTE	– Office des Tunisiens à l'Étranger
OTTEEFP	– Office des Travailleurs Tunisiens à l'Étranger de l'Emploi et de la Formation Professionnelle
PLO	– Palestine Liberation Organization
PSD	– Parti socialiste destourien
RCD	– Rassemblement constitutionnel democratique
SAP	– structural adjustment program
SSNP	– Syrian Social Nationalist Party
TD	– Tunisian dinar
TME	– travailleur marocain à l'étranger
TRE	– Tunisien résidant à l'étranger
TTE	– travailleur tunisien à l'étranger
UAE	– United Arab Emirates
UNFP	– Union Nationale des Forces Populaires
USFP	– Union Socialiste des Forces Populaires
VAT	– value-added tax
WLCU	– World Lebanese Cultural Union
WLU	– World Lebanese Union

1 States and their citizens abroad

While scholars remain divided as to whether population movement in the post 1945 period in fact surpasses the magnitudes of earlier periods, the issues of who, why, when, how, and to what effect people move from farm to city, town to town, or country to country have received increasing scholarly and policy attention in recent years. Researchers across disciplines have sought to answer these and related questions, focusing on a variety of levels and units of analysis, and drawing upon myriad theoretical frameworks and empirical tools. While some have looked at the micro-level questions of individual decisions to migrate and their impact, often emphasizing economic cost–benefit calculations or push-pull factors, others have posed community or societal-level questions, as they have sought to understand the cultural impact of immigration, various historical aspects of the immigrant experience, or the possibilities for integration or assimilation in the new host country. In the fields of political science and international relations, explanations have often been sought for governmental response to immigration, with some analysts locating their explanations at the level of the state, others in the international political economy, and still others in changes in international norms.[1]

If migration or immigration studies have been remarkable in terms of the diversity of treatment and disciplinary interest noted above, they have, conversely, been, in their majority, surprisingly limited geographically: most of the work that has been done on the question of the permeability of borders, border controls, citizenship and migration or immigration (as opposed to work solely on citizenship) has dealt with Western Europe and the United States. The focus has therefore been on issues related to security or sovereignty understood in terms of border control; the impetus behind immigration (often with the goal of suggesting policy remedies to encourage people to stay in place); how the immigrants are received; in what sorts of jobs they work; how they organize their social, political and

---

[1] Caroline Brettell and James F. Hollifield (eds.), *Migration Theory: Talking Across Disciplines* (New York: Routledge, 2000). "Introduction," p. 3.

economic lives; and their possibilities/desire for socio-cultural integration. This focus on Western Europe and the United States is even more striking given that the vast majority of international or transnational population movement is in fact South–South, not South–North migration.

Thus, not only are receiving states of the global South understudied in this context, but even more strikingly, although immigration obviously requires a prior *emigration*, little work has in fact focused on the state/country of origin. There are exceptions in the anthropological literature, in which we find studies of the impact of emigration on the families and communities left behind. Furthermore, with the dramatic increase in writing on transnationalism and globalization, attention has focused on a variety of networks – social, cultural, economic and, increasingly, political – that link sending and receiving countries. There are also economic or political economy studies that discuss the importance of remittances, as well as a few international relations or political science works that discuss questions of border control from both the sending and receiving sides. Nevertheless, even with the attention that a handful of scholars has devoted to various aspects of the sending country's economy, social structure or culture, one cannot really talk about a developed literature on sending-state *emigration* policy or practices in the way one can cite myriad works on receiving-state *immigration* policy. Thus, as Hollifield, who has done a great deal of work on immigration and the question of borders (and sovereignty) from the point of view of European states,[2] has noted, "Very little has been written about the politics of control from the standpoint of the sending countries."[3]

This paucity of detailed treatment of the home state in the literature is particularly striking given the increasing interest sending states have manifested since the 1980s in their nationals (and in some cases their descendants) abroad. To cite just a few examples, from various parts of the world: in 1982, the Office of Overseas Chinese Affairs began sponsoring a youth festival for young people of Chinese descent who are citizens of foreign countries. In 1995, the Russian Duma established a Council of Compatriots, an analytical–consultative body charged with representing the interests of Russians (and their descendants) residing abroad. In 2000, the newly elected Mexican president, Vicente Fox, created a cabinet-level

---

[2] See, for example, James F. Hollifield, *Immigrants, Markets and States: The Political Economy of Postwar Europe* (Cambridge, MA: Harvard University Press, 1992).

[3] Hollifield in Brettell and Hollifield, p. 143. Rainer Bauböck notes a "growing empirical literature" on sending-state involvement with emigrant groups (although he provides no direct citations), but also states that there have been few theoretical attempts to explain sending-country behavior, in "Towards a Political Theory of Migrant Transnationalism," *International Migration Review* 37 (2) Fall 2003: p. 703.

office, the Office of the President for Mexicans Abroad, charged with promoting closer ties between Mexican emigrants and both the USA and Mexico. In 2002, Syria established its first Ministry of Expatriate Affairs.

These examples are but four of what is, upon broader examination, a growing phenomenon: the establishment of state institutions charged with responsibility for some aspect of expatriate community affairs. While embassies and consulates, with their mission of serving the needs of their citizens abroad, have long been a feature of international politics (if not a common focus of study), other institutions, with such charges as language training, investment advice and parliamentary representation of emigrants, have proliferated only in recent years. Clearly international migration and, more specifically, state emigration policy are key frameworks within which to begin to evaluate such developments. It is precisely with issues in this realm, the goals and the implications of policies of the *sending* states toward their nationals who depart for extended periods abroad, that this work is concerned.

Setting policy regarding the exit (and re-entry) of nationals – a subset of border control – has long been understood to be a basic part of the definition of sovereignty as exercised by the territorially bounded entities we call states, and hence properly falls within the realm of international politics. Perhaps it is because the majority of sending countries are in the global South that the field of international relations, long preoccupied with great powers, which in this case are the receiving states, has largely ignored questions related to home state policy toward emigrants, except insofar as border policing is concerned. Whatever the reason, the contours and role of sending-state policy form the other side of the emigration–immigration nexus, and raise many critical questions, a number of which are simply the reverse of questions that have been posed by those studying the receiving states: what are the elements that drive or shape states' policies toward various forms of emigration? To what extent have sending states been proactive or simply reactive in the realm of emigration? Whichever stance has been most characteristic, what sorts of institutional forms have characterized state responses? Finally, what may such responses tell us about how sovereignty, understood not only as border control, but also as defining the boundaries of the "national community" or the nation, is practiced in the context of a world system in which growing numbers of people live outside the country of their birth or citizenship?

The literature on Emigration

Myron Weiner, one of the few political scientists to address emigration seriously, argued for a synthesis of international political economy explanations of migration – which focus on global inequities, economic ties between labor-exporting and importing states, and changes in the international division of labor – and international security explanations. He contended that while traditional economic explanations – push-pull and cost–benefit analyses – explain a great deal, they neglect two critical political factors: "that international population movements are often impelled, encouraged or prevented by governments or political forces for reasons that may have little to do with economic conditions"; and that "even when economic conditions create inducements for people to leave one country for another, it is *governments* that decide whether their citizens should be allowed to leave and *governments* that decide whether immigrants should be allowed to enter, and their decisions are frequently based on non-economic considerations" (emphasis added);[4] "An examination of both historical and contemporary population movements ... demonstrates that countries of emigration have more control over international population flows than is usually accounted for by political analysts, and that what often appear to be spontaneous emigration and refugee movements may represent deliberate emigration policies on the part of sending countries."[5]

The various non-economic considerations he cites – internal political disorder, global networks of communication and transportation, political constraints on the admission of migrants and refugees – suggest the need for what he terms a "security/stability framework" for the study of international migration. Both this framework and the international political economy approach focus on the larger social, political and economic context within which individuals act, rather than on individual decision-making. Both also pay close attention to the behavior of states and to the importance of borders, but the security/stability framework places greater emphasis on the role of state decision-making than does a political economy approach, which often regards the state as a weak or less significant actor.[6]

Weiner's focus on the importance of the state and state decision-making is a welcome corrective to some political economy and other studies that downplay or underestimate the role of the state in international migration. However, even Weiner's approach does not go far enough, for two reasons. First, his primary concern remains the *receiving* states of the North and their response to cases of expulsion / forced emigration, and he therefore does not engage in a deeper consideration of the motives

---

[4] Myron Weiner, "Security, Stability and International Migration," *International Security* 17 (3) winter 1992/93: pp. 96–97.

[5] Ibid., p. 103.   [6] Ibid., p. 95.

or strategies of sending governments that resort to such policies. Second, expulsion suggests (and often is) a final break in the state–citizen relationship. At this point, we begin talking about refugees, asylum, statelessness, etc. However important in increasing our understanding of conflict and security, such a focus obscures or ignores the much more common case of continuing state involvement in the lives of its expatriates. A consideration of emigration policy should not be limited to those cases in which the state–citizen (or state–subject, in the case of authoritarian states) bond is completely severed. Indeed, as much of the recent migration/immigration literature now shows and the surge in diaspora studies indicates, the more common relationship today is one of continuing, if reconstructed, ties between the emigrant and the homeland.[7]

Most of the diaspora literature deals only in passing with the home *state* and its role, preferring instead to focus on the family, community, village or immigrant association level. Yet, the perpetuation or reconfiguration of ties between the expatriate and his/her homeland must be understood to take place in the context, not only of unequal North–South political economy relations or new forms of mobility and contact that facilitate the maintenance of a range of ties with the home society, but also in the context of a *state* that at its most basic level continues to control citizenship and to allow entry and exit as part of its exercise of sovereignty. Hence, given the current foci of the literature, the challenge is two-fold: to think more systematically about *state* policies and institutions (as opposed to focusing on developments in the international political economy), and to think about such policies in terms of the *sending*, as opposed to just the *receiving*, state.

Emigration policy

Emigration policy is not a term that is widely used – again an indication of the overwhelming focus by scholars and policymakers on the receiving states of the global North which, as wealthy democracies, have not to date viewed as necessary or politically appropriate careful control or encouraging the *exit* of citizens.

As noted above, border control has long been understood to be a prerogative of the sovereign state. The most basic elements of such a policy are the means and possibility for exit (and re-entry). Here, of course, the

---

[7] See, for example, Robin Cohen, *Global Diasporas: An Introduction* (Seattle: University of Washington Press, 1997); Nicholas Van Hear, *New Diasporas* (Seattle: University of Washington Press, 1998); Jana Evans Braziel and Anita Mannur, *Theorizing Diaspora* (Oxford: Blackwell, 2003); Helena Lindholm Schulz, *The Palestinian Diaspora* (New York: Routledge, 2003).

availability of travel documents, usually passports, is the most common element, and states may be classified according to regulations regarding how nationals obtain and renew passports, as well as how they deal with nationals who have left and/or entered another country illegally and are repatriated. In addition, while most travelers are familiar with the need to obtain visas to enter some foreign countries, the policy of requiring exit visas is a related matter. For example, pre-revolutionary Russia had never had a tradition of freedom of movement because of serfdom. With the revolution in 1917 and the foreign intervention against it, the regime feared that those who left would join the enemy ranks. Anyone who wanted to leave was seen as an enemy, and hence permission to travel, through the requirement of exit visas, was imposed.[8] In addition to other communist regimes,[9] a similar policy subsequently emerged under a number of authoritarian regimes, such as fascist Italy and Nazi Germany:

generally, prohibition of emigration arises as a concomitant of state-directed economic autarky, particularly in the case of states that seek to catch up by imposing great sacrifices on the current generation. But the prohibition also serves more purely political objectives; since exit is tantamount to 'voting with one's feet,' an alternative to protest, authoritarian regimes which claim to rest on democratic consent cannot afford such concrete evidence of deep alienation.[10]

A related practice is that of confiscating passports, a more targeted policy than an across-the-board denial of exit. Accordingly, individuals who have engaged in political activities deemed threatening by the state are stopped at points of exit or have their passports impounded upon their return to the country from abroad. In both cases the outcome is the same: the individual is prevented from leaving the country legally until such time as the state decides that the menace s/he poses has receded.

Whatever the system of exit regulations put in place, a second element of emigration policy involves states' decisions to enter into contractual relations with other states to provide labor power. In this case, special recruiting bureaus and, in some countries, training centers are established to locate and prepare workers to go abroad. This may be in addition to, or in place of, free outmovement of nationals seeking employment abroad, something which the state may also implicitly or explicitly encourage through a variety of training/educational policies and employment

---

[8] See Alan Dowty, *Closed Borders: The Contemporary Assault on Freedom of Movement* (New Haven: Yale University Press, 1987).

[9] For example, following the war, Vietnam had what was called the ODP: orderly departure program.

[10] Albert O. Hirschman, "Exit, Voice and the State," in *Essays in Trespassing: Economics to Politics and Beyond* (Cambridge: Cambridge University Press, 1981), pp. 246–65.

services. The state's involvement may be that of a more or less active facilitator: it may leave the oversight of contractual elements in the hands of the foreign recruiter; or it may play a more interventionist role by overseeing the placement of its nationals abroad.

This is not the end of the story, however, for the sending state's role continues beyond the window of passport control. Indeed, this study argues that the understanding of emigration policy should be much broader and include the entire range of sending-state policies and institutions that may play a role in the national's life while s/he is abroad. The underlying assumption is that while one aspect of state sovereignty is in play in the control of borders (exit and entry of nationals and others), another aspect of sovereignty – the implicit contract between sovereign state and citizen – continues to be active when the citizen is outside the territorial boundaries of the state. Thus, emigration policy should be understood to include not only the state's approach to exit, but also its policies toward those who have exited.

Embassies and consulates, whose grounds have legal status as extra-territorial extensions of the home state, have long been the most obvious manifestation of this sovereign concern with nationals abroad, whether as individuals or as larger groupings. The extent and type of services offered by such government offices abroad are important indicators of a state's interest and involvement in its expatriate communities. Embassy/consular responsibilities generally include matters related to passports and civil status (registering marriages, births, deaths, etc.). Ideally, they also include assistance/advice on a range of legal problems back home, as well as a certain degree of advocacy for the rights and protection of nationals abroad. In practice, the provision and quality of such services has depended upon home country and host country forms of government, the size of community, its relationship to the home state (political, ethnic sensitivities, etc.), as well as the level of professionalism and resources of consular officials.[11]

In addition to these functions, with which most citizens of advanced industrial democracies are familiar, embassies/consulates have at times served to organize or host individuals or institutions whose primary function is to *monitor* the communities of nationals abroad. Expatriate or diaspora communities – especially, although not exclusively, students

---

[11] As Weiner noted, "While some countries are prepared to take armed action in defense of their overseas citizens, others prefer not to antagonize a government that has enabled its citizens to find employment and a country that is a source of badly needed remittances": "Security," p. 104. Examples are legion in the Middle East and Persian Gulf region, for instance, of abused Sri Lankan and Filipina domestic workers whose embassies have refused or been hesitant to help them for precisely this reason.

and workers – have often provided support for political agitation back home. When the host state offers greater freedoms than the sending state, expatriates may also be in a position to attract media attention to pressure or embarrass the home regime. On the other hand, the embassy of the sending country may also seek to mobilize its supporters abroad. In either case, the expatriate groupings may become "a focal point of controversy between the home and the host countries, among contending groups within the diaspora, or between sections of the diaspora and the home government. Thus, struggles that might otherwise take place only within a country become internationalized if the country has a significant overseas population."[12] Recent revelations regarding the 1965 Paris kidnapping and murder of Moroccan political opposition figure Mehdi Ben Barka, as well as examples of political assassinations of expatriate Iranians by the revolutionary regime or the assassinations of Southern Cone citizens abroad as part of Operation Condor, are extreme examples of this darker side of state policy toward emigrants.

In a more positive vein, embassies may offer or facilitate expatriate access to banking and remittance transfer services, with the goal of facilitating expatriate investment of funds back home. On the occasion of important national holidays, they often hold parties or celebrations which serve to bring members of the expatriate community together and reinforce a sense of identity and belonging. They may also play a role in the establishment and direction of schools for the children of their nationals abroad.

As the discussion above suggests, ministries of foreign affairs, of which embassies and consulates are an extension, have traditionally held the governmental portfolio on expatriate community affairs. Nevertheless, important and increasingly numerous examples of state institutions and initiatives in the emigration realm have appeared that do not fall completely within the realm of embassy or Ministry of Foreign Affairs responsibilities. Some of the best-known have been labor recruitment or coordination offices, but institutional manifestations of state interest have often played a role well beyond the realm of labor contracting. From Japan and India to Morocco and Mexico, new institutional forms of state interest in expatriates have proliferated in recent years.

The question is: why? What factors have led governments to develop new institutions (or restructure existing ones) designed to take an active role in the lives of nationals abroad? How may we explain these new or transformed expressions of state emigration policy? Finally, may they be

---

[12] Ibid., p. 108.

indicative of changes in the contours of the nation, in the practice of sovereignty, and perhaps even more broadly, in the world system?

The literature from transnationalism

The only literature to date that has discussed state institutions involved in expatriate communities or affairs is that of transnationalism.[13] This field of scholarship traces its origins to the 1992 work of Basch, Glick Schiller and Szanton Blanc, who later defined transnationalism "as the processes by which immigrants forge and sustain social relations that link together their societies of origin and settlement."[14] Transnationalism arose at least in part as a reaction to the inability of existing theoretical approaches to immigrant incorporation, namely the cultural assimilationist and the ethnic pluralistic models, to accommodate the multiplicity of trans-territorial affiliations that transnational migrants seem to possess.[15]

---

[13] Early writings in the field of transnationalism suffered from problems of definition, scope and problematique. See David Fitzgerald, *Negotiating Extra-Territorial Citizenship: Mexican Migration and the Transnational Politics of Community*. CCIS Monograph 2 (La Jolla: University of California, San Diego, Center for Comparative Immigration Studies, 2000). First, it was not clear what in fact was new (aside from scholarly interest in it), although some scholars stressed the "high intensity of exchanges, the new modes of transacting and the multiplication of activities that require cross-border travel and contacts on a sustained basis." See Alejandro Portes, Luis E. Guarnizo and Patricia Landolt, "The Study of Transnationalism: Pitfalls and Promise of an Emergent Research Field," *Ethnic and Racial Studies* 22 (2) March 1999: p. 218.

Second, there were problems with the unit of analysis – the individual, the community, the network, etc. Moreover, how many communities can truly be said to live transnational lives in the sense Basch, Glick Schiller and Szanton Blanc meant – lives that seem to pass easily back and forth between two countries? See Linda Basch, Nina Glick Schiller and Cristina Szanton Blanc, *Nations Unbound: Transnational Projects, Postcolonial Predicaments, and Deterritorialized Nation-States* (Langhorne, PA: Gordon and Breach, 1994). There also seemed to be little consideration in the transnationalism literature – which looks almost exclusively at Western Hemisphere communities with a foot in the United States – of situations of marginalization or cultural and social displacement in these communities.

Third is the implicit normative evaluation of the various transnational institutions, that as members of civil society they are by definition representative and dynamic, and that by transgressing established structures of power they are by needs counter-hegemonic. As the work of Fitzgerald on Mexico shows, the success of transnational associations often owes to the relationships that they develop with the state of origin.

[14] Basch *et al.*, p. 7. It is interesting that none of the works in this field that I have encountered expresses an intellectual debt to the much earlier work of Robert Keohane and Joseph Nye on interdependence. This may well owe to the fact that those writing on transnationalism tend to be sociologists and anthropologists, not students of international relations.

[15] Luis Eduardo Guarnizo, Arturo Ignacio Sanchez and Elizabeth M. Roach, "Mistrust, Fragmented Solidarity, and Transnational Migration: Columbians in New York City and Los Angeles," *Ethnic and Racial Studies* 22 (2) March 1999: p. 389.

The transationalism literature criticizes traditional works on migration for their assumption of a clear dichotomy between sending and receiving states, arguing that such an approach does not offer the tools necessary to deal with the more fluid, transnational (although not *deterritorialized*)[16] existence that characterizes many of today's migrants.

The majority of the work in this area has been concerned with civil society and its myriad transnational extensions, whether through business, village associations, or other activities. A few of the early works give at least passing consideration to state institutions involved in expatriate affairs, although they are not the primary analytical focus. Basch *et al.*'s point that transmigrants "take actions, make decisions, and develop subjectivities and identities embedded in networks of relationships that connect them simultaneously to two or more *states*," (emphasis added)[17] is helpful in reminding us that the relationships are not just with networks of family or civil society institutions. Transmigrants are in fact located in a particular historical, political, social and economic context,[18] part of which is the "states in their lives."

Nonetheless, in general, Basch *et al.* miss a number of key elements in the relationship between the migrants and states. For example, they contend that "migrants and political leaders in the country of origin are engaged in constructing an ideology that envisions migrants as loyal citizens of their ancestral state." Such an ideology, they argue, "recognizes and encourages the continuing and multiple ties that immigrants maintain with their society of origin" but ignores "the ongoing incorporation of these immigrants into the society and polity of the country in which they have settled."[19] The first problem with such a contention concerns what sort of "ideology" is in fact in the process of being developed. The authors assume that there is an intersection of state interest with that of the migrants on the point of constructing the migrants as loyal citizens. That, it would seem, is an hypothesis requiring empirical testing, rather than something to be assumed a priori. True citizenship (not just passport holding, but real rights and inclusion), rather than subjectness, has been quite limited in most developing countries over the years. Hence the whole notion of "loyal *citizen*" in the context of many sending countries, especially generally poorer, authoritarian states of the global South, needs to be interrogated.

---

[16] Smith and Guarnizo argue that in a context in which states continue to maintain the legitimate means of coercive force within their borders, "deterritorialization" of the state is a problematic concept. See Michael Peter Smith and Luis Eduardo Guarnizo (eds.), *Transnationalism from Below*. Comparative Urban and Community Research, 6 (New Brunswick, NJ: Transaction Publishers, 1998), p. 9.

[17] Basch *et al.*, p. 7.   [18] M. Smith and Guarnizo, p. 177.   [19] Basch *et al.*, p. 3.

Second, regarding the ongoing incorporation of the migrants into the new society/polity, empirical material in the case studies that follow as well as elsewhere demonstrates that far from being ignored by the sending country, the possibilities for assimilation – particularly as expatriates become increasingly economically successful – may in fact constitute a primary impetus behind increased state interest in the migrants: "The power now wielded by transmigrants has not escaped the notice of national governments, many of whom have launched initiatives varying from relatively benign cultural exchanges to full-fledged campaigns designed to institutionalize and control transnational ties."[20] In other words, the state of origin is keen to maintain or to reassert influence over the resources of these people, or over these people as resources. At the same time, countervailing pressures from the host state cannot be ignored: initiatives, whether originating from the state or civil society in the receiving country, may aim "at recuperating and reifying a mythical national identity . . . as a way to eliminate the penetration of alien 'others.' "[21] Thus, sending-state responses will be shaped not only by forces in the receiving society that promote emigrant integration but also by those groups advocating marginalization of the émigrés, a phenomenon that transnationalism seems largely to overlook.

As Robert C. Smith sums up, "the problems with the classical models for understanding immigration and transnational life lie with their two assumptions regarding the clean break [with the sending country] and full and exclusive membership [in one or the other]"; on the other hand, the post-national model is also deficient in that it "neglects the continued and even increased importance of the home state . . . in creating transnational forms of political and social life, and in maintaining local, ethnic and national identities linked to the home country."[22]

Recently, a number of studies have begun to examine manifestations of what has now come to be called political transnationalism, the various means by which nationals abroad participate in politics (especially elections) back home. These works look at the intersection of or interaction among three main institutional actors: "the administration of the sending

---

[20] Sara Mahler, "Theoretical and Empirical Contributions Toward a Research Agenda for Transnationalism," in M. Smith and Guarnizo, p. 89.

[21] Luis Eduardo Guarnizo and Michael Peter Smith, "The Locations of Transnationalism," in M. Smith and Guarnizo, p. 10.

[22] Robert C. Smith, "Transnational Localities: Community, Technology and the Politics of Membership within the Context of Mexico and US Migration," in M. Smith and Guarnizo, p. 200. Of all the writers in the transnational field, Smith demonstrates the greatest sensitivity to the role of the sending state. See, for example, his "Migrant Membership as an Instituted Process: Transnationalization, the State and the Extra-Territorial Conduct of Mexican Politics," *International Migration Review* 37 (2) Summer 2003: pp. 297–343.

states; political parties in the country of origin; and immigrant organizations in the receiving country."[23] Thus, they are particularly concerned
with how states and political parties court migrants, what factors lead
migrants to participate in politics back home (generation, degree of
integration or exclusion from the host society), how they may serve as
lobbyists for the home state abroad, and the like. As Smith argues writing
about Mexicans in the USA,

some level of engagement with the state is a crucial aspect of transnational life . . . this
engagement with the state of origin helps migrants create the conditions for transnational life in a variety of ways. It provides [a means] for migrants and their children to
register demands (which they often feel they do not have in the United States) and
receive recognition; and, it creates a public sphere within which to create alternative
identities to the stigmatized ones the dominant society often assigns them.[24]

What seems clear is that both the sending state and its expatriates are in
the process of adjusting behavior and expectations, and not necessarily in
linear ways. Just as transmigrants, "living in a world in which discourses
about identity continue to be framed in terms of loyalty to nations and
nation-states, . . . have neither fully conceptualized, nor articulated a form
of transnational identity,"[25] neither have states fully come to terms with how
traditional tools (embassies, consulates) may be modified or new institutions (expatriate representation in parliament, separate expatriate ministries, and the like) developed as a way to address the same phenomena.

Whatever the nature and extent of the policies they pursue toward their
nationals, states cannot be viewed simply as passive exit and entry points
for migrants, much of whose lives are spent abroad. Joppke's observation
regarding the state's role in immigration policy – that it is not a passive
receiver of voluntary immigrants, but also a set of institutions that plays a
"constitutive role" in international migration[26] – should be applied to
considerations of the sending states as well: they, too, should be seen, not
as passive exit points, but also as a set of institutions whose policies and
practices play a constitutive role in emigration. The leaderships of these
states have taken steps in the political, security, religious, social and
cultural realms to reinitiate, reinforce and shape ties with those who live
abroad. Moreover, it is not just the recent arrivals who are targeted, but,
in many cases, other, longer-settled members of the community as well.

---

[23] José Itzigsohn, "Immigration and the Boundaries of Citizenship: The Institutions of
Immigrants' Political Transnationalism," *International Migration Review* 34 (4) Winter
2000: p. 1131.
[24] Robert C. Smith, pp. 302–3.   [25] Basch *et al.*, p. 8.
[26] Christian Joppke, *Immigration and the Nation-State: The United States, Germany and Great
Britain* (New York: Oxford University Press, 1999), p. 1.

Explaining state institutional responses

While the literature in the field of transnationalism does increasingly contain some treatment of the sending state and its institutions, the focus remains on the level of the migrants, their networks, affiliations and activities. With the exception of Robert C. Smith's work, noted earlier, there is virtually no study of problematiques derived from a focus on the sending state, rather than the emigrants themselves. Thus, while there is some overlap of interest between this study and the transnationalism literature, the intent here is first and foremost to understand *state* behavior, concerns, claims and demands regarding membership and resources, rather than emigrant behavior. Certainly, sending-state behavior is affected by the domestic and international context, just as is the behavior of the emigrants. However, it is expected that a focus primarily on the state will suggest new questions and answers, just as it will tell a part of the story that is largely missed by studies whose primary focus is the emigrants, their networks and their behavior.

In one of the few explicit considerations of the origins of state interest in expatriates, Bauböck has outlined what he calls "three instrumental reasons: human capital upgrading, remittances, and the political lobbying of receiving-country governments."[27] Similarly, Itzigsohn specifies three state interests in developing this transnational political field: guaranteeing the flow of remittances; promoting investment by migrants; and mobilizing the support of immigrants as lobbyists in the host country.[28] Mahler discusses attempts by states with large diasporas to mobilize the various communities on behalf of their homelands, and uses examples that illustrate both the economic and lobbying arguments.[29] Finally, Levitt seconds the economic and lobbying arguments, while adding, without further elaboration or examples, that "symbolic purposes" – demonstrating modernity, democracy, development or power to their citizens abroad – often motivate states.[30]

These goals are clearly central to sending-state activity. However, the works in transnationalism have also been overwhelmingly limited to Western Hemisphere countries and to their migrant communities' recent experiences in the USA. Such a focus introduces a number of specificities that may or may not be operative in the cases in this study, which are

---

[27] Bauböck, "Towards a Political Theory of Transnationalism," p. 709.

[28] Itzigsohn, Table 2, p. 1140.

[29] Sarah J. Mahler, "Constructing International Relations: The Role of Transnational Migrants and Other Non-state Actors," *Identities* 7 (2) 2000: 200.

[30] Peggy Levitt, "Transnational Migration: Taking Stock and Future Directions," *Global Networks* 1 (3) 2001: p. 204.

examined over a longer period of time and in which neither the USA nor the Western Hemisphere plays much of a role. Indeed, detailed research into several cases as well as reading on a number of others suggest that the factors driving and shaping state involvement are and have been more complex and varied than these works suggest.[31] Hence, for the purposes of this study, a broader range of possible explanations has been developed. Each will be detailed briefly below, and will then be reconsidered in the individual country case studies. The categories of explanations to be used in this work will be termed: macro-historical, international politics, economic, domestic political, and security/stability.

Macro-historical explanations

A broad hypothesis, found in the work of Basch *et al.* – in its simplest form – is that transnationalism as a phenomenon (and hence state response to it) has been produced by a particular stage of (unequal) capitalist development between the global North and South,[32] which has drawn/pushed increasing amounts of labor from the poorer states to the wealthier ones, in the context of greater possibilities for communication and travel between home state and host state. While this hypothesis may be intuitively appealing on a certain level, particularly to those with a preference for structuralist explanations, for those with a knowledge of emigration outside the context of the US orbit, it appears ahistorical, or at best regionally (Western Hemisphere) specific. A cursory reading of the evolution of older diasporas (as exemplified by the Lebanese case in this work) reveals that many organizations and institutional phenomena similar to those discussed by Basch *et al.* were discussed, put in place, or contested well before the current phase of "globalization."

On a less grand scale, the history of the emigration itself, meaning the evolution of the distribution and size of the community/ies, their degree of

---

[31] For works that have treated some aspect of the state, if only tangentially, see: Basch *et al.*; M. Smith and Guarnizo; José Itzigsohn, Carlos Doré Cabral, Esther Hernandez Medina and Obed Vazquez, "Mapping Dominican Transnationalism: Narrow and Broad Transnational Practices," *Ethnic and Racial Studies* 22 (2) March 1999; Manuel Garcia y Griego, "The Importation of Mexican Contract Laborers to the United States, 1942–1964," in David G. Gutierrez (ed.), *Between Two Worlds: Mexican Immigrants in the United States* (Wilmington, DE: Scholarly Resources, Inc., 1996). Luin Goldring, "Disaggregating Transnational Social Spaces: Gender, Place and Citizenship in Mexico–US Transnational Spaces," in Ludger Pries (ed.), *New Transnational Social Spaces: International Migration and Transnational Companies in the Early Twenty-first Century* (New York: Routledge, 2001); Igor Zevelev, *Russia and Its New Diasporas* (Washington, DC: US Institute of Peace Press, 2001); Itzigsohn; and R. C. Smith.
[32] Basch *et al.*, pp. 11–12.

economic integration (and success) in the receiving state, and their self-perception may explain state institutional interest in them. That is, to understand state interest, a consideration of length of residence abroad, socio-economic composition of the communities (diverse class structure or not, family-based or largely single male emigration), as well as their developing relationship (legal, cultural, economic, social) with the new host society may be key. In other words, it may be that certain state institutional expressions are associated with particular "stages" of expatriate community development. For instance, state institutional interest may be dependent simply upon at least one of its émigré communities' (among perhaps many) reaching what would be defined as numerical critical mass in a certain host state. The perception that the émigré community's residence has become long-term may also serve to trigger state interest. Perhaps relatedly, states may launch émigré-oriented institutions when the possibility of significant emigrant integration into a host state leads the state to fear for its control over the émigrés and their resources.

For example, in discussing the Haitian case, Laguerre divides state policies into three main phases. First came the "directorate phase," during which diaspora affairs were the responsibility of the Ministry of Foreign Affairs, and the main thrust of governmental efforts was to defend the interests of Haitians abroad rather than to undertake anything more proactive. Next was the "representative phase," which began with Aristide's arrival to the presidency and during which a special envoy of the president was responsible for coordinating relations between the communities abroad and the state. The third phase, the "ministerial phase" was marked by the creation of a ministry dealing with Haitians abroad headed by a member of the Haitian diaspora.[33] Such a progression would seem to indicate a gradual, positive evolution in the degree of interest and involvement of the Haitian government in the affairs of its expatriate communities.

That said, it remains an empirical question as to whether the development of such institutions is linear. While not looking specifically at the state, Guarnizo insists that his findings

suggest that transnational relations and activities do not follow a linear path and are not necessarily and inevitably a progressive process ... the reach, scope and effects of transnational activities are contingent on the interaction of multiple contextual and group factors. Accordingly, the interaction among these factors might induce the expansion, stagnation, or reversal of transnational activities and relations over time.[34]

[33] M. S. Laguerre, "State, Diaspora and Transnational Politics: Haiti Reconceptualized," *Millenium Journal of International Studies* 28 (3) 1999: pp. 633–51.
[34] Guarnizo in M. Smith and Guarnizo, p. 391.

Robert C. Smith's detailed work certainly reveals a non-linear pattern in the Mexican government's relations with its nationals in the USA,[35] a confirmation of which came with the Mexican government's July 2002 decision to collapse into the Ministry of Foreign Affairs the special office representing Mexicans living abroad that had been an early initiative of the Fox administration.

International politics explanations

Migrants/expatriates must also be considered within the complex of regional or international relations. In the first place, one may look to the treatment by host states of the expatriates as a source of sending-state policy toward their communities. In other words, the impetus to provide changed assistance or services may be triggered by, for example, incidents of discrimination or harassment (or worse) against emigrants in the host state. Conversely, the sending state, if it fears a loss of power over emigrants due to increasing possibilities for assimilation or enfranchisement, may mobilize to maintain expatriate loyalty.

A second explanation in the international realm may relate to the possible development among emigrants, noted above, of ethnic lobbies that could exert influence in certain bilateral relationships.[36] A number of sending states have developed the impression, rightly or wrongly, that their expatriates can push for special consideration of their needs by the host state.[37] The examples that are generally cited are those of the Irish, Jewish and Armenian lobbies in the United States. A final possible explanation concerns the use of immigration-related issues in other spheres of a bilateral relationship. For example, the question of clandestine emigration is a point of contention in Mexico's relations with the United States and in Spain's ties with Morocco. In both of these cases, one can point to the use by one side or the other of the illegal immigrant "card" in negotiations over other, perhaps unrelated, issues. Hence a state may initiate institutional outreach to its émigrés as a way of highlighting their importance in a bilateral or regional relationship.

---

[35] "The dramatic resurgence and expansion in the scope and intensity of the Mexican state's professed interest in Mexicans in the United States follows [a] pattern of waxing and waning interest determined by the political importance and definition of US-residing migrants": R. C. Smith, p. 305.

[36] See, for example, Yossi Shain, *Marketing the American Creed Abroad: Diasporas in the U.S. and their Homelands* (New York: Cambridge University Press, 1999).

[37] Mexican officials openly discuss the possibility of their expatriates in the United States developing into a lobby comparable in weight to that of the American-Jewish lobby.

Economic explanations

The economic explanation for such institutions appears to be the most obvious and easiest to make. At base, in the realm of emigration, states have two powerful economic incentives – often interrelated – which may vary in importance over time and across context. The first concerns what can be called the employment effect, the fact that exporting workers can serve as an economic safety valve in a situation of high or potentially high unemployment. In such a context, the state may seek to develop institutions both to facilitate the movement/placement of its nationals abroad and to assist them in leading economically productive lives in their new societies. The second incentive concerns remittances.[38] Here, the concern is not so much the employment effect in the sending state, but rather the impact that the émigrés' hard currency transfers have on the balance of payments back home. When remittances play an important role, states may be expected not only to promote conditions enabling their nationals to lead productive lives, but also to seek to maintain close ties with them – a concern that may or may not apply in the first case.

One may think of the loss of home state control over the expatriate through his/her settling abroad, but particularly through increasing integration in the new host society, as an indication of loss of state control over a resource. For some expatriates, economic loyalty may evolve or exist naturally as a result of attachment to family or village in the homeland. In other cases, and especially with the passage of time, such ties may weaken, or may not exist to the same extent among those of the second or third generation. Here, in order to maintain the same level of remittances, the state may deem it necessary to undertake special efforts to reach out to its nationals (or their descendants), to cultivate their loyalty. In this way, one may view the institutional development as a response to the basic economic concern of maintaining a certain level of transfers or investment.

Domestic political explanations

Developments in the domestic political system may also play a role in changing state perceptions of or interest in expatriate communities. Movement toward more open or participatory political systems after years of authoritarianism may render the expatriates potential sources

---

[38] For a thorough discussion of the many facets of the remittance issue, see Luis Eduardo Guarnizo, "The Economics of Transnational Living," *International Migration Review* 37 (3) Fall 2003: pp. 666–99.

of support (political and financial) for new or ascendant political forces. In such cases one may expect the new regime/government to introduce institutions or programs to harness this power. In addition, the political changes underway may energize the expatriates themselves into seeking to play a role in bringing about or consolidating change back home. In response, the sending state may thereby be "inspired" to capture or co-opt this interest. Such was certainly the case in Haiti's relations with its nationals in the USA after the election of Aristide in 1991. The responses of Mexicans in the USA to the 2000 presidential campaign and the initiatives of the Mexican government and political parties to win the support of the communities of Mexicans north of the border as a result are other, obvious examples.

Part of what is at work here are changes that give new meaning to the very concept of citizenship, to the content of political, rather than just cultural or social, belonging. As noted earlier, the political systems of many sending states of the global South have long been characterized by varying degrees of authoritarianism, and hence by treatment of the "citizen" as subject rather than participant: "Citizenship has a different meaning in countries of emigration and countries of immigration, in old and new states ... in totalitarian and liberal democratic states."[39] Part of the definition of political opening or liberalization is a gradual process of institution-related recognition that repressive/exclusivist politics as usual will no longer work. To the extent that such a process may be underway in the sending state, there may be a relatively automatic response by the state also to change its behavior toward expatriates, or the expatriates themselves may take action to force the state to deal with them on changed bases.

Security/stability explanations

Expatriate communities have long served as places of refuge for political exiles. Whether because the receiving state is a more open political system that allows dissent, or because it seeks to oppose or destabilize the sending country, expatriates may find fruitful organizing, fundraising and agitating ground abroad. As a result, the sending country may decide that existing institutions, such as embassies and consulates, need to expand their activities to include effective surveillance, or it may decide to establish new institutions to carry out related tasks.

---

[39] Tomas Hammar, "State, Nation, and Dual Citizenship," in William Rogers Brubaker (ed.), *Immigration and the Politics of Citizenship in Europe and North America* (New York: University Press of America, 1989), p. 86.

A government may, therefore, conclude that a more proactive approach than simply monitoring the communities abroad is in order. Such an approach may involve establishing branches of a ruling party (with extensions into the various sectors of the community, such as women and youth), or initiating cultural or other information-oriented programs and activities intended to provide a particular image of the home state regime. The function of these activities may be understood as largely propaganda-related, intended to mobilize people within the framework of an approved institution, or it may be part of a more (or less) subtle policy to intimidate through manifestation of home-state power abroad.

Related to these two elements but worthy of separate mention are efforts by the government of the state of origin to convey a message about its expatriates. Particularly in the European context, where a number of expatriate communities have been associated with high levels of delinquency and crime, sending states may initiate special policies to dissuade their nationals from becoming involved in such activities, in large part because of the negative repercussions such behavior may have for the continued, successful residence of the vast majority of its expatriates abroad. This is security-related image control aimed at maintaining the various advantages that the expatriate communities enjoy and from which the sending state, by extension, benefits.

Methodology

My country cases – Morocco, Tunisia, Jordan and Lebanon – all have at least one state-sponsored expatriate-related institution, although the histories and functions of these institutions differ considerably, as the chapters that follow demonstrate. The countries chosen may disappoint the methodological purist in that they do not represent a carefully structured set of cases, either from the point of view of the number and function of the institutions, or along the lines of type of domestic political system, emigration policy, size of expatriate communities, relationship with host states or colonial legacy. Case selection for studies requiring fieldwork in the Middle East North Africa (MENA) region is in large part shaped by the realities on the ground. First was the question of feasibility. Algeria, with its large communities in France could have been one choice, but continuing security concerns regarding living in Algeria led to its exclusion. Egypt, a country with a large expatriate presence, particularly, but not exclusively, in the Gulf region, might have been chosen; however, I was denied research permission by the Egyptian government. Yemen and Syria also now have such institutions, but they were barely initiated at the time this research was conducted. Turkey could have been another choice, but I do not have Turkish as a research language.

There was also the issue of comparability: I wanted sovereign states, as well as states whose legal approaches to their citizens were roughly comparable. Such considerations led to the exclusion of the Palestinian National Authority, since it has been at best a quasi-state, with no finally defined borders, minimal sovereignty, given the continuing Israeli occupation, and the destruction of its incipient institutions since the beginning of the second intifada in 2000. In the case of Israel, the fact that it defines itself not as a state for its citizens, but as a state for Jews worldwide, and that it has never declared its borders, raised other problems of comparability regarding sovereignty and citizenship. Finally, Iraq is – as of this writing – occupied (US government insistence upon its post June 30, 2004, sovereignty notwithstanding) and in political transition (although it does have a Ministry of Immigration and Refugees). None of the other oil producers has a significant population of nationals abroad. Hence, exploring cases in which no such institutions existed in order to explore the "why not" question seemed limited to examples where the lack of such organizational state interest was fairly easily explained by the lack of expatriate communities. That said, Jordan, one of the four cases explored here, had only one, very limited "institution" (a series of conferences) which lasted only four years. Given the size and importance of the kingdom's expatriate population, the question of "why so little attention" must be addressed, and may offer insights regarding cases in other regions in which there is a complete absence of state institutional concern.

The result of these various research constraints was the choice of four countries which exhibit a number of key differences as well as some interesting similarities. In all four, the histories of the emigrations are examined from their beginnings, to allow for sufficient historical sweep to determine the depth of the origins as well as possible successive reconfigurations of institutions. They fall into two pairs: Morocco and Tunisia, whose emigration has been overwhelmingly to (relatively) nearby, but culturally different, Western European democracies; and Lebanon and Jordan, whose migrations, while increasingly diverse, have been largely to authoritarian states of the global South, with important communities in the culturally similar Arab world.

Both Morocco and Tunisia are former French colonies which retain strong economic ties to France. Both these North African countries have had similar histories of migration, beginning in response to colonial need, but then continuing as a safety valve to relieve domestic unemployment, ultimately developing into a key source of remittances that have helped to offset what would otherwise be serious balance of payments deficits.

Their largest expatriate communities are in the former metropole, while the next largest concentrations are also in Western Europe: in the Netherlands, Belgium and Germany for Morocco; and in Italy and Germany for Tunisia. These Europe-based communities have had increasing access to social, economic and civic rights, including, in some cases, full enfranchisement in the form of citizenship.

Morocco is a kingdom whose monarch traces his line to the Prophet Muhammad. Its heavy-handed authoritarian system, which has seen some liberalization since the late 1980s, has been infused with laws and practices grounded in what for years was a feudal monarchy, jealous of tradition and drawing legitimacy from the king's self-proclaimed position of religious authority as Amir al-Mu'minin (the commander of the faithful). Tunisia, on the other hand, secured independence led by a group of secular nationalists in the French republican tradition. The small, relatively homogeneous country has resisted the militarizing tendencies of its neighbors and, thanks to the developmentalist approach of its first president, Habib Bourguiba, managed to avoid the tremendous income disparities that have characterized other MENA countries. That said, its repressive political system has made Tunisia, a country with a relatively large middle class and generally well-educated population, an anomaly as a continuingly highly authoritarian state.

The third case country is Lebanon. Of all the countries examined here, Lebanon is the smallest (in terms of both land surface and population), but has the longest history of emigration, and the largest and most widely scattered expatriate presence. Lebanon's oldest communities are in North and South America (and to some extent Africa), while, more recently, important communities have developed in the Persian Gulf, Europe and Australia. Lebanon's communities abroad have been, since the days of the French Mandate (1921–46), an integral part of the numerical calculus that produced and has maintained the country's political system, generally referred to as "confessional," meaning that representation is based on religio-ethnic affiliation. Lebanon has also enjoyed a more open political system over the years than any other Arab country, but it was in part that openness that paved the way for its fifteen-year civil war. The presence of literally millions of Lebanese (and their descendants) abroad has continued to shape and be shaped by politics in the homeland, with the 1975–90 conflict only the most tragic and obvious example.

The final case is Jordan. Here the emigration story is the most recent of the four cases, beginning in the wake of the dismemberment of Palestine in 1948 and the annexation by the Hashemite Kingdom of the rump of eastern Palestine, now known as the West Bank. With many of Jordan's emigrants originally from the part of Palestine that became the state of Israel, the Hashemite Kingdom's history of emigration is the only one of the four with a significant domestic refugee component: one which, although overwhelmingly citizen, has nonetheless faced political and structural obstacles to full enfranchisement. While Jordanian communities are now found around the world, the majority of Jordan's expatriates live and work in the Persian Gulf region. In the case of Jordan, the culture in which the majority of its expatriates (and the Lebanese resident in the Gulf) live is overwhelmingly Arab and Muslim, and hence reasonably familiar, even if permanent settlement is not possible, owing to highly restrictive Gulf state policies regarding naturalization. Both of these factors distinguish the Jordanian communities from those of the Maghrebis in Europe, who live in a European/Christian context but in which citizenship is increasingly an option.

The initial questions that arose as I embarked on this research were: whence the impetus to establish new or reconfigure old institutions? Is it located in the domestic realm, in international politics, or at their intersection? Can it be traced to a particular stage of migration driven by the structure of the present international political economy, or are its origins to be found elsewhere? In order to answer these questions a two-pronged approach was followed. The first, which was the primary thrust of the work, was to identify the state institutions involved in expatriate affairs and then examine in detail their origins and development. The second was to attempt to construct a history of state emigration policy over the years and then to use it, as well as a more general socio-economic and political history of the country's development, as backdrop, but also as potentially explanatory material for the developments in the institutional realm. After completing the fieldwork and engaging in the writing, the role of these institutions in the context of historical challenges to various aspects of state sovereignty also became clear. The sovereignty–security–identity nexus, which therefore served to guide the final framing of the study, will be further discussed in the next chapter.

A final word: while I believe strongly in the importance of region-specific knowledge in studying the MENA area, or any other region for that matter, I do not believe in Arab, Muslim or MENA exceptionalism. Each region has its specificities, yet many social, economic and political phenomena have clear or close parallels in other regions. I am only too painfully aware of how certain historical developments have shaped this region in ways different from others, but I do not as a result feel the need to make a special case for, for example, drawing comparisons between MENA country examples and examples from South America, the Caribbean or Asia. Similarly, readers expecting a central consideration of Islam or Arab culture in my analysis will be disappointed. While acknowledging the role of religion in regional politics, and discussing some aspects of its place in the Maghrebi communities in Europe, I did not at any time in the course of my fieldwork encounter evidence suggesting that Islam itself constituted a variable that would set MENA cases apart for this study. I do note the importance of sectarianism in the Lebanese system and for Lebanese expatriate relations, just as I discuss the fact that, for example, Arab expatriates in the Gulf states entered societies with which they had a religious affinity. However, just as Lebanon can be analyzed as an example of a more general phenomenon, that of a multi-confessional society, so in terms of cultural and religious affinity, Arab guest workers in Saudi Arabia may be compared with Latin American emigrants in Spain. MENA studies can only benefit from greater integration into comparisons with other regions.

In each of the four case studies that follow, several state institutions responsible for aspects of expatriate affairs are examined in detail. The stories of their founding and evolution tell a great deal about the immediate catalysts of formal and expanded state involvement in the lives of nationals abroad. The narratives reveal a complex mix of international, domestic and bureaucratic politics, all of which contribute to our understanding of the bases and evolution of state emigration policy. However, behind these developments are larger or more basic questions related to the importance of borders, security and state identity. What is the relationship between emigration and the demands of state-building? How may reinventing or restructuring relations with nationals – sovereign concerns – abroad in fact "produce different forms of state, states of sovereignty, and conceptions of territoriality"?[40] What role do the institutions examined here play in this nexus, and what may answers to such questions tell us about how sovereignty, understood not only in narrow terms of border control but also as it relates to the contours of the political community, is practiced and changes? It is to a consideration of sovereignty and its role in explaining state behavior in the context of growing expatriate and diaspora communities that this study now turns.

---

[40] Thomas J. Biersteker, "State, Sovereignty, and Territory," in Walter Carlsnaes *et al.* (eds.), *Handbook of International Relations* (Thousand Oaks: Sage, 2002), p. 167.

2   State sovereignty, state resilience

The now voluminous literatures on globalization and the new security agenda intersect in their discussion of whether the state is waning in importance or manifesting forms of resistance in the face of contemporary challenges.[1] There is no question that many issues formerly understood as being under the control of the state or falling within its sovereign realm can no longer be accurately portrayed in such a way. Environmental threats in the oceans and the air admit no boundaries; developments in military technology have rendered national boundaries vulnerable in an unprecedented way; economic restructuring in response to neoliberal dictates has reconfigured the role of the state in the domestic economy and opened the way to broader and deeper foreign investment that is less controlled by national authorities; and the speed and development of communications have rendered virtually impossible tight governmental control of information flows across borders. In the realm of population movement, the evolution of the global economy has led employers to seek low-cost (often illegal) labor, thus rendering increasingly difficult the prevention of undocumented flows. Moreover, despite state efforts to stem the tide, the numbers of refugees, displaced and asylum seekers have been steadily rising.

In addition, some argue that state power is waning owing to the growth in numbers and importance of a variety of transnational actors – some of them of a supranational sort, others sub-national in origin – which engage in coordination and advocacy work on such issues as human rights, the environment, indigenous culture and women's rights, supported by like-minded activist groups abroad. These groups, such theorists argue, have

[1] For only three, classic, examples see: Arjun Appadurai, *Modernity at Large: Cultural Dimensions of Globalization* (Minneapolis: University of Minnesota Press, 1996); Saskia Sassen, *Globalization and Its Discontents* (New York: The New Press, 1998); Barry Buzan, Ole Waever, Jaap de Wilde, *Security a New Framework for Analysis* (Boulder: Lynne Reinner, 1998). Basch *et al.* also have as a basic premise the idea that it is no longer the nation-state, but rather global capitalism that is the driving force in international, now transnational, relations.

been able to work around the state (from below and above) in order gradually to force changes in state norms and, ultimately, practice in a variety of issue areas.[2]

Those on the other side of the debate, while generally admitting of the presence and importance of the factors mentioned above, nonetheless argue that the state has historically shown remarkable resilience and remains the most basic unit in international politics. For example, using a structuralist argument, Spruyt explores how and why the sovereign state bested other contenders, notably city-states and city-leagues, to become the predominant political organizing form in Europe.[3] Philpott, whose argument is based in the causal force of historical revolutions in ideas, also traces the sovereign state's arrival and expansion from Westphalia through colonial independence to becoming a universal organizing principle.[4] Murphy's approach is somewhat different, although also historical: "Over the years sovereignty as a systemic notion was repeatedly thrown into crisis when social, technological and economic developments challenged the theoretical and functional bases of particular territorial arrangements";[5] nevertheless, the inertia of the sovereign territorial ideal has been great enough to prevent an enduring alternative from taking root. Thus, while representing different intellectual traditions, all three concur that despite periods of challenge to the sovereign state, it has developed as a universal form and has manifested enormous staying power.

Focusing more exclusively on the notion of sovereignty itself rather than the staying power of the state (which he would also endorse), Krasner argues that some of the confusion over whether the state's sovereign authority has been waning owes to the fact that sovereignty has always been violated, and deliberately so, by the rulers involved. For that reason he calls it "organized hypocrisy."[6] The ideal type that some

[2] See, for example, Thomas Risse, Stephen C. Ropp and Kathryn Sikkink (eds.), *The Power of Human Rights: International Norms and Domestic Change* (Cambridge: Cambridge University Press, 1999); Thomas Risse-Kappen (ed.), *Bringing Transnational Relations Back In: Non-State Actors, Domestic Structures and International Institutions* (Cambridge: Cambridge University Press, 1995); and Sanjeev Khagram, James V. Riker and Kathryn Sikkink (eds.), *Restructuring World Politics: Transnational Social Movements, Networks and Norms* (Minneapolis: University of Minnesota Press, 2002).

[3] Hendrik Spruyt, *The Sovereign State and Its Competitors: An Analysis of Systems Change* (Princeton: Princeton University Press, 1994).

[4] Daniel Philpott, *Revolutions in Sovereignty: How Ideas Shaped Modern International Relations* (Princeton: Princeton University Press, 2001).

[5] Alexander B. Murphy, "The Sovereign State as Political Territorial Ideal," in Thomas J. Biersteker and Cynthia Weber (eds.), *State Sovereignty as Social Construct* (Cambridge: Cambridge University Press, 1996), p. 83.

[6] Stephen D. Krasner, *Sovereignty: Organized Hypocrisy* (Princeton: Princeton University Press, 1999).

have in mind in discussing sovereignty has never existed in practice, he contends. Thus, according to this view, what one sees today is not the beginning of the end, but, rather, simply new forms of how sovereignty is violated purposefully. This is not to ignore the reality of failed states or the impact of a range of non-state actors, whether of a political, economic or cultural nature. The international system clearly includes new and growing forces that may undermine traditional state authority. Nevertheless, it remains the prerogative of states to adhere to or reject international conventions. It is in states that most political life is ordered; states continue to have responsibility for the legislation that most broadly and deeply affects the world's populations; and, most important for this discussion, states continue to be responsible for borders, for emigration and immigration policy as well as for extending (or withdrawing) citizenship. States face a range of challenges and challengers to their power and authority; but their demise is far from imminent.

In the context of the concerns of this study, Bauböck contends that "if we theorize migrant transnationalism as a challenge to the nation-state system itself, we are likely to exaggerate its scope and misunderstand its real significance."[7] However, one way to interpret the emergence of state institutions charged with expatriate affairs is to place them in the context of the historical development of the principle of sovereignty, as it has been shaped and reshaped over time through the interaction and clashing of forces and actors in the international system. In this way, on the one hand, one has the actors described by the literatures on transnationalism, NGOs and international political economy – individual and group actors operating either from above or below the state who seem to be whittling away at or reshaping state power. On the other hand is the state itself, which responds by reasserting itself, resisting or reconfiguring the intrusion or attempted ap/expropriation of aspects of its sovereignty. Paradoxically then, we can theorize the emergence of these varied expatriate-related institutions with their differing histories and functions as indicators of state resilience:[8] through these institutions, states manifest one aspect of their robustness by attempting to renegotiate their role, thereby reshaping and reasserting sovereignty, in the context of the development of ever larger groups of nationals (and even their descendants) who live for extended periods beyond their territorial boundaries, the traditional limits of their sovereign reach.

---

[7] Bauböck, p. 701.
[8] Joppke reaches a similar conclusion regarding state resilience rather than attrition or retreat through his examination of US, British and German immigration policy: pp. 262–71.

The question of sovereignty and nationals abroad

While authors differ regarding how sovereignty has developed and what its meanings are, they are in accord on the point that there is no single, unchanging and valid historical formulation of the concept. For example, the notion of sovereignty as found in Hobbes (absolute subjection to the sovereign) differs from popular sovereignty, based in participation, formulated by Rousseau, and even more so from Locke's attempt to ground sovereignty in constitutional theory by reviving the idea of a partnership between ruler and ruled.[9] Today, Ruggie's definition of sovereignty as "the institutionalization of public authority within mutually exclusive jurisdictional domains"[10] is broadly accepted as a succinct formulation. In a similar definitional vein, Philpott, arguing that the definition needs to be sufficiently broad to allow for the observed diversity over time and space, terms sovereignty, at its most basic, "supreme authority within a territory." The word "supreme" is critical, he contends, so that the holder of this authority is immune to rival claims from both within and without its territory.[11]

Of course, authority itself has many bases. As Camilieri notes, the state's authority viewed from the point of view of the citizen/subject may be moral (in keeping with one's conscience), customary (obeyed as part of upholding social norms, customs or conventions) or coercive (backed up by force). Indeed, many would agree that "what distinguishes the state from other institutions is its coercive authority, or as others have labeled it, supreme coercive power,"[12] although Rodney Hall, for example, downplays the importance of state coercive force, stressing instead the state's moral authority as key to its legitimacy and order: "The notion of enfranchised citizenship, the citizen as an individual with a material stake in the well-being of the nation and a voice in the regulation of its affairs, in many ways constitutes a fundamental legitimating principle of the national-sovereign system."[13]

[9] Rainer Bauböck, *Transnational Citizenship: Membership and Rights in International Migration* (Brookfield, VT: Edward Elgar, 1994), pp. 55–69.
[10] John Gerard Ruggie, "Continuity and Transformation in the World Polity: Toward a Neo-Realist Synthesis," in Robert O. Keohane (ed.), *Neo-Realism and its Critics* (New York: Columbia University Press, 1986).
[11] Philpott, pp. 16 and 254.
[12] Joseph A. Camillieri, "Rethinking Sovereignty in a Shrinking, Fragmented World," in R. B. J. Walker and Saul H. Mendlovitz (eds.), *Contending Sovereignties: Redefining Political Community* (Boulder: Lynne Reinner, 1990), p. 15.
[13] Rodney Bruce Hall, *National Collective Identity: Social Constructs and International Systems* (New York: Columbia University Press, 1999), pp. 40–41, 72.

Biersteker and Weber argue that sovereignty is the "product of a normative conception that links authority, territory, population (society, nation), and recognition in a unique way and in a particular place (the state)."[14] They are interested in how various sovereign ideals and resistances to them have been constructed, reproduced, reconstructed and deconstructed over the years. By introducing historical context, Biersteker additionally claims that there is no necessary unilinearity in the evolution of sovereignty; indeed, he insists that at the end of the twentieth century there was evidence in a number of countries (Chile regarding Pinochet, and Russia regarding Chechnya) of attempts to reverse the redefinition of their sovereignty.[15] Careful examination reveals that the conception and practice of sovereignty over time have been no more static than have been conceptions about what constitutes the state itself.

A number of authors have explored in detail the structural, technological and ideational background to changes in the understandings of sovereignty over time. Hall, for example, seeks to show how the transformation from what he calls the sovereign-territorial state to the national sovereign state took place, what that implied for changing notions of "the national interest," and what the systemic consequences of such changes were. According to his argument, each type of state relied upon a different legitimating principle: dynastic in the first case and the "imagined community" of the nation in the second. Just as important, he argues, "the rules of the game, and not a few of the objectives of international relations, have changed with variations in socially constructed conceptions of sovereignty."[16]

Murphy argues that across the centuries the prevailing understanding of the concept has swung back and forth between two notions. The first is sovereignty as a principle governing relations among states, defining what states are and are not allowed to do in the international arena. The second is sovereignty as a territorial ideal, meaning the degree to which the map of individual states is also the map of effective authority.[17] At times, the understanding of sovereignty has been that of a principle permitting rulers to do anything that they defined as being in their own interest, including attacking a neighboring state. At others, although the state has been no less autonomous, sovereignty has been widely understood as a

---

[14] Thomas J. Biersteker and Cynthia Weber, "The Social Construction of State Sovereignty," in Biersteker and Weber, p. 3.
[15] Thomas J. Biersteker, "State, Sovereignty and Territory," in Walter Carlsnaes *et al.* (eds.), *Handbook of International Relations* (Thousand Oaks: Sage, 2002), p. 160.
[16] Hall, p. 299.   [17] Murphy in Biersteker and Weber, p. 87.

principle limiting the rights of states to pursue territorial claims.[18] The importance of this for the present discussion is two-fold: one, the understanding of sovereignty has not been fixed; and two, at least since the eighteenth century, territorial claims have been preeminent.

Krasner, whose presentation does not include considerations of historical context, argues that much of the confusion over the waxing or waning of sovereignty derives from what he regards as misunderstandings regarding its nature. To clarify the issue, he delineates four separate or identifiable types of sovereignty. The first, *international legal* sovereignty, refers to the practices of mutual recognition, usually between territorial entities that have formal juridical independence. The second is *Westphalian* sovereignty, by which he means political organization based on the exclusion of external actors from authority structures within a given territory. *Domestic* sovereignty, on the other hand, is the formal organization of political authority within the state and the ability of public authorities to exercise effective control within the borders of their own polity. Fourth is *interdependence* sovereignty, which refers to the ability of public authorities to regulate the flow of information, ideas, goods, people, pollutants or capital across the borders of their state.[19] He further argues that these four forms do not covary. A state may have one and not another, and the exercise of one may undermine another.[20] On the other hand, Philpott, among others, makes a distinction between what he calls "internal" and "external" sovereignty, which are complementary, not distinct types. In his formulation, while internal sovereignty means supreme authority within a bounded territory, it also implies immunity from external interference. In contrast, "external sovereignty of the state is what international lawyers have in mind when they speak of sovereignty, and what the United Nations Charter means by 'political independence and territorial integrity.' "[21]

In all these considerations of sovereignty, the border, whether crossed or not, is basic and critical. Indeed, regardless of their divergence on other elements, writings on sovereignty converge on the crucial nature of territoriality:

This is a principle that defines the set of people over whom the holder of sovereignty rules. They are to be identified, territoriality says, by virtue of their location

---

[18] Ibid., p. 109.   [19] Krasner, *Sovereignty*, pp. 1–2, 10.

[20] Biersteker and Weber do not differ from Krasner's analysis; rather, they argue that he has not gone far enough. What is missing is a sense of history, the context that would explain the provenance of change. Otherwise, they argue, sovereignty seems timeless: if it involved or required hypocrisy in the present, it has in fact required hypocrisy all along. Such a view explains a reproduction of, but not the transformations in, the understanding and practice of sovereignty that have taken place across the centuries: p. 6.

[21] Philpott, p. 18.

within borders. The people within these borders may not necessarily conceive of themselves as a 'people' or a 'nation' with a common identity ... But their location within boundaries requires allegiance to their sovereign.[22]

That said, for most writers on the question of sovereignty, human beings – those subject to the sovereign – are generally left un(der)explored.

One exception is Barkin and Cronin, who do take populations, and not just borders, seriously. They note that "international relations scholars rarely examine how definitions of populations and territories change throughout history and how this change alters the notion of legitimate sovereignty."[23]

Sovereignty in international relations has been ascribed to two different types of entities: states, defined in terms of the territories over which institutional authorities exercise legitimate control, and nations, defined in terms of 'communities of sentiment' that form the political basis on which state authority rests ... Legitimation stems not from the boundaries but from the community of sentiment ... State sovereignty ... stresses the link between sovereign authority and a defined set of exclusive political institutions, and national sovereignty ... emphasizes a link between sovereign authority and defined population.[24]

As we know, in the international system, there are myriad examples in which the boundaries of the state do not coincide with those of the nation, imagined or real.

While Barkin and Cronin's work helps to problematize the territorial component of sovereignty, their historical cases do not directly address the question of the sovereignty of "the nation" when it may comprise numerous and sometimes far-flung communities well beyond the borders of the state. Nor does Krasner, although noting a number of cases of states or juridical units that do not fit the Westphalian model of sovereignty,[25] really offer us a way to think about the millions of *people* around the world who do not fit neatly into the contours of this territorially bounded state. We live in a world of (hypocritically) sovereign *states*, yet there are countless people who are in fact or in effect state*less*: refugees, the forcibly expelled, as well as large numbers who are marginalized

---

[22] Ibid., p. 17.

[23] J. Samuel Barkin and Bruce Cronin, "The State and the Nation: Changing Norms and the Rules of Sovereignty in International Relations," *International Organization* 48 (1) Winter 1994: p. 107.

[24] Ibid., pp. 111–12.

[25] He notes, for example that the leaders of states that joined the European Union in effect undermined their Westphalian sovereignty by entering into an agreement recognizing authority structures outside their borders. Conversely, Taiwan has Westphalian sovereignty, but not international legal sovereignty, that is, formal international recognition of its juridical independence: *Sovereignty*, p. 4.

by lack of enfranchisement in their countries of residence. At the same time, to return directly to the topic at hand, there are millions of people who live on a long-term, if not permanent, basis outside their home country, just as there are increasing numbers of people who carry dual nationality. How may one fit such people – the stateless, expatriates, guest workers, and dual nationals – into an analysis which, even in a less rigid form, is still based on a dichotomy of "inside or outside the political community" based on the territorial boundaries of the state? While handfuls of people could perhaps be written off as exceptions, under-standing how states react to growing communities of such "anomalies" in a system of sovereignty based on territorially bounded units would seem to be critical. The transnationalism literature provides a sociological basis for understanding people whose lives, families and activities (whether business or personal, whether economic, social, political or cultural) cross or span more than one country; it does not, however, theorize the nature of the various states' relationships with those who inhabit such "spaces."

R. B. J. Walker focuses his discussion on the level of society or the individual, calling sovereignty a principle that "offers both a spatial and a temporal resolution to questions about what *political community* can be, given the priority of citizenship and particularity over all universalist claims to a common human identity."[26] In his formulation, the territorial principle long so crucial to state sovereignty marks *one* type of boundary between who and what is inside and outside the political community. Citizenship is another. Its extension is related to, but it is not fully coincident with, the territorial boundary marker. Ideally, or in theory, those who are citizens are inside the boundaries of the state and covered by or included in its sovereignty; those who are not are outside the community (and the territorial borders). In practice, however, we see that a disjuncture between the two bases – territory and citizenship – is increasingly common.

In the Middle East and North Africa there is a long tradition of European state involvement in the affairs of foreign nationals and what were called "protected minorities." In the 1600s, the Ottoman Empire began to enter into a series of agreements called "Capitulations," most of the earliest of which were economic in nature and originated as enticements to Western merchants at a time when the Ottoman Empire was militarily dominant. During the eighteenth century, with Ottoman power waning, these agreements were renegotiated, and additional

[26] R. B. J. Walker, *Inside/Outside: International Relations as Political Theory* (Cambridge: Cambridge University Press, 1993), pp. 62–63, emphasis added.

privileges were granted to the European powers. One such privilege was the power to grant certificates of protection – *barats* – to non-Muslim Ottoman subjects. These certificates afforded their holders the same protection enjoyed by European nationals: they were exempted from taxation and from the legal jurisdiction of the empire. When they ran into trouble they were able to seek protection from European consular officials and, in the event of criminal activity, it was the consuls who in effect tried their cases in accordance with the law of the European country. European representatives freely granted the *barats* to minority subjects of the empire, and through them these minorities were able to gain control of important sectors of Ottoman external trade.[27]

Here, of course, we are interested in examining relations from the other direction – the degree of Arab state involvement in the lives of their nationals abroad – but the example is relevant nonetheless, as it highlights several important issues. First, it suggests that what constitutes both the "inside" and the "outside" of the sovereign realm of the *sending state* needs to be rethought. Just as Soysal in her work on post-national membership attempted to explain how European states dealt with this disjuncture from the perspective of the host,[28] this work attempts something similar, but with a focus on the states of origin. Given the large numbers of people resident in countries in which they do not hold citizenship (or in which they hold a second citizenship), how are we to think about the notion of political community and sovereignty? An appreciation of the distinction between a sovereign state-territorially bounded political community and one bounded by the possession of citizenship (or perhaps only national attachment) is critical to this work.

Obviously, sovereign, bounded territorial entities – states – no longer (if they ever did) contain just their own citizens, just as increasing numbers of states have come to witness the growth of communities of their nationals (and descendants) beyond their borders. More important, a sending state's attempts to maintain or reassert sovereignty over those outside its physical boundaries take place *within* the physical boundaries of another sovereign entity, the receiving state. Clearly, then, physical presence within bounded units alone is insufficient to define a person or group of people as falling within the sovereign state's full range of

---

[27] For annotated presentations of the documents that constitute the Capitulation agreements, see J. C. Hurewitz, *The Middle East and North Africa in World Politics: A Documentary Reader* (New Haven: Yale University Press, 1979, 2nd edn.).

[28] Yasemin Nuhoğlu Soysal, *The Limits of Citizenship: Migrants and Postnational Membership in Europe* (Chicago: University of Chicago Press, 1994).

responsibilities or, on the other hand, to require that such people undertake the full range of obligations of those who are included within the political community. Tourists abroad are expected to obey or abide by the laws of the lands they visit, but they are in no way, thereby, considered members of the political community encompassed by the country they are visiting. Similarly, but a bit more problematic and closer to the concerns of this work, although guestworkers are subject to a range of host state laws, their work and extended residence do not automatically qualify them for full political membership in the receiving state. The potential for a clash of sovereignties or at least a kind of tug of war should be clear. Indeed, the argument here is that states' initiatives aimed at reincorporating expatriates (and their descendants) should be seen as a part of their efforts to assert or maintain authority in the ongoing processes of redefining and reconfiguring sovereignty in the international system.

Maintaining sovereignty

In this context, it is critical to consider why – if the inside/outside dichotomy is so basic to the principle of sovereignty, and the sovereign state has had such staying power – states do not simply "relinquish" or largely ignore citizens who reside for extended periods abroad and who, in some cases, become citizens of another state. Many of today's emigrants are people politically or economically disaffected, those who were unable to find (suitable) work at home and hence chose or felt compelled to go elsewhere to build a decent life. Why would a state seek to continue to hold on to such people as citizens? What are the origins of governments' willingness to engage in practices that challenge the traditional insider/outsider dichotomy seemingly so basic to sovereignty in matters related to maintaining ties with citizens abroad? These questions overlap to a certain degree with the question posed in the previous chapter regarding why states establish expatriate-related institutions. Here, however, we focus on explanatory elements as they relate to the principle of sovereignty. Four possible explanations suggest themselves.

The first is the notion from modern political theory of popular sovereignty: that it is the people themselves who constitute the basis of sovereignty. If this notion is central to the legitimacy of the sending state, then the obligation to tend to the needs of those who may be within the political community but outside the territorial entity would seem clear. To lose contact could jeopardize the state's claim to authority, even at home. More generally, implicit in sovereignty, particularly since the emergence of the modern welfare state, is the state's obligation to "do its best for" its citizens[29] (a target of which many states, nonetheless, fall far short). Part of a state's power derives from how it is viewed both domestically and by other members of the international community; and part of its reputation – at least today – is based on how it treats its citizens, the services it provides and the rights it accords. If maintaining sovereign power involves protection of, or looking after, nationals, not just at home, but also abroad – what Krasner calls the "script of modernity, something that a modern state does,"[30] i.e., what evolving norms suggest they are supposed to do – then this would seem to constitute a basis for maintaining ties of protection and assistance. The extensive outmigration and enfranchisement abroad of a large number of citizens of a particular country may well brand the sending country as, at best, incompetent, and is likely an indicator of a lack of Krasner's domestic sovereignty, the public authorities' inability to exercise effective control.

Less straightforward, perhaps, but also important in this context is the image of the communities abroad in the eyes of their hosts. Are the immigrants socio-economically successful? Are they good residents/citizens of the host state? Do they project a positive image of the sending country? Sending-state prestige may be intimately bound up in the perceptions that serve as answers to these questions. To the extent that the sending state is capable of positively shaping the image of its nationals abroad, its own image may be enhanced. These considerations are all related to the moral (and perhaps the customary) bases of state authority.

A second explanation is related to history. Particularly where there has been regime change or transformation of the political system, the government may seek, in effect, to right the wrongs of the past. In other cases, where economic circumstances triggered the emigration, leaderships may feel a certain responsibility for not having been able to create jobs at home during an earlier period. In either case, reaching out to those who left may be a way of rehabilitating the state image both domestically and abroad, and of laying the bases for a new state–society relationship in the future. Again, to a certain degree, the state's moral authority is in question here.

Third is security. As noted in the previous chapter, expatriate communities have often been a source of agitation or support for opposition back

---

[29] Weiner uses this expression in "Ethics, National Sovereignty and the Control of Immigration," *International Migration Review*, 30 (1) Spring 1996: p. 171.

[30] Krasner, *Sovereignty*, p. 33. He uses this specifically in reference to states' willingness to sign conventions, defined as "voluntary agreements in which rulers make commitments to follow certain kind of practices involving relations between rulers and rules within their borders; commitments that are not contingent on the extent to which other signatories honor the same accord": p. 30.

home. Monitoring them may be part of a strategy of protecting the home front, part of the state's coercive authority. The fourth element – economic need and the desire to mobilize the resources of the communities abroad – was also discussed in chapter 1. Inyatullah has argued that sovereignty requires a right to wealth: projects that construct identities as states as well as express differences from other states require financial means.[31] In addition, of course, part of being sovereign involves creating wealth with one's own resources.[32] Those writing in the field of transnationalism would likely argue that certain actions by states of the global South toward their expatriates are part of a process of renegotiating their place in the international economy so as to increase revenues. Attempting to secure or increase remittance levels can easily be understood as part of this same process of trying to reinforce a state's economic sovereignty, an element related to strengthening both its moral (providing for welfare functions) and coercive authority. As Østergaard-Nielsen has noted, migration provides sending countries, particularly those "peripherally positioned in the global economy, with new options for reconfiguring the reach of the nation-state through transnational economic, social and political ties with nationals abroad."[33]

A final point that needs to be made here is that, regardless of the source of the impetus to establish such institutions, there is the question of state capacity. The nature and extent of available resources – human, material and bureaucratic – will enable or constrain the state in its efforts. If a state is weak, financially strapped or lacking trained cadres, it will be in an inferior position in trying to build ties with its expatriate communities, regardless of the need they may fulfill.

These are the major factors shaping sending states' desire to continue to assert sovereignty over their nationals abroad. Nevertheless, the home state does not act in a vacuum. An additional consideration – the sovereign prerogative of the receiving state – will certainly shape sending-state actions. For example, why and to what extent may receiving states allow their territorial sovereignty to be infringed upon by sending states that seek increased involvement with their expatriates? A related question concerns what steps the host states themselves may take in response – either in defense of their sovereignty or in deference to this apparent evolution in the practice of sovereignty.

---

[31] Naeem Inyatullah, "Beyond the Sovereignty Dilemma," in Biersteker and Weber, pp. 51–2.

[32] Ibid., p. 59.

[33] Eva Østergaard-Nielsen, "The Politics of Migrants' Transnational Political Practices," *International Migration Review* (*IMR*) 37 (3) Fall 2003: p. 767.

In answer to the first question, it must be stressed that the establishment of foreign, government-sponsored institutions seeking to serve diaspora communities has not been uniformly welcome. As we will see in the case of Lebanon, even the quasi-statal Lebanese World Union had to add "cultural" to its title to make its activities among the large Lebanese community in Brazil acceptable to the Brazilian government, while some countries – usually, but not always more authoritarian in nature – simply refused to allow branches to be established. Not surprisingly, concern over such institutions' infringement upon sovereignty through their engagement in political activities has been the most basic objection of receiving states. In some instances, institutions have been granted permission to operate, but only from the grounds of the embassy or consulate, thus limiting them to areas already legally recognized as territory of the sending state. In other cases, however, shared host-state–sending-state interests in issues that may broadly be defined as security-related have led to concessions. For example, initially as a way of trying to ensure that the immigrants would be prepared to return home rather than remain long-term, several European states cooperated with North African governments in instituting Arabic language and culture classes for expatriate children.

The political system in the host states is a key variable here. Because of traditions of freedom of organizing and expression, democratic host states would be loathe to circumscribe initiatives among immigrants to organize – whether in NGO or political party form – as long as such institutions did not pose a security threat to the state. The United States, for example, allows some institutions registered as agents of foreign governments to operate within its borders. The USA also, like many European states, allows residents to engage in a variety of forms of political fundraising and politicking aimed at the countries of origin. While not all countries are this open, at least among the world's democracies historical traditions of participation and equality, along with the forces continuing to militate for their expansion at least in theory, make such states more open to accepting immigrant activity in the framework of institutions formally or informally sponsored by other states.[34]

Some receiving states have devised policies intended to address various aspects of the complicated question of what is inside or outside the polity. For example, a number of European states have accorded long-term resident, non-national communities sets of less than full citizenship rights

---

[34] For a discussion of the case of Turks in Germany, see Nedim Ögelman, "Documenting and Explaining the Persistence of Homeland Politics among Germany's Turks," *IMR* 37 (1) Spring 2003: pp. 163–93.

in the economic, social, but especially the political, realm. In this way, denizens, as they were termed,[35] were not fully excluded from the polity for lack of full citizenship, although neither were they fully incorporated. Soysal's argument was that this "solution" constituted a new form of membership whose emergence was a result of changing international norms about human and immigrant rights.[36] Her view of these developments as the harbinger of even greater positive transformations in the making seems to have been overtaken by anti-immigrant backlash, and, in any case, they were clearly specific to the European Union experience. Nonetheless, they are worth considering in the context of possible steps states may take that modify or, as Joppke terms it, "self-limit" sovereignty[37] as they attempt to address the demise of a clear boundary-based distinction regarding who is considered to be inside or outside the political community.

Part of what is at work here is the result of the spread of norms related to human, and especially immigrants', rights, thanks to the work of a variety of non-governmental and transnational organizations. It may also be that the provision of some rights and benefits to long-term non-citizen residents constitutes part of the struggle by receiving states to preserve sovereignty and to maintain order in circumstances of increased migration and movement. That is, the drive to reassert sovereignty, combined with the desire for social peace and order, has led some states to offer denizens benefits and/or rights that were traditionally associated only with citizenship. This kind of inclusion, however limited, reduces the impact of at least some of the elements that may lead to immigrant marginalization. At the same time, it does not challenge the sending state's "right" to these people in its most basic manifestation, that of citizenship.

Dual citizenship, dual nationality

The Westphalian principle of sovereignty preceded the development of modern notions of citizenship. Nevertheless, modern conceptions of citizenship may be traced to two basic understandings that developed in the classical period. According to the Greek model, citizens were free men

---

[35] See Hammar, "State, Nation and Dual Citizenship," in Brubaker, *Immigration*.
[36] Soysal.
[37] Joppke, ch. 8. He rejects the notion that such changes have been triggered from outside by the forces of globalization, hence constituting further evidence of the decline of the state. Instead, he argues forcefully for the internal origins, through existing liberal traditions in the USA, as well as Germany, Britain and other European states, of changes in laws that have led to greater incorporation of immigrants and refugees.

who participated in the public life of the polis. Indeed, the work of non-citizens (women and slaves) in the private sphere in effect enabled the male citizens to have sufficient time to be involved in the public sphere. The most important element of this Greek model for our purposes is that it implied *active participation* as part of a community of citizens. The second type of citizenship, which developed under the Roman Empire, was quite different. Instead of providing for participation in decision-making, citizenship became a legal status that afforded the citizen protection from the emperor and arbitrary rule. Roman citizenship was defined, not by the right to participate, but by the right to be a proprietor.[38] These two conceptions correspond roughly to what have been referred to, depending upon author, as participatory versus formal, democratic versus passport, or republican versus liberal, citizenship today.

With the emergence of the modern nation-state, individual polities have determined how membership in the community and hence eligibility for citizenship (as well as losing it) are governed. The two most basic principles have been *jus sanguinis* (citizenship that is passed along according to blood line, often only of the father, but in some countries of either parent), or *jus soli* (citizenship that is obtained by virtue of birth in a particular territory). A basic division can be observed between countries that tend to export large numbers of emigrants, like those covered in this work, whose laws are generally based in *jus sanguinis*, and settler colonial countries like the United States or Australia, where the law is generally a combination of *jus soli* and *jus sanguinis*.

The presence of large numbers of citizens abroad does not, in and of itself, challenge the rules according to which citizenship is awarded or maintained, the rights of expatriates to cross back and forth into the homeland, or the larger concept of border passage through the use of passports. However citizenship may be obtained and whatever effective content it may have (participatory or mere formal membership), it is still the state that controls such laws as one of its sovereign prerogatives: "Nationality is a legal–political category that constitutes the most basic legal nexus between an individual and a state. It involves a reciprocal relationship, obligating a state to protect the individual and investing that individual with allegiance to the state";[39] "The 'classic' view is that

---

[38] See J. G. A. Pocock, "The Ideal of Citizenship since Classical Times," in Gershon Shafir (ed.), *The Citizenship Debates* (Minneapolis: University of Minnesota Press, 1998), pp. 31–41.

[39] T. Alexander Aleinikoff and Douglas Klusmeyer, "Plural Nationality: Facing the Future in a Migratory World," in Myron Weiner and Sharon Stanton Russell (eds.), *Demography and National Security* (New York: Berghahn Books, 2001), pp. 154–55.

individuals swear allegiance to a sovereign and in return the sovereign provides protection to its citizens and subjects, including those who live abroad."[40]

According to Westphalian theories of the sovereign state, multiple ties of loyalty have been unthinkable, nor could one transfer allegiance from one sovereign to another. Therefore, clearly, dual citizenship was to be avoided

in order to protect the unity, cohesion, and strength of the state ... The people of a state consists of the sum of all the citizens. The territory of the state is their territory; indeed, the state itself is their state ... Traditional theories of constitutional government and democracy presume that there is no significant incongruence between this people and the actual population living in the country.[41]

Moreover, "To be a citizen is not simply to be assigned in a purely neutral way to one state or another. It is to be – or to be presumed to be – engaged on the side of one particular state in its latent or manifest conflicts with other states. Citizenship involves loyalty to the state."[42] As late as 1930, the Hague Convention[43] reconfirmed the traditional view that nationality should be singular.

While the actual laws affecting the administration of citizenship fall under Krasner's field of domestic sovereignty, their implications for the control of the flow of people certainly affect interdependence sovereignty as well as international legal sovereignty, to the extent that passports are recognized as providing for legal entry and exit. However, in the context of this discussion of expatriates, perhaps the most important component of citizenship falls under both Krasner's Westphalian and his domestic sovereignty categories, as the former implies the exclusion of external actors from domestic authority structures, and the latter derives from the ability of public authorities to exercise singular control within the borders of their polities.[44]

Proponents of dual nationality argue that "in an increasingly mobile and interdependent world, the strict policing of the demarcations of national membership seems increasingly futile and counterproductive"; "dual nationality is simply the recognition of a changing world" and "can be a means to reconcile memberships in both the countries of residence

---

[40] Myron Weiner and Michael S. Teitelbaum, *Political Demography, Demographic Engineering* (New York: Berghahn Books, 2001), p. 81.
[41] Hammar, "State, Nation and Dual Citizenship," in Brubaker, *Immigration*, p. 87.
[42] Ibid., p. 85.
[43] The International Convention on Certain Questions Relating to the Conflict of Nationality Laws, 12 April 1930.
[44] Krasner, *Sovereignty*, p. 20.

and of origin."[45] Ole Waever has gone as far as to claim that, at least in the EU context, increasing acceptance of dual nationality represents "a collective redefinition of sovereignty."[46] From the perspective of the migrant, securing a second nationality facilitates residence and movement, opens new economic opportunities, secures greater participation rights, and lays the basis for a fuller identification with the host society while preserving some ties with the sending country. However, from the perspective of the receiving state, hosting significant numbers of nonnationals or dual nationals in the context of home state involvement in their affairs would seem potentially to violate both Westphalian and domestic sovereignty. For, unless the activities of the sending state are minimal or outlawed, how could one continue to argue that "the domestic political authorities are the *sole* arbiters of legitimate behavior"?[47]

Bauböck argues that the tolerant attitude of increasing numbers of countries toward dual nationality derives from their understanding of its value as primarily symbolic.[48] Yet, if contentions that dual nationality is symbolic or a mere convenience are true, how then are we to understand, for example, the Iraqi-American who voted in Iraq's January 2005 elections, the Indian-American who contributes to the BJP (Bharatiya Janata, the Hindu nationalist party), or the Mexican-American who sends her extra earnings back to her home village through a PRI (Partido Revolucionario Institucional) organized community-of-origin club? These are far from merely symbolic activities. While none of these people is breaking the law, their actions demonstrate that their sense of political community is not fully encapsulated, nor can it be fully expressed, in the country of residence, which may or may not be the country of sole citizenship. The emergence of such multiple ties of political loyalty would seem to take us back to the pre-sovereignty, pre-Westphalian system.

An argument based in Westphalian exclusivity would militate either for complete exclusion of the outsider or for a rather liberal policy of enfranchisement so as to remove the anomaly of the "outsider within," but states have a range of reasons for resisting such approaches. First of

---

[45] Michael Jones-Correa, "Under Two Flags: Dual Nationality in Latin America and Its Consequences for Naturalization in the United States," *IMR* 35 (4) Winter 2001: p. 1014.

[46] Ole Waever, "Identity, Integration and Security: Solving the Sovereignty Puzzle in E.U. Studies," *Journal of International Affairs* 48 (2): pp. 417–18.

[47] Jones-Correa, p. 1014, emphasis added.

[48] Indeed, he contends that "apart from the right to return, most of the other external citizenship rights of dual nationals can be deactivated": Bauböck, "Towards a Political Theory of Transnationalism," p. 715.

all, near blanket exclusion implies a political, economic and cultural isolation of the immigrant that virtually all countries today eschew. Its practice in the past was limited to some of the most repressive of states, since only through substantial coercion could such a policy be maintained. As for the more liberal policy, it, too, is clearly problematic, for awarding citizenship does not solve the problem of dual loyalty or dual jurisdiction. If an individual takes a second citizenship, s/he in effect is expected to be loyal to both states just as s/he enjoys rights and responsibilities in both. As opponents of dual nationality have argued, depending upon circumstances, such rights/obligations may be impossible to fulfill or may even come into conflict. Similarly, now two states have obligations to this person: which takes priority? Which state is responsible if the person encounters difficulties or violates the law? States' laws on dual nationality are not uniform, and in any case, are changing, but traditionally, most states have not permitted dual citizenship: in keeping with Westphalian exclusivity, a national of country X had to give up his/ her citizenship (or would be stripped of it) upon acceptance of citizenship in country Y.[49]

Another reason why dual nationality can be problematic derives from the potential negative reaction from the sending state, whose sovereign claim of allegiance from the expatriate is undermined by the offer of citizenship. For the sending state, therefore, one way to try to normalize the situation of having large numbers of nationals with (or with the option of) dual citizenship living abroad is to make them *more* a part of the inside, rather than in effect relinquishing them to the host state. In attempting to maintain control over its nationals, the sending state in effect seeks to expand the boundaries of its extraterritorial activity to reimpose some elements of domestic sovereignty over its nationals abroad. As Aleinikoff and Klusmeyer have noted, countries of immigration such as the USA "have the strongest interest in encouraging the effective transfer of allegiances from former homelands to the new countries of permanent residence," whereas the countries of origin have "traditionally shown the strongest interest in preserving ties of affiliation with their emigrant nationals."[50] Given current levels of mobility and migration, sending states may increasingly find it in their interest to recognize a second nationality for their emigrants rather than risk alienating them through

---

[49] For a discussion of changing state practices and the evolution of international norms regarding dual nationality, see Rey Koslowski, *Migrants and Citizens: Demographic Change in the European State System* (Ithaca: Cornell University Press, 2000), ch. 7.

[50] T. Alexander Aleinikoff and Douglas Klusmeyer, "Plural Nationality," in Weiner and Russell, p. 161.

laws that insist that adoption of a new nationality nullifies their original citizenship. In such cases, some sending states may opt to permit dual nationality, but not dual citizenship, meaning that many rights are preserved, but that political participation would not automatically be one of them.

A third problem with dual citizenship as an answer to the problem of encroachment upon domestic sovereignty is the well-known and well-publicized fear in some receiving countries that a large-scale inclusion of "the other" will constitute a threat to the identity of the national political community. Current examples in Europe and the United States make clear that socio-economic and cultural differences between immigrants and the host societies have rendered the prospect of terminating the immigrants' outsider status through full enfranchisement unacceptable to significant parts of the host state citizenries. In this light, concessions short of citizenship – the denizen status discussed above – may be seen as promoting a particular notion of state security: the sense of marginalization among immigrants and the consequent possibilities of societal conflict are thereby reduced, but the question of a fundamental reconstruction of the identity of the nation is not posed.

Sovereignty and the cases to come

All four of the countries examined in the following chapters experienced external imperial control in the form of the Ottoman Empire and/or direct European colonization in their pre-independence periods. All four have also struggled with economic solvency, with only Lebanon escaping the implementation of an IMF-designed program of structural adjustment. Indeed, in all four, the early stages of emigration were indicators of serious imbalances in their domestic economies, just as migrant remittances gradually assumed greater and greater importance in the sovereign task of generating wealth. In these respects none of the four differs substantially from others of the developing world that have struggled to assert sovereignty in the wake of colonial withdrawal.

Internal security challenges have also marked their histories, but to quite different degrees. Tunisia has experienced a number of incidents of domestic unrest in the form of riots and a military mutiny, and Morocco witnessed two high-profile assassination attempts against Hassan II as it combated armed revolt in the early 1970s, but these challenges to their domestic sovereignty did not play a significant role in the evolution of emigration (although opposition to the regimes did find support in the communities abroad). In this respect the two North African countries' experiences depart markedly from those of Lebanon and Jordan. Jordan lost effective sovereignty over the West Bank (into which the Israeli military had previously made periodic raids) to Israeli occupation in 1967; it experienced continuing Israeli military assaults against the East Bank from 1967 through 1971; and it suffered a multi-episode civil war from 1970 to 1971. Lebanon's case is even more extreme, as it suffered two civil wars, one in 1958 and the other spanning the period 1975–90. Moreover, beginning shortly after independence, Lebanon became the terrain on which larger inter-Arab, regional and East–West rivalries were contested. Examples of outside intervention were lethal and legion: US marines in 1958; the arrival and development of the PLO (1971–82); Israeli invasions in 1978 and 1982; Syrian interventions in 1975, 1976 and as "peace keepers" according to the Ta'if accords following the civil war in 1990; Iranian presence and support for the Shi'i militia Hizballah in the 1980s; and an Israeli occupation of the south from 1982 until 2000. Clearly then, according to the criteria most commonly used to determine sovereignty, that of both Jordan and Lebanon has been *significantly* compromised over the years. As we shall see in the case studies that follow, the instability that has been both cause and effect has played a key role in triggering emigration and in shaping the respective states' responses to it.

Finally, there is the question of allegiance and national identity. In the cases of Morocco and Tunisia, although they have been independent states only since 1956, the sense of a shared identity anchored in the homeland (if not necessarily in the regime) is relatively strong. Tunisia is the most homogeneous and has the strongest sense of shared national identity. Moroccans also share an identity that places them in the Arab/Muslim world, but with strong connections to both Europe and Africa. That said, the divide between Arab and Berber remains – indeed, it is growing – and constitutes an important line of discrimination, if not disenfranchisement, that has had an impact on migration.

Nevertheless, one cannot compare the situation in Morocco to that in Lebanon or Jordan, in which communal divisions have figured prominently in domestic political and military struggles. In Jordan, it is the divide between Transjordanians and Palestinians, in which Palestinians have long felt the sting of second-class citizenship. In Lebanon the situation is even more complex, with seventeen official confessional groups whose relationship to the state and sense of attachment to it are conditioned by different understandings of what the identity and history of the polity are.

Thus, the case studies may be placed along a spectrum of the degree to which the state's authority is viewed as legitimate and nationals feel a loyalty to it, beginning with Tunisia, enjoying the most solid such base, and Jordan or Lebanon falling well toward the other end. While the impact of the degree of affinity and loyalty to the state is more difficult to measure than some of the other criteria that sovereignty comprises, consideration of it is nonetheless critical to a study of state institutions seeking to work with or through communities of nationals (and their descendants) who live in other cultures and may have access to rights and privileges that compete with those available in the state of origin.

Many of the issues raised by dual nationality or dual citizenship – political rights, conscription, taxation, and property rights – can be and have been addressed by bilateral treaties over the years between sending and receiving states.[51] Such regulation is not insignificant, and provides another example of the sovereign state's response to challenges to its realm. However, the larger issue here, and, therefore, the challenge for all parties – the sending state, the receiving state and the peoples involved (migrants, home state nationals and host state nationals) – continues to be (whether and) how to (re)define the bases – territory, identity, citizenship – of national membership, a basic component of sovereignty. According to Doty, "When it is no longer clear who makes up the nation, a state's internal sovereignty and the existence of the state itself is threatened. When the criteria for differentiating the inside of states from the outside become blurred and ambiguous, the foundational premise of state sovereignty becomes shaky."[52] Given the continuous re- and de-constructing of sovereignty over the years, it seems reasonable to conclude that the process through which this challenge to the inside–outside dichotomy regarding immigrant and emigrant communities is addressed will constitute an important step in the further evolution of the understanding and practice of sovereignty. It is to our four case countries' experiences with such issues that we now turn.

---

[51] See Jones-Correa. He notes that both US and international law "have evolved over the years in the direction of increased ambiguity or outright tolerance in favor of dual nationality": p. 1012.

[52] Roxanne Lynn Doty, "Sovereignty and the Nation: Constructing the Boundaries of National Identity," in Biersteker and Weber, pp. 122–23.

3   Morocco: expatriates as subjects or citizens?

Of the four countries covered in this work, Morocco's history as a distinct entity (as traced through its Alaouite monarchy)[1] is the longest and its experience with outside intervention the shortest. Unlike Tunisia, Lebanon and Jordan, it was never a part of the Ottoman Empire, and it was the last of the three to come under external control, succumbing for economic and political reasons to the imposition of a protectorate with French, Spanish and international zones in 1912. It secured formal independence in 1956 following an independence struggle that produced the bases of one of the few multiparty political systems in the region, just as it transformed Mohammed V, the grandfather of Mohammed VI, into a beloved national hero. A strong sense of national identity – at least among the elite and the city-dwellers – notwithstanding, Morocco entered the community of nations with a significant divide between rural and urban which coincided to a certain extent with that between Berbers[2] and Arabs.

Hassan II succeeded his father Mohammed V in 1962 and ruled until his death in 1999 using a governing formula that combined the traditional authority of religion (the royal family's claims to be from the line of the Prophet Muhammad), the power of the state apparatus with its attendant patron–client relations (called the *makhzen*), and at times brutal coercion. It was a formula that preserved the monarchy, but which did little to promote socio-economic development. Much of the kingdom's rural population lived in severe poverty and, even before independence, sought

---

[1] The Alaouites arrived in the southern part of the country (Rissani) in the 1300s from Arabia. They were formally invited by the people of Fez to take over the throne of Morocco in 1660. However, it was the second Alaoui ruler, Moulay Rashid (1666–72), who came to be known as the unifier of Morocco.

[2] While their origins are disputed, the Berbers are the descendants of the tribes living in North Africa before the arrival of the Phoenicians. Today, it is language which serves as the primary marker between Berber and Arab. The Berber language, which has several distinct dialects across North Africa, and which was acknowledged as a legitimate idiom by the state in the mid-1990s, is a distant cousin of, and hence quite distinct from, Arabic.

45

to escape its harsh living conditions by leaving for the cities or points beyond.

Official institutional involvement in emigration was initiated by Paris during the protectorate period, and was aimed at labor recruitment. Following independence, France (and later Germany and the Netherlands) continued, along with new Moroccan bureaus, to play an important role in this aspect of emigration policy. Not until Moroccan laborers and students became politically active in France in a way that had security implications for the Alaouite throne did Rabat move to establish institutions responsible for more than the worker placement aspect of expatriate affairs. The state's involvement then gradually expanded as the nature and future prospects (not to mention size) of the communities abroad also changed. Domestic political developments in France in particular, which challenged Hassan II's sovereign claim to the allegiance of his subjects abroad, triggered what became a series of bureaucratic moves that should be understood as part of the state's ongoing attempts to reinforce the boundaries of the national community by insisting upon the economic, political and cultural "Moroccanness" of those living outside the territorial frontiers of the kingdom.

The European context for immigration

Moroccan emigration to Europe began prior to the Second World War. Those involved were overwhelmingly of rural origin, and the large cities – Casablanca, Meknes and Rabat – usually constituted the first stop in a search for employment that generally ended beyond the Mediterranean.[3] Differing perceptions of the value of the outmovement were apparent from its beginnings. For example, as early as 1933, the Chamber of Commerce of Casablanca expressed concern about the "hemorrhage" that it felt the first migratory flows northward represented. On the other hand, with the pacification of Morocco still to be completed, the French résidence-générale took a more positive view of the emigration, considering each Moroccan who left as one less rifle that might be used against the European presence, as well as one less mouth to feed. An additional bonus, in the view of the French administrators, was the positive economic impact the money sent home by the emigrants would have on "pacifying" those who stayed behind.[4]

---

[3] Catherine Wihtol de Wenden, Les immigrés et la politique (Paris: Presses de Sciences Po, 1988), p. 140.
[4] Hassan Bousetta, "Comment Hassan II a organisé l'immigration des Marocains," Demain 68 15–21 June 2002: p. 9.

With independence in 1956, migration from the Rif (the northern region that had formed part of the Spanish protectorate and which had staunchly resisted the Spanish presence) was particularly encouraged, because of its reputation for both opposition and limited economic possibilities.[5] Indeed, the Rif and Souss (the southern area around Agadir), both Berber areas referred to as '*le Maroc inutile*' because of their marginal agricultural value, became the largest sources of migrants. Rifans headed overwhelmingly to Germany, Belgium and the Netherlands, whereas Soussis went largely to France.[6]

The first generation of migrants, that of the 1970s, was marked by labor struggles, an identity of "immigrantness" (*l'immigritude*), and an orientation toward the countries of origin. During this period, it was French support organizations and foreign associations, not the Moroccan state, that demanded and fought for immigrant rights. There were also extramunicipal consultative commissions of migrants and organizations established in opposition to home state structures, some of which were close to French labor unions or to opposition parties in the home country. Following the establishment of the first Secretariat of State for Immigration in 1974 the French government in effect mobilized these associations as mediators between itself and the Maghrebi workers.[7]

France continued to be open to immigration until the oil price hikes of the early 1970s culminated in the embargo that accompanied the 1973 Arab–Israeli war. Even before the full dimensions of this crisis became clear, government discontent over the high levels of remittances transferred abroad led to the passage of a law allowing for family reunification in hopes that more francs would remain in France.[8] Subsequently, all Western European host states were forced to re-examine their policies of labor importing and, as a result, moved to close their borders to immigrant labor. In 1977, a scheme was introduced in France to provide financial inducements to immigrants to return home, but the state also began to deport workers without documents, moves which were met with

---

[5] The one product for which the Rif has become famous and which brings millions of dollars into the Moroccan economy is kif.

[6] Noureddine El-Aoufi, "Trajectoires et regulation de la politique d'émigration," in Kacem Basfao and Hinde Taarji (eds.), *L' Annuaire de l'émigration marocaine* (Rabat: Fondation Hassan II pour les Marocains Résidant à l'Etranger, 1994) – hereafter, *AEM* – pp. 590–91.

[7] Catherine Wihtol de Wenden and Remy Leveau, *La bourgeoisie: les trois âges de la vie associative issue de l'immigration* (Paris: CNRS Editions, 2001), pp. 8, 16, 19.

[8] However, instead, the additional family members (notably wives) in some cases then took jobs themselves, driving up remittance levels even further. Interview with Fouad Isma'il, Director of Marketing, Banque Populaire (al-Bank al-Chaabi), Tangiers, 28 June 2000.

a wave of hunger strikes. Worse, migrants were publicly labeled a social problem, which then fueled racism and led to increased attacks on North Africans.[9] Nevertheless, no mass exodus ensued. In 1969 Algerians, Moroccans and Tunisians in France had numbered 608,000, 143,000, and 89,000 respectively (26.4 percent of the foreign population). By the end of 1981, their numbers were 817,000, 444,000 and 193,000 (34.4 percent of the foreign population).[10]

Immigrant rights finally emerged as an electoral issue in France in 1981 when the Socialist Party platform included a plank to grant long-term residents municipal voting rights, a new form of greater, if partial, inclusion. Not surprisingly, many French objected to the granting of such rights. More interesting, particularly in the context of considering challenges to sovereignty, both the Moroccan and Algerian governments opposed the participation of their citizens in French elections.[11] In the end, upon assuming the reins of government, the party retreated from this position on the grounds that such an innovation would have necessitated constitutional amendments.

More important for the long term was the law of 9 October 1981. Prior to its passage, according to a decree of 1939, all foreign associations had been required to obtain prior authorization from the Ministry of the Interior, and numerous associations of immigrant workers had therefore been denied authorization. Moreover, the fact that their authorization could be withdrawn at any time exposed some associations to police harassment and threats of dissolution. The 1981 law, which lifted all restrictions on foreigners' rights of association and put them under the jurisdiction of the common right of associations (regulated by Law 1901), marked a turning point for France, for immigrant groups, and for immigrant associations and their relationship with the home country. Legislation of this type had been one of the basic demands of the young of the immigrant communities and their supporters,[12] and this new law opened the way for a second generation of associational development, not only of a secular nature, but also of religious organizations, the importance of which we will consider below. The law's passage was accompanied by attempts by the government and the political elite to institutionalize ethnic/communal collective expression in secular and

---

[9] Stephen Castles, *Here for Good: Western Europe's New Ethnic Minorities* (London: Pluto Press, 1984) p. 53.

[10] Ibid., p. 55.

[11] Mark J. Miller, "Political Participation and Representation of Noncitizens," in William Rogers Brubaker (ed.), *Immigration and the Politics of Citizenship in Europe and North America* (New York: University Press of America, 1989), p. 132.

[12] Wihtol de Wenden and Leveau, p. 7.

republican forms aimed at renewing citizenship around such themes as anti-racism, cultural diversity and multiple citizenship. The law also sought to create new electors and mediators capable of responding to the rise of both the nativist Front National and the violence in the heavily immigrant suburbs (*banlieues*).[13]

It has been argued that it was precisely this legal change that created the Beur movement,[14] which reached its apogee between 1983 and 1993. Among the young Beurs, the impossibility of assimilation or their rejection of it led them to search for a cultural and political identity distinct from that of their parents, all the while intent upon preserving the advantages they enjoyed in France. Their refusal to accept the living conditions of their parents raised concerns in a society that, regardless of the recent changes, was not yet ready to accept them on a different basis. The economic woes of the heavily immigrant suburbs of Paris, Marseille and Lyons at the beginning of the 1980s, as well as the numbers involved – 2.2 million if one includes those of foreign origin 26 years of age and under in 1980 – torn by dual nationality, the inadequacy of educational institutions, and residential ghettoization, only exacerbated the problem. The bases for a new militancy had been laid, and the principal instrument of the new generation was the freedom of association acquired through the 1981 law.[15]

Two of the most important organizations that emerged shortly thereafter were SOS Racisme and France-Plus. But the real launching of the Beur movement can be traced to the march for equality against racism of December 1983, for none of the other important immigrant communities – the Portuguese, Italians, Spaniards or Africans – were present in large numbers. At the same time this march marked a break with the activists of the first generation and, more or less, with the countries of origin as well. The movement's reference points were less and less the past and more and more the future.[16]

By the 1990s, the third associative generation had developed, one that, by virtue of length of residence, had a different educational and professional profile than the two previous generations. A small political-economic or economic-cultural elite of merchants and entrepreneurs emerged symbolizing the image of success and upward mobility. This group sought a synthesis between community-based identification and

---

[13] Ibid., p. 10.
[14] The term "Beur" comes from French slang for the word "Arabe." However, it gradually entered into common usage, hence the title of the Wihtol de Wenden and Leveau book, *La beurgeoisie*. It refers specifically to Arabs of North African, rather than Middle Eastern, origin.
[15] Ibid., pp. 24–26.　　[16] Ibid., pp. 34–37, 45, 59.

association on the one hand, and individual integration on the other. Their religious education was rather weak, but they felt drawn by Islam and the Arab–Islamic world, even if they seldom knew classical Arabic and often spoke Berber better than a dialect of Arabic. Culturally, they found themselves opposed to both the outdated conception of the émigré oriented toward the country of origin, and to the "right to difference" that was stressed at the beginning of the 1980s. Their objective was a convergence of cultures, the creation of a social tie that would serve as a bridge between Europe and North Africa.[17] While this did not offer the sending states the opportunity to reassert their claims to and over the immigrant communities in quite the same way as in the past, it did provide an opening for a reconstructed form of belonging which involved elements of the state's sovereign interest.

Other countries of Western Europe

The beginnings of North African migration to the Netherlands, Germany and Belgium date to the 1960s, while in the cases of Italy and Spain, the population movement is even more recent. Thus, North Africans may be considered part of the second wave of migration, gradually supplementing or replacing laborers of Southern European origin. Nonetheless, regardless of host country, their migration was viewed as temporary, and hence it was their status as workers, and not potential members of the community, that underpinned the various bilateral labor accords that were concluded.

As in France, the economic crisis that began in 1973 also led these countries to put a brake on labor recruitment from outside the European Community. In some cases incentives were offered to immigrant workers to return home, but, at the same time, most states followed a fairly liberal family reunification policy. Thus, despite efforts to decrease the immigrant presence, by the late 1970s, the numbers of immigrants resident in Europe were actually growing, and the North African presence was increasingly family-based, with all that that meant for new political, socio-economic and cultural challenges related to identity, integration, and to the development of a second (and subsequent) generation.

In the case of the Netherlands, the recognition of the long-term character of immigration came later (1980) than in France, but led to the implementation of a coherent policy adapted to an immigration of settlement. Initially, the immigrant groups were referred to as ethnic minorities

---

[17] Ibid., pp. 84, 90–91.

(a term that was later replaced by *allochtones* – "those born elsewhere") and were considered to be like other groups who sought to integrate into Dutch society.[18] In 1984, in the name of a policy toward minorities, the government created a consultative body in which representatives of different minority communities held seats and which the government was obliged to consult on anything related to minority policy.[19] The new approach involved some measures to preserve elements of immigrant identity, including, for North Africans, the introduction of Arabic language as a regular part of the academic day in primary and secondary schools.[20] It also included a number of denizenship-related elements: the right to vote in municipal elections (granted in 1985 to non-Dutch residents with valid residence permits and five years' residence), the right to associative life, and socio-economic rights such as housing, education, work, and social security.

Beginning in 1986, non-Dutch citizens became eligible to run in municipal elections, and it was hoped that this would lead to a larger participation of eligible immigrants. That year, forty *allochtone* candidates were elected, although none were Moroccan, and the community's participation level was quite low. Indeed, an air of distrust pervaded Moroccan–Dutch relations during the 1980s. The Dutch looked unfavorably on the activities of the *amicales*[21] (see below), which were considered forms of home state control and intimidation. For their part, the Moroccans were suspicious that the Dutch wanted to assimilate them, for they refused active Moroccan participation in Arabic language instruction and insisted upon the application of Dutch law in personal status matters (matters governed largely by *shari'a*, Islamic law, in Morocco).[22] Another aspect of Dutch policy was to facilitate the acquisition of Dutch citizenship, while not obliging the person to renounce his/her nationality of origin: by 1994, more than 30,000 had exercised this option.[23]

For its part, Belgium moved to terminate non-EC worker immigration in 1974, but the ban took time to become effective, and significant clandestine immigration continued until 1976.[24] At approximately the same time, the state recognized Islam on a par with other religions, an indication that the authorities understood that the Muslim community

---

[18] Zoubir Chattou, *Migrations marocaines en Europe: le paradoxe des itinéraires* (Paris: L'Harmattan, 1998), pp. 108–9.

[19] Paul Brasse, "Participation politique: un test pour l'intégration," in *AEM*, p. 502.

[20] Herman Obdeijn, "Hier travailleurs invités, aujourd'hui citoyens," in *AEM*, p. 490.

[21] These "friendship" associations, built on the Algerian model, constituted the first generation of home-state-sponsored institutions.

[22] Obdeijn in *AEM*, p. 491. [23] Ibid. [24] Castles, p. 47.

was there to stay;[25] and, while restrictions on new immigration were tight, the policy toward family reunification was quite liberal.[26] In 1980, a new law granted foreigners the right to form political associations and demonstrate, as long as there was no challenge to the public order. Thus, again denizen-related rights were expanded, although naturalization remained highly restricted.

During the 1980s the North African (overwhelmingly Moroccan) presence elicited increasing negative reactions from Belgian society. It became a major issue in political debates, and consequently radicalized certain elements in the Maghrebi community. The rise of the extreme right (Vlaams Block) and a growth in racist crimes increased young Moroccans' desire for respect for and recognition of their culture. In response, in 1988–89 the state took a number of steps to address the problems associated with immigration: a royal commission for immigrant policy was created, charged with developing and implementing immigration policy; government measures, including easier access to Belgian nationality, were initiated; and regional policies were put in place aimed at various forms of integration or fighting against exclusion. Unfortunately, most of these measures were characterized by a lack of continuity: programs implemented in some areas were not extended to others, or were extended much later, thus indicating either differences of opinion on the initiatives or a lack of political will.[27] In May 1991, anger among Maghrebi youth erupted in riots in several parts of Brussels, the seriousness of which led the government to create a special fund to address a range of problems faced by immigrant youth.[28]

In the realm of representation and participation, foreigners with a valid work permit have since 1949 had the right to participate in committee or delegation elections at the factory / work establishment level. (In 1971, foreign workers also obtained the right to run in such elections.) In the second half of the 1960s, immigrant communal consultative councils were constituted in districts where there was a significant foreign worker presence and where the political powers were favorable to such a development. In this way, foreigners were offered a kind of participation in the context of laws that prevented anything more; at the same time, since such councils were seen as temporary, they were also understood as a kind

[25] Rashida Attar, "Après les Polonais, les Italiens, et les Grecs, les Marocains ..." in *AEM*, p. 21.
[26] Castles, p. 49.
[27] Pierre Blaise, "De l'immigration à l'intégration: l'évolution des concepts et des politiques," in *AEM*, pp. 23–24.
[28] Attar in *AEM*, p. 21.

of experiment or democracy training for those who were otherwise outside the political system.[29]

In the case of Germany, borders were also closed to non-EC workers in the wake of the oil embargo. At least initially, this led to a drop in the number of foreign workers from 2.6 million in 1973 to 1.9 million in 1976.[30] However, by the late 1970s, the numbers began to rise, owing to family reunification, workers remaining longer, and the emergence of a second émigré generation born in Germany.[31] Like its neighbors, Germany concluded that a long-term approach to immigration was needed. In 1977, while the government reiterated that Germany was not a country of immigration, provisions were made for the further integration of foreign residents who wished to remain. The most important of these was the granting of residence permits of unlimited duration after five years' stay. Nonetheless, concern regarding the immigrant population continued, and in 1982, with the coming to power of a right-leaning coalition, Chancellor Helmut Kohl emphasized restricting immigration and encouraging repatriation.[32] The possibility of naturalization, on the other hand, was beyond the reach or desire (as it required renunciation of existing citizenship) of the majority of immigrants until the change in German nationality law in January 2000.

As noted above, Italy was itself long a country of emigration, so it was not until the 1980s that immigration began to be an issue. Italian immigration law was a carry-over from the fascist period, but its non-application meant that clandestine immigration helped to provide industry with needed labor, while at the same time keeping the immigrants in a position of insecurity. In 1986 a new law recognized the rights of immigrants who were already employed, through regularizing their situation. However, since many employers were not keen to have their foreign workers employed legally, only about 100,000 immigrants took advantage of this opportunity. Given the failings of this law, in 1990 a second law (known as the Martelli Law) was passed, which sought to regularize those who had come illegally seeking political asylum as well as those who did not have regular jobs (small vendors, etc.). It is estimated that another 100,000 were regularized under these provisions, but this still left perhaps as many as 500,000–700,000 without papers. Italian policy continued to

---

[29] Pierre Blaise, "Participation politique: hors la naturalization, point de salut," in *AEM*, pp. 46–48.

[30] Castles, p. 42.

[31] Germany did not host a significant number of North Africans at this time. ("Africans" is an undifferentiated category in German statistics and accounted for only 1.7% (69,000) of the foreign population in 1974 and 2.7% (124,000) in 1982: ibid., p. 79.

[32] Ibid., p. 81.

lack coherence, vacillating between a tolerant and a hardline approach.[33] Between the passage of these two laws, the Maghrebi population in Italy increased dramatically. The numbers of Moroccans rose from 15,705 in 1987 to more than 98,000 in 1993.[34] The Tunisian/Algerian community grew from just over 3,000 in 1981 to just over 49,000 in 1993, and the Moroccan and Tunisian communities were among those who benefited most from the regularizations of 1986 and 1990.[35]

Like Italy, Spain had also long been a labor-exporting country. However, the hardening of immigration policies in other European countries, the end of Spanish emigration thanks to increasing economic development following Madrid's accession to the European Community in January 1986, and the absence of a Spanish border control policy before 1985 led to its gradual transformation from a transit into a migrant-receiving country.[36] The 1985 Ley de Extranjería ("Law on Foreignness") did not provide for equal treatment of foreigners and nationals, and participation in political life was conditioned by the principle of reciprocity. The law embodied an intent to defend the Spanish labor market through restrictions on entry into the country, but it also indicated a desire to integrate those whose situation was legal. Unfortunately, the integration thrust has failed to be realized in practice, and North African immigrants continue to live in largely marginal economic and social circumstances.[37]

In December 1990 Rabat and Madrid signed an accord which established the requirement that, as of March 1991, Moroccans would need a visa to enter Spain. Indeed, as of May 1991, all citizens of the Arab Maghreb Union states (Morocco, Tunisia, Libya, Algeria and Mauritania) needed visas for Spain, as part of Spain's preparations for entering into the Schengen group[38] on 25 June 1991. But not until two years later did immigration begin to play a more central role in Spanish national political debates. In the general elections of 1993 the center-right PP (Partido

---

[33] Alessandro da Lago, "Politiques migratoires: les lois Martelli," in *AEM*, pp. 396–97.

[34] Ottavia Schmidt di Friedberg, "Historique de l'immigration marocaine en Italie," in *AEM*, pp. 407–8.

[35] Francesco Carchedi, "Caractéristiques générales de l'immigration marocaine," in *AEM*, pp. 409–10.

[36] Chattou, p. 112.   [37] Ibid., p. 113.

[38] This treaty was first signed in 1984 by Belgium, the Netherlands, Luxemburg, Germany and France in order to accelerate the process of community integration in the area of borders, customs and the circulation of people. In June 1990 these same countries adopted a convention applying the original accord, the content of which had three major parts: border control and circulation of people, regulations regarding visas, and rights to asylum; police cooperation and shared information; and mutual aid in the area of international justice. Italy, Spain and Portugal signed on in 1991.

Popular) campaigned on a platform seeking a revision of the 1985 Ley de Extranjería in order to facilitate the expulsion of clandestines, whereas the PSOE (Partido Socialista) called for reform of the 1985 law, but in the direction of expanding residency permits. There was also discussion of control of the borders – whether it should be tighter or not – and of fighting racism. Most parties' programs also made some mention, whether openly or discreetly, of the threat to Spanish identity posed by non-European (and non-Christian) immigrants.[39] The potential for such feelings to explode into violence was manifested clearly in the riots against the Moroccan community in El Ejido in February 2000.[40]

It is worth noting that, in addition to labor conventions with France and Germany signed within days of each other in 1963, Morocco signed conventions with a number of other European states over the years as well. In 1969 a convention was signed with the Netherlands, which then opened an employment office in Rabat, although the economic slowdown in Europe led to its closing four years later. (The kingdom also signed a series of agreements with Arab states, largely in the 1980s, but Moroccan emigration to these states has never been of substantial size.) Various provisions for social security were covered in subsequent, separate accords, with France (1965), the Netherlands (1972) and Germany (1981), just as social security agreements were concluded with countries with which Morocco had no labor convention: Spain (1979), Sweden (1980), Denmark (1982), Italy (1994) and Canada (1998).[41] Finally, Morocco has signed a series of cultural accords with host countries regarding Arabic language and Moroccan culture instruction: Belgium (1975 and 1998), Spain (1980), the Netherlands (1983), France (1983, applied in 1990) and Germany (ratified in 1991).[42]

Thus, in sum, while European state and societal responses have not been uniform, several common strands are clear. First, state and NGO institutions were established whose function has been to protect immigrant human and other rights, particularly in the context of the rise of anti-immigrant racism. Second, a variety of fora have evolved to provide

---

[39] Carlos Celaya, "L'émergence de l'immigration dans la politique," in *AEM*, pp. 206–7.

[40] The riots, referred to by some as pogroms, were triggered by the murder of a Spanish woman by an apparently deranged Moroccan. The violence and destruction of property that ensued in the Moroccan community were widely covered in the Spanish press.

[41] Abdelkrim Belguendouz, *Les marocains à l'étranger: citoyens et partenaires* (Kenitra: Boukili Impressions, 1999), pp. 102–9.

[42] Ibid., p. 147. There are some agreements to include language and culture instruction in the formal curriculum, and there are other agreements to use educational facilities to provide instruction outside of normal class-room hours. In some cases, such as that of the Netherlands, the instructors are in large part Moroccan, responsible to the local community and the Dutch authorities, with Morocco paying neither salaries nor allowances.

for some degree of political participation, at least on the municipal level, just as a host of immigrant and host-state-initiated organizations have emerged to address various questions related to the immigrant presence. These institutions have accorded status approaching citizenship in some cases, while in others full enfranchisement has been possible. These attempts and the responses by the sending states should be understood as examples of evolving approaches to the challenge to identity and sovereignty posed by the "insider without" and the "outsider within."

The role of Islam

Although immigrant identity and its relationship to the sending country has been continually evolving, from the European point of view the primary defining characteristic of the Maghrebis has not been that they are Tunisian or Moroccan, but that they are Arab or, increasingly, with the rise of political Islam, Muslim.[43] As time has passed, and owing to changing conditions and length of stay, increasing numbers of these North Africans are also European citizens. As noted above, the Beur movement emphasized fighting racism and marginalization, but in a context in which assimilation was impossible. Indeed, by the late 1980s the movement's affiliated associations had made little headway in addressing the marginalization of immigrant youth. The ensuing credibility crisis left a gap that by the early 1990s began to be filled by organizations promoting the Muslim aspect of second-generation North African identity.[44]

It is not that Islamic organizations had not existed before; indeed, their origins may be traced to the mid-1970s and to the efforts of the first generation of immigrants, who at that time were bringing their families to join them in the context of family reunification programs. However, the Islam of the first generation appeared far removed from the challenges that immigrant children began to face as they grew up in the marginal conditions of the *banlieues*. A few religious activists of university age at the time sought to recruit student sympathizers who would return home after their studies and militate for the establishment of Islamic states. To these activists, the Beurs were lost to Islam because of their integration into French culture. However, in the mid-1980s some second-generation

---

[43] Although in countries where one community is far larger than the others, the term "Muslim" may become largely synonymous with the nationality: for example, Algerians in France or Moroccans in Belgium.

[44] Gilles Kepel, *Allah in the West: Islamic Movements in America and Europe*. Trans. by Susan Milner (Stanford: Stanford University Press, 1997), p. 175.

youth began attending mosques, and their numbers gradually began to grow.[45]

The year 1989 constituted a watershed for a number of reasons. First was the rise of the Front Islamique du Salut (FIS) as Algeria's one-party system began to unravel. The FIS's rapid development of hegemony over the Algerian religious field attracted the attention of all North African Muslims. Second, this was the year of the controversy over the wearing of the veil in a school in Creil, just north of Paris.[46] Islamist activists served as advisors to the parents of the pupils concerned, and it was the following year, at the congress of the Union of Islamic Organizations in France, that Rachid al-Ghannouchi, the leader of the Tunisian Islamist party al-Nahdah and its French networks, laid out the goal of re-Islamizing the populations of Muslim origin in France. The 1991 Gulf War only reinforced the growing sense of reconstruction of identity among the second generation.[47] Thus, like the host states, the Islamist organizations also came to the realization that these communities were in Europe to stay. Hence, they needed to be addressed with this in mind, and not in terms of preparing them ultimately to return to North Africa.[48] In this respect, as we shall see, the Muslim organizations did not differ significantly from the governments of the home states.

The growth in importance of an explicitly Muslim identity component has forced the long-term resident or enfranchised immigrants to confront the issue not only of how to be, for example, Muslims in France, but also of how to be Muslims *and French*,[49] although the Islamist alternative promoted by the FIS, as well as some other groups, was based in part upon a rejection of the West. For the Maghrebis in Europe, focusing on religious identity has proved one way to maintain integral ties with the society of origin, while reducing the dissonance of the increasingly common holding of two political identities. Part of the challenge involves training prayer leaders, imams, from within the European Muslim communities rather than relying on recruitment from abroad, the result of which in some cases has been the arrival of men unfamiliar with the country or the language and more inclined to extremism.[50]

Much of the writing on the Maghrebi communities in Europe addresses them under the general heading of "Muslims in Europe,"

---

[45] Ibid., pp. 150–51.   [46] Ibid.   [47] Ibid., pp. 152–53.

[48] W. A. R. Shadid and P. S. van Konigsveld, *Religious Freedom and the Position of Islam in Western Europe* (Netherlands: Kok Pharos, 1995), pp. 24–25.

[49] For detailed discussion of this problematique, see the works of Tariq Ramadan, among others, *To Be a European Muslim* (Leicester: Islamic Foundation, 1999).

[50] Elaine Sciolino, "Europe Struggling to Train New Breed of Muslim Clerics," *New York Times*, 18 October 2004.

instead of giving them separate treatment according to country of origin. Nonetheless, this literature also stresses the presence of many different nationalities and languages, not to mention the Shi'i–Sunni divide, among Muslims: one finds numerous references to the fragmentation of these communities and the consequent paucity of centralized bodies to serve as effective interlocutors with the state. Indeed, except where the numbers of Muslims are quite small, people tend to organize themselves ethnically for worship. In some cases, sending states have sought to provide imams to their own communities, owing in part to a desire to maintain ties with the emigrants but also in order to ensure that a religious line approved by the home regime – in terms of both politics and doctrine – is conveyed through Friday sermons.[51]

Césari argues that there is significant competition between ethnic and Islamic ties in Europe, and that it plays a large part in shaping cleavages among Muslim communities on the continent.[52] In France, competition between Moroccans and Algerians for control of mosques has been particularly clear, especially for the Paris Mosque, to which the French appointed an Algerian Director, Si Hamza Boubaker in 1957. Upon his retirement in 1982, despite the protests of the French and the Moroccans, he made sure that control passed to the Algerian government.[53] This competition has also played out in the Conseil Français du Culte Musulman (CFCM), founded by the French government in 2002 to provide a channel of communication with France's Muslim population. Since 2003 this body has been controlled by Muslims of Moroccan origin, but since his re-election in 2004 Algerian President Bouteflika has renewed Algiers's efforts to increase Algerian influence in the body. Unfortunately, while the states of origin jockey for position, the CFCM's ability to serve France's Muslims is compromised, and many young Maghrebis are in fact alienated by these North African states' attempts at asserting control.[54]

---

[51] Although not a source of emigrants, owing to its wealth and its identity as the origin of Islam and the keeper of its holy places, Saudi Arabia has also played a major role in supporting the construction of mosques, Islamic centers and schools in Europe. Indeed, countering Saudi influence among their expatriates is a central concern of some of these Muslim-majority sending states.

[52] Jocelyn Césari, *Être musulman en France: associations, militants et mosquées* (Aix-en-Provence: Karthala-IREMAM, 1994).

[53] See Jørgen Nielsen, *Muslims in Western Europe* (Edinburgh: Edinburgh University Press, 1992), p. 13. Nielsen notes that "while the mosque has sought to attain recognition as the general representative of Islam in France ... recognition by Africans other than Algerians has been ambivalent, while Turkish groups have tended to ignore it completely": p. 14.

[54] Jeremy Landor, "Hearts and Minds," *Middle East International*, 21 January 2005.

In sum, to understand the evolution of Moroccan emigration policy, a series of actors must be considered. Governmental policies of the European host states which offer citizenship or packages of rights just short of it have threatened to undermine Rabat's claim on the loyalty and resources of its nationals abroad. In addition, non-state actors in the form of NGOs have emerged within the host societies as well as within the emigrant communities themselves to respond to a range of expatriate needs left unfulfilled by both home and host state. Finally, also clearly competitive with the sending state for emigrant identification are Islamic or Islamist institutions offering a supranational identity which enables the Maghrebi emigrant to maintain the most basic elements of his/her cultural heritage, while at the same time holding European citizenship. In the context of an authoritarian home state whose policy long treated nationals abroad as simply subjects, these institutions have emerged as serious competitors in the struggle to redraw the lines of sovereign control over extra-territorial communities.

Moroccan state emigration policy

What is the record of the Moroccan state vis-à-vis its emigrants? A review of government documents reveals that, like their French colonial predecessors, in the early post-independence period Moroccan policy-makers saw a clear link between emigration and the regulation of the domestic labor market. Faced with growing unemployment, the government first moved to create the Bureau of Emigration in the Ministry of Labor and Social Affairs. This bureau had two objectives: to centralize offers coming from foreign countries and to propose recruitment zones; and to supervise the selection of workers according to both professional and health criteria. The actual recruitment was accomplished through the intermediary of placement bureaus (or local authorities in the administrative areas where there were no such bureaus), which selected candidates from among the registered unemployed. The Bureau of Emigration was also supposed to ensure the application of the labor power conventions concluded by the Moroccan government (beginning in 1963).

Morocco concluded its first labor conventions with Germany on 28 May 1963 and with France on 1 June 1963. In both cases, the need for miners was specified, while for France, other economic sectors, such as agriculture and metallurgy, were also mentioned. The conclusion of the convention with France was accompanied by the opening in Casablanca of a mission of the French Office National d'Immigration (ONI). The ONI then proceeded to recruit Moroccan labor for French factories according to two types of contracts: by name, when the employer requested a particular person; and anonymously, when solely the number of workers needed and the qualifications required were specified. While the economic value of such employment to both the worker and the kingdom should not be ignored, neither should the fact that the accords concerned the commercial/instrumental, not the human, value of the workers: no consideration was given at this stage to expatriate treatment or rights abroad.[55]

Not surprisingly, such conventions alone were incapable of solving the kingdom's problem of excess labor supply, and a reading of successive development plans demonstrates the state's continuing concern with (un)employment. The first such plan, the five-year plan of 1960–64, focused on the needs triggered by the then-recent independence (1956) and the departure of large numbers of French: finding sufficient numbers of trained cadres and developing integration among economic sectors became imperative.[56] To the extent that unemployment was discussed, it was argued that it needed to be solved through a policy of industrialization, spurred by domestic investment.[57] The only mention of related themes was that of the need to limit *im*migration – for at that time there was movement from an Algeria still in the throes of its independence struggle into the country – to those cases of workers for whom no qualified Moroccan alternative could be found.[58]

A few sources hint at how the regime dealt with emigration and border control outside the framework of formal conventions during this period, and they are instructive as well. Boukhari, for example, discusses how, beginning in 1961, the Moroccan security services worked with the Israeli Mossad to facilitate the emigration of Moroccan Jews. He describes Morocco at the time as a country in which the processes of obtaining a passport and the papers necessary to leave the territory were complex and intrusive. Moroccan Muslims had to prove they had a minimum income to obtain a passport, and a kind of security clearance was required before one was allowed to cross the frontier. Moreover, several levels were involved in the process: the provincial, to facilitate rapid delivery of passports; the *arrondissement* to obtain certificates of residence; the Sûreté Nationale to speed up the policy investigations; and the border police and customs services.[59] Obtaining a passport cost money and took

---

[55] El-Aoufi in *AEM*, pp. 590–91.
[56] Royaume du Maroc, Ministère de l'Economie Nationale, Division de la Coordination Economique et du Plan, *Plan quinquennal, 1960–64* (Rabat, 1960), p. 46.
[57] Ibid., p. 57.   [58] Ibid., p. 60.
[59] Ahmad Boukhari, *Le secret: Ben Barka et le Maroc, un ancien agent des services spéciaux parle* (Neuilly-sur-Seine: Editions Michel Lafou, 2002), pp. 111–12.

time, and could not be taken for granted. It was also a way for certain parts of the Moroccan administration to line their pockets. While the case of the Moroccan Jews was no doubt exceptional, Boukhari claims that General Mohammed Oufkir, and to a lesser extent General Ahmed Dlimi and Minister of the Interior Reda Guedira, pocketed several million dollars for the exit of some 120,000 Jews.[60] Bensimon argues that King Hassan was also a primary financial beneficiary, while his brother Moulay 'Abdallah (nicknamed "Sa Altesse 51%") skimmed a percentage for each departure, since it was transport owned by him that was used by the Jewish emigrants to depart the country.[61] The larger lesson is that passport issuance as part of emigration policy was characterized by extortion and corruption.[62]

To return to policy as expressed in official documents, it is not until the 1968–72 plan that one finds mention of a "temporary emigration policy" under the section on population.[63] Levels of remittances are not included in the accounts provided; however, the document does state that certain psychological and administrative factors had, so far, obstructed the extension of emigration. The plan called for a strategy of targeting other European, especially certain Mediterranean, countries, with the expectation of thereby triggering three results: a growth in foreign currency reserves, which were to help finance a part of domestic investment; employment for part of the population which could not be absorbed by the domestic market; and the development of a large group of nationals who would have acquired abroad professional qualifications favorable to the spirit of business and economic development.[64] In addition, a network of social attachés located at embassies and consulates was to be developed. The document states clearly that the objective was to achieve an augmentation in the number of workers abroad at the end of the five-year period.[65] However, nowhere in the document were the concrete steps needed to achieve these goals even discussed, much less decided upon.

At this stage the government was well aware of the contribution of the Moroccan worker abroad or TME (*travailleur marocain à l'étranger*), as he

---

[60] Ibid., p. 112.

[61] Agnes Bensimon, *Hassan et les juifs: histoire d'une émigration secrète* (Paris: Editions du Seuil, 1991), pp. 165–67.

[62] See also Omar Bendourou, *Le régime politique marocain* (Rabat: Dar al-Qalam, 2000), pp. 149–50.

[63] Royaume du Maroc, Premier Ministre, Ministère des Affaires Economiques du Plan et de la Formation des Cadres. Division de la Coordination Economique et du Plan, *Plan quinquennal, 1968–72*, Volume I (Mohammedia: Fedala, n.d.), p. 32.

[64] Ibid., p. 93.   [65] Ibid.

was then called,[66] and in response devised a number of institutional arrangements to capture remittances. During the early years of emigration, there was no real system in place to facilitate remittance transfers. At times people simply returned with francs in their pockets; at others, they sent money through the mail in "billets de poste."[67] To rectify this situation, in 1968 the Banque Populaire (BP) was charged by the state with organizing the repatriation of hard currency. This did not mean a monopoly: other banks such as the BMCE, BCM, and Wafa Bank were also involved, but it was the BP that opened offices on embassy or consular grounds, and hence it secured the lion's share. In 1968 the bank transfers of the Moroccan workers abroad represented only 8.7% of the total funds transferred from emigration. Ten years later these bank transfers accounted for more than 50% of repatriations. By 1988 it was 72%. BP's share of those transfers rose from 30% in 1970 to 77% in 1977. Other measures taken to encourage transfers were the development of correspondence banking between European and Moroccan banks and the state's tying of the exchange rate of the dirham to the franc.[68]

In the 1973–77 plan, one finds the first accounting of expatriate remittances, which are credited, along with tourism and export encouragement, with producing a positive balance of payments.[69] Indeed, under the category of private transfers, more than half the sums involved are attributed to MREs (*marocains résidant à l'étranger*).[70] The plan includes projections of the number of Moroccans likely to go abroad, with a goal of 155,000 expatriates by the end of the plan period (1977), although there is a clear admission that half that number might be more realistic.[71]

This plan was drafted prior to the European cutback in immigration, so the projections must be understood as the result of conditions prevailing in 1972. Given the positive outlook for Moroccan emigration to Europe

---

[66] The terminology used to refer to the emigrants changed over the years. This first appellation, TME, underlined the fact that it was primarily a community of workers abroad (before family reunification), and that these people were understood first and foremost to be laborers in the context of government policy.

[67] Isma'il interview.

[68] Groupe d'Etudes et de Recherches Appliquées de la Faculté des Lettres et des Sciences Humaines, "Etude des mouvements migratoires du Maroc vers la Communauté Européenne. Résumé du rapport final." Etude pour le compte de la Commission des Communautés Européennes 5 January 1992, pp. 75–76, 88.

[69] Royaume du Maroc, Premier Ministre, Secretariat d'Etat au Plan, au Développement Régional et à la Formation des Cadres, *Plan de développement économique et social, 1973–77*, Volume I (Casablanca: Dar El-Kitab, n.d.), p. 90.

[70] Ibid., p. 112. MRE, "Moroccan resident abroad," is the term that gradually replaces TME. At times one also finds RME – *resortissants marocains à l'étranger* – "Moroccan nationals abroad."

[71] Ibid., p. 122.

at that point, several measures were proposed. First was the development of emigration-related services in Morocco as well as a network of attachés abroad. (These social attachés had been discussed in the previous plan, so clearly little or nothing had been done on that front.) Second, social action to benefit the emigrants was to be reinforced through organizing activities for them, and through concluding labor accords with the countries that hosted them.[72] Third was the establishment of an Emigration Fund designed to assist emigrants by advancing them the cost of settling abroad.[73] This is all very interesting, and certainly represents a broadening of the range of Rabat's concerns, but there are not, in the sections of the documents that detail individual ministry expenditures, any line items for these things. Hence it is not clear whence the money was to come.

In 1974, during this plan period, Spain announced its intention to withdraw from what has come to be known as the Western Sahara, and in October 1975 Hassan II launched his famous Green March to assert Moroccan rights to the former colony. What ensued was increasing Moroccan military involvement in an armed conflict over the territory with the Polisario (Frente Popular para la Liberación de Saguía El-Hamra y Río de Oro). As a result, the economic strains on the Moroccan budget increased dramatically, giving the monarch all the more reason to be concerned with the state's ability to attract hard currency, from remittances or foreign investment. Yet it was precisely at this time that the slowdown in Europe came, and with it the virtual closing of the borders of the traditional recruiting states of Western Europe to foreign labor.

The long-term direct and secondary effects of such a dramatic change were not obvious at the time. Up to this point, Moroccan state officials had not yet realized (or acknowledged) that unemployment and emigration had become structural characteristics of the Moroccan economy. There had been no planning based on the possibility that the emigration would be long-term, but neither had policymakers contemplated an abrupt halt to recruitment. At the same time, as we saw above, European state policy virtually across the board shifted to encourage immigrant return, while allowing for family unification. Thus, circumstances quickly changed the relationship between Morocco and the host states from one of a certain confluence of interest, to one where, at least initially, Morocco's need to

---

[72] Belguendouz, "Les marocains à l'étranger," p. 83. In fact, in April 1976 a cooperation accord was signed by Morocco and the then EEC, recognizing certain rights for Moroccans in the member states: equality of treatment; the right to free transfer to Morocco of pension and/or retirement of the disabled or the deceased; the payment of family allowances for children, and so on.

[73] Royaume du Maroc, *Plan de développement économique et social, 1973–77*, Volume I, p. 123.

continue to alleviate unemployment at home clashed with a European state desire to close the doors to immigration and send many migrants home. These shifts begin to lay the basis for challenges to various aspects of sending- and receiving-state sovereignty that a long-term expatriate presence triggers.

While some immigrants took the financial incentives and returned home, the arrival of wives and children joining their husbands and fathers as part of family reunification provisions actually increased the size of the communities abroad. As a result, the composition of the communities also changed, as did their social, cultural, religious, linguistic, economic and educational needs, along with their "residence horizons," with the question of a second (and eventually a third) generation gradually posed. The character of the communities was being transformed, as were their relationships with the host states and societies as well as their ties of loyalty and affect to Morocco. That these developments should then serve as a trigger for changes from the side of the sending state as well should therefore not be surprising, for they posed a direct challenge to the Moroccan state's ability effectively to claim its subjects.[74] We will examine state institutional responses later in this chapter. However, in terms of the planning documents, there is no change in the state's view of MREs as *devisards*[75] or unemployment alleviators until the 2000–4 plan. Indeed, rather surprisingly, the 1978–80 plan makes only brief mention of TMEs, although it *is* of their remittance levels, for the period 1973–77.[76]

The 1981–85 plan, on the other hand, discusses the great importance of MRE transfers, and notes that, in the interest of encouraging them, a bonus was instituted by the banking system in July 1978.[77] It also voices particular concern over what it calls the "employment equilibrium." Given the retrenchment in Europe, there was concern that MREs might return to Morocco in substantial numbers and upset the balance. The plan therefore states that employment would occupy a privileged place in the economic and social development strategy.[78] It also notes that, although temporary emigration had increased, permanent emigration had become negligible. Greater efforts needed to be exerted in the realm of job creation domestically, and hence there is a strong focus on investment.[79]

---

[74] El-Aoufi in *AEM*, pp. 593–4.

[75] This term comes from the French "devise" or currency, implying that the basic worth of these people was their hard-currency-earning capability.

[76] Royaume du Maroc, Premier Ministre, Secretariat d'Etat au Plan, et au Développement Régional, *Plan de développement économique et social, 1978–80*, Volume I (n.p., n.d.), p. 128.

[77] Royaume du Maroc, Premier Ministre, Ministère du Plan et du Développement Régional, Direction de la Planification, *Plan de développement économique et social, 1981–85* (n.p., n.d.), p. 56.

[78] Ibid., p. 103.   [79] Ibid., pp. 231–22.

The years 1981–85 were particularly difficult ones for Morocco: drought increased food deficits and triggered further rural–urban migration; the price of phosphates, Morocco's most important export, tumbled; the war in the Western Sahara continued to take its toll; debt was rising; and, as a result, in 1983 the kingdom was forced to implement an International Monetary Fund(IMF)-dictated program of structural adjustment. As with other structural adjustment agreements, this one required serious belt tightening through reductions in state subsidies and other services as well as drastic cuts in domestic investment, a combination which had further negative effects on employment levels.

Given the dire state of the government's budget, the 1988–92 plan's note that domestic saving had financed 51% of investment in 1981–85 and 72.5% in 1986 *and* that the presence of sufficient domestic savings to finance such a large portion of investment had come through private sector, particularly MRE, resource mobilization, is not surprising.[80] The plan anticipated that MRE transfers would contribute significantly to keeping the current account in balance or in the black.[81] Thus, Morocco had reached a point at which the MRE contribution to the domestic economy had far surpassed solely domestic unemployment alleviation: remittances were now clearly understood to be a key factor standing between relative solvency and economic crisis.[82] (See Table 3.1.) As a result, asserting an effective sovereign claim on these resources also became critical.

In 1989 a new development bank, the Bank al-'Amal, was established, three-quarters of the capital of which was to be made available in shares to Moroccans working abroad to encourage more investment from the expatriate community.[83] In the meantime, the BP and its services expanded, so that in addition to the possibility of transferring remittances, it began to offer

---

[80] Kingdom of Morocco, Prime Minister, Ministry Attached to the Prime Minister's Office in Charge of Planning, Directorate of Planning, *Orientation Plan for Economic and Social Development, 1988–92* (Mohammedia: Imprimerie de Fedala, 1988), p. 46.

[81] Ibid., p. 123.

[82] Moustafa Kharoufi, "Les effets de l'émigration sur les sociétés de départ au Maghreb: nouvelles données, nouvelles approches," an article from *Correspondances, bulletin scientifique de l'IRMC*, from the website of l'Institut de Recherche sur le Maghreb Contemporain, www.irmcmaghreb.org/corres/textes/karoufi.htm, p. 5.

[83] Fadlallah Mohammed Fellat, "Le Maroc et son émigration," in *L'Annuaire de l'Afrique du Nord*, Volume XXXIV (Paris: CNRS, 1995), p. 988. Bank al-'Amal was also envisaged by Hassan II in 1990 as a new institution meant to serve exclusively the MREs, but the royal directives were not fully executed. It has a problem of hybridity, as the only "bank" aspect to it is its name. It does not receive deposits, nor is it a commercial bank. It has no presence in the host countries and, in Morocco, exists only in Casablanca. It is in effect simply an informal branch of the Bank al-Maghrib. (See Belguendouz, "Les marocains à l'étranger," p. 271.) Its administrative council still has *amicale* presidents as its representatives of the MRE communities.

Table 3.1. *Moroccan expatriate remittances (in millions of dirhams)*

Year	Amount	Percentage change
1975	2,159.6	38.7
1976	2,417.8	12.0
1977	2,652.1	9.7
1978	3,176.0	19.8
1979	3,696.5	16.4
1980	4,147.6	12.2
1981	5,242.0	26.4
1982	5,114.5	−2.4
1983	6,515.4	27.4
1984	7,680.9	17.9
1985	9,732.2	26.7
1986	12,730.6	30.8
1987	13,267.9	4.2
1988	10,700.4	−19.4
1989	11,344.1	6.0
1990	16,537.2	45.8
1991	17,328.1	4.8
1992	18,530.7	6.9
1993	18,215.9	−1.7
1994	16,814.4	−7.7
1995	16,819.9	0.03
1996	18,873.8	12.2
1997	18,033.4	−4.5
1998	19,161.6	10.6

Source: Royaume du Maroc, *Les Marocains résidant à l'étranger,* p. 188.

credit to invest, buy a house or an apartment; insurance and assistance in the event of road accidents (since problems on the road in Spain were common); and electronic banking. It further reinforced its presence with the creation of new delegations in Europe and two branches in France and Belgium, and each year it undertakes a campaign to present its products to MREs. As of 1999, it handled 60% of the total MRE transfers and disposed of 65% of MRE global resources collected by the national banking system.[84]

By the time of the 2000–4 plan it appears that the state had finally acknowledged the centrality of the MREs, as this document has the most serious and multi-faceted consideration of the expatriates to date. It first

---

[84] *La Vie Economique,* 14–20 May 1999, "SMAP 99" (special edition), p. 55.

notes some fluctuations in MRE transfer levels: from 1986 to 1992 transfers grew an average of 9.6% annually, whereas from 1993 to 1998, they grew only 2.1% annually.[85] Regardless of past fluctuations, the plan assumes that the transfers will continue and will keep the current account deficit low.[86] The document argues that the consolidation of relations between the MREs and Rabat contributed to the inflow of foreign currency, just as these ties have helped cement other forms of economic exchange between Morocco and the host countries. Given the importance of these relations, the plan's strategy calls for the creation of an emigration research unit to enable Morocco to understand emigration flows, to follow the development of MRE ties with Morocco, and to put in place a more dynamic policy regarding MRE savings, including simplifying investment procedures.[87] MREs now enjoy all the rights of citizens, but, because of their place of residence, they also enjoy the full range of facilities available to non-residents. As citizens they can hold title to internal accounts (*comptes intérieurs*), benefit from bank credits, invest with dirhams, etc. As non-residents they benefit from such advantages as the right to open accounts in convertible dirhams or in foreign currency, to invest in hard currency, and to transfer the revenues generated by these investments.

The real innovation of the 2000–4 plan, however, is found under the section "Sectoral Development, General Administration," where, for the first time, there is a separate section devoted to the MREs. This section in effect affirms state sovereignty over the MREs, by stressing that relations between what it calls the CME (*communauté marocaine à l'étranger*) and Morocco are very deep, and hence, implicitly unseverable. The CME remains deeply attached to its identity, the plan asserts. To preserve these ties, the government is to oversee efforts intended to reinforce that identity in order to avoid Moroccans' opting for integration into their host countries. Further, the nature of Morocco's relations with the host countries, notably those of the EU, is understood to depend at least in part upon the type of relations the kingdom has with the CME. The Ministry of Foreign Affairs and Cooperation (MFA) is thereby charged with overseeing the preservation of the rights and the interests of the CME, but also with consolidating their ties with Morocco. One objective for the planning period is, therefore,

[85] Royaume du Maroc, Ministère de la Prévision Economique et du Plan, Direction de la Programmation, *Le plan de développement économique et social, 2000–2004*, Volume I, *Les orientations et les perspectives globales de développement économique et social*" (Sale: Print-Diffusion, 2001), p. 73.

[86] An IMF report released in summer 2004 indicated that while remittances were equivalent to about 5% of GDP in the 1990s, more recently they have increased to represent 9% of GDP: "What Drives Remittances in Morocco?" *Daily Star* (Beirut), 29 July 2004.

[87] Royaume du Maroc, *Le plan de développement économique et social, 2000–2004*, p. 225.

to devote greater attention to things that affect MREs; to defend their rights and to preserve the lines of attachment/belonging to Morocco. A second is to work to associate the CME with the process of development and encourage its participation in financing social and economic projects in Morocco.[88] In this way, the Moroccan state is not only reaffirming its claim to the loyalty of its nationals abroad, but also laying claim to their resources as key to domestic development efforts.

There is also mention in this plan of the role of the Ministry of Human Rights (MHR). The document argues that the MHR gives MREs (which it calls *immigrés marocains à l'étranger*) particular attention through establishing relations of cooperation and dialogue with a range of actors, notably associations and NGOs, as well as government institutions in the host country. The principal objective has been to inventory the problems they face and the types of discrimination of which they are victim. The MHR has then sought to identify the best ways to defend them, to focus the attention of the host countries on these problems, and to concretize a policy of non-discrimination in the domain of human rights.[89] This document is thereby the first to treat MREs as full human beings and fuller citizens, in the sense of the state's manifesting a serious concern for their welfare and success. The state implicitly seems to have understood that for its call to maintain identity to generate a positive response, it must demonstrate its commitment to provide something akin to the protection or concern for its citizens that underpins the moral authority of the sovereign state.

There were in fact great hopes among some that, given the emigrant experiences of a number of members of the 1997–2002 government, including Prime Minister 'Abd al-Rahman Youssoufi himself, this team would formulate serious responses to MRE concerns. Youssoufi did establish an interministerial committee consisting of sixteen members (representing concerned ministries) to address the MRE issue. However, given that this committee met only once a year, its accomplishments were limited.

Summary

While the detailed consideration of institutional developments to come will provide an additional part of the story of emigration policy not included in the planning documents consulted for this section, the successive plans do provide important insights into state thinking. As the discussion shows, over time there was a gradual evolution in the state's

---

[88] Ibid., Volume II, "Le développement sectoriel," pp. 60–62.   [89] Ibid., p. 92.

view of the emigrants, from that of a Moroccan abroad as one less unemployed worker at home, to that of a contributor to the national economy, and finally that of a multi-faceted asset with economic, social and cultural ties to the kingdom. Given that these are economic development plans, one should expect their emphasis in the MRE domain to be on the emigrants' financial role and contribution, as opposed to other areas. Nevertheless, even here, the last plan indicates a clear shift in state thinking regarding the need to incorporate these workers as real (contributing) members of the polity as the state's need for them to generate economic wealth (a key element of sovereignty) increases. They thereby undergo a transformation from being expendable, minimally endowed subjects, to a valuable resource that generates additional scarce resources. As the sections to follow demonstrate, evidence of the transformation of state thinking regarding the role, identity and allegiance of the emigrants is even more abundant when one examines institutional developments.

The evolution of government institutions dealing with Moroccan expatriates

Despite the long history of emigration, it was not until the 1970s that the *makhzen*, the Moroccan state, initiated its first institutionalized activities aimed at involvement in the expatriate communities, beyond its role in the labor recruitment process. State concern over growing labor union activism in which TMEs were involved might be sufficient to explain the timing of the state's first organizational initiative, but a careful examination of domestic politics offers other possible reasons.

Since his accession to the throne in 1962 Hassan II had sought to tame domestic opposition, as manifested through a number of key political parties, while maintaining the façade of a parliamentary monarchy with an opposition. The privileged target of regime/monarchical ire at the time was the UNFP (Union Nationale des Forces Populaires), a leftist political formation that had split from the mother Istiqlal (Independence) Party in 1959. Continuing state repression against the UNFP, including charges in 1963 that some of its leaders had been involved in a plot to assassinate the king, led to jail and exile for a number of its members.

In March 1965, a new challenge in the form of student and worker strikes rocked Casablanca, the kingdom's commercial capital and its largest city. Bloodily suppressed by the security forces, the unrest led to the imposition of a state of emergency, as a result of which the king appropriated even greater powers. A few months later, in October, with French assistance, Moroccan security services abducted and murdered the powerful UNFP leader Mehdi Ben Barka in Paris. To strengthen his position, Hassan moved to reinforce the role of the army and its top leaders as his most trusted counselors. However, coup attempts in July 1971 and August 1972, the first an assault on the royal palace at Skhirat south of Rabat and the other an attempt to down the plane in which the king was returning from Europe – both hatched by top members of his armed forces – must have left the king badly shaken.

Indeed, by 1970, politics in Morocco had been radicalized: the major opposition parties were preparing to reject for the second time the king's proposed constitutional reforms and boycott legislative elections. Although Ben Barka was gone, another major UNFP figure, al-Fiqh Basri, was based in Europe and had at his disposal substantial resources to support anti-regime activity, including military training in other Arab countries of volunteers who sought to overthrow the monarchy. Many of those recruited were from the ranks of the Union Nationale des Etudiants Marocains (UNEM), largely from branches in Europe. Indeed, the regime finally decided to shut down the UNEM in Morocco in January 1973. Two months later, an insurgent group associated with Basri launched an armed insurrection in several parts of the kingdom, which was suppressed militarily.

The other key mobilization force in the country, the Union Marocaine de Travail (UMT), a labor union, was also closed in 1973. Thereafter, the Moroccan left remained active primarily through the communities abroad. In Europe, student activists sought to politicize and mobilize the far more numerous workers, many of whom were already members of labor unions.[90] In the climate of domestic political security challenges in the kingdom, controlling the student movement abroad became essential. Moroccan state security services penetrated and constantly monitored student groups not only in Moroccan universities, but also in the émigré communities;[91] "A large number of Moroccan students abroad were informers: in exchange for a passport which opened up for them the doors to go abroad, they had to provide regular reports of students' comings and goings."[92]

Growing expatriate student and worker communities; vociferous, radical opposition abroad; coup attempts and subversion at home: it was in this climate of multiple challenges to the state that the first *makhzen*-sponsored associations abroad – *amicales* (in French) or *widdadiyyat* (in Arabic), "friendship societies" – were established.

---

[90] Mehdi Bennouna, *Héros sans gloire: echec d'une révolution, 1963–73* (Casablanca: Tarik Editions, 2002), pp. 145–46.
[91] "La 'migration' estudiantine," *Le Journal*, 29 June – 5 July 2002.   [92] Bennouna, p. 167.

The amicales

The Moroccan *amicales* were based on an Algerian model, the Amicales des Algériens en Europe (AAE), which had evolved out of the Fédération de France du Front de Libération Nationale (FFFLN). The FFFLN had been intended, in principle, to organize the departure of migrants, but in fact was devoted to tasks of social integration, control, and defense of the Algerian population.[93] Its successor, the AAE, fulfilled a variety of functions. In its efforts to protect and promote the interests of Algerians in France it frequently mediated between the Algerian community and French institutions. The AAE also tried to represent emigrant interests in Algerian national policymaking, and to maintain governmental control over the emigrant community. An additional function has been to maintain the political loyalty of Algerians residing abroad.[94]

In 1973 a conference of Moroccan ambassadors and consuls in Europe was held in Paris, at which it was decided to create Moroccan associations called "Amicales des travailleurs et commerçants" ("Workers' and Businessmen's Friendship Societies") throughout the expatriate communities. Such an initiative apparently also had the support of the French business establishment, since it sought to oversee and rein in the more activist or "radical" elements in the Moroccan worker community.[95] Officially, the *amicales*' principal objectives were to establish contacts with the consulates, the administrations of the two countries, and in a general way all the bodies concerned with the social situation of emigrants and their families. In addition, in the Netherlands, for instance, many mosques were associated with the *amicales*, although the Moroccan government did not provide the imams.[96] The broader goal was to maintain a certain control of the community abroad and to use these institutions to inform the expatriate populations of the political decisions of the Moroccan government directly concerning them. At the same time, there was a desire to urge the emigrants to continue to repatriate funds, while furnishing social services, including the establishment of non-profit associations such as mosques.[97] By the early 1990s the federation of *amicales* grouped together 128 associations in France alone.

---

[93] Wihtol de Wenden, *Les immigrés et la politique*, p. 138.
[94] Mark J. Miller, "Political Participation and Representation of Noncitizens," in Brubaker, *Immigration*, pp. 135–36.
[95] Wihtol de Wenden, *Les immigrés et la politique*, p. 180.
[96] Nielsen, *Muslims in Western Europe*, p. 63.
[97] Abdelatif Saidi, "Les Stratégies des associations marocaines bruxelloises une comparaison avec les Noirs Americains et les Franco-Maghrebins," from www.users.skynet.be/suffrage-universel/bmar02.htm.

For a Moroccan there were a number of advantages in joining an *amicale*. First, given its close relationship with the consulate or embassy, the *amicale* afforded access to a range of practical information – exchange rate information, the price of land back home, investment opportunities, and so on. The *amicale* was also a place where deals could be negotiated: purchases and sales, loans, translation of documents, and the like. Arabic classes for children, as well as other classes for adults, were offered, and football teams were organized. Some of their best-publicized activities were the celebrations they sponsored on the occasion of Moroccan national festivals.[98]

There were also disadvantages to *not* joining an *amicale*. Moroccans who were active in labor union struggles in Europe often had troubles upon returning home, having been denounced either by consular authorities or by the *amicales*. Far from being "faithful intermediaries between the government and the communities abroad, whose power derived from the Moroccan community's trust," as they were described by the kingdom's official *Le Matin du Sahara*,[99] from their beginnings they served as antidemocratic recruiting or training instruments. As such they were programmed by the Moroccan consulates to infiltrate, intimidate and monitor the emigrants in order to prevent them from participating in worker struggles and activism.[100] Concerned about the image of the country abroad, which could affect worker recruitment, the regime sought to limit agitation among its expatriates. It also feared a possible contagion effect in the kingdom from MRE involvement in democratic processes and labor unionization in Europe.[101]

A look at the Moroccan press offers some additional insights into the functioning of the *amicales*, and underlines the mixed record. A 1982 article lists the activities of the *amicales* as: parties on the occasion of the 'Eid al-'Arsh (Throne Day); soccer games, trips for children and showing movies; a club for youth; meetings with some municipal and political party leaders; various forms of awareness raising; the provision of support for the local mosques; and visiting the sick.[102] Another, more charitable, article argues that the *amicales* began as a means of structuring relations between the émigré worker and his home country in addition to what the embassies or consulates did. The problem came, it contends, with the appointment of leaders who worked for a completely different goal, as instruments of repression against Moroccan workers. They worked in

---

[98] Abdelkader Belbakri, "Commerçants: un rôle à la fois économique, culturel et social," in *AEM*, pp. 303–5.
[99] As cited in Belguendouz, "Les marocains à l'étranger," p. 52.   [100] Ibid.
[101] Ibid., pp. 52–53.   [102] *Al-Anba'*, 6 May 1982.

concert with the French authorities and institutions, and helped to break the strikes at Citroën in 1982.[103] There are also repeated claims of the lack of democracy, and embassy/consular interference in *amicale* elections.[104] Another article published just prior to the 1984 Moroccan parliamentary elections, in which MREs were allowed to elect representatives,[105] called upon the *amicales* not to interfere. It asked specifically that their offices not be used as voting places, as had been the case with the 1980 constitutional referendum, in which MREs had been allowed to vote.[106]

The USFP (Union Socialiste des Forces Populaires, a majority offshoot of the UNFP) deputy 'Akka al-Ghazi criticized the *amicales* for not doing their job in the cultural, sports, religious or educational realms. He did not demand that they be closed, but he did call for a re-examination of their statutes.[107] An article entitled "Amicales: Failure and Lack of Legitimacy" argued that in dealing with the communities abroad, the Moroccan authorities had failed to take into account the pluralist reality of emigrant organizations. Instead, the government wanted to implement its policy of interaction with MREs through a single party – the *amicales*. The *amicales* were playing no role in defending the rights of emigrants with the host countries, and other organizations stepped into this vacuum. The article insisted that the government was obliged to realize this and deal with these organizations instead.[108]

Amicales were associated with the slander of a large number of association activists, and they created a climate of fear, suspicion and threat in the communities. They thereby generated a bad reputation for themselves, not only within the MRE community, but also among democratic popular opinion in Europe. In Holland, for example, they became well-known as fascist organizations which would use violence against those who opposed them.[109]

In late 1985, in a speech to the community given during a visit to France, King Hassan admitted that the *amicales* had not done their job in serving the needs of the community, and declared himself disappointed with the favoritism and nepotism that had plagued their

---

[103] *Al-Bayan*, 28–29 December 1982.   [104] *Al-Bayan*, 9 March 1983.

[105] In 1984, Morocco initiated an experiment of having representatives of the MREs in the parliament. These five seats were cancelled in the following round of parliamentary elections (1992) for reasons which remain unclear.

[106] *Al-Bayan*, 1 September 1984.

[107] *Al-Ittihad al-Ishtiraki*, 31 October 1985. Al-Ghazi was one of the MRE representatives elected in 1984.

[108] *Al-Ittihad al-Ishtiraki*, 8 November 1985.

[109] *Al-Ittihad al-Ishtiraki*, 11 November 2001.

operation.[110] He promised that, in response, a royal initiative had been undertaken to place the *amicales* on truly democratic foundations. To that end, a conference was to be held to define a new basis for the relationship in accordance with the will/desire of each Moroccan worker.[111] Hassan's primary message to the community was that they "remain Moroccan." As noted earlier, he had objected when the Socialist Party had suggested a fuller inclusion of immigrants in the electoral process in France. Thereafter, the 1981 Associations Law helped launch the Beur movement along with a series of other immigrant civil society associations. Hence, his claims to his subjects abroad – according to Moroccan law a Moroccan cannot renounce his/her citizenship, s/he is always a subject of the Alaoui throne – were being challenged both by community-based civil society activity outside the bounds of home state control *and* by the offers of greater integration or participation available to the Moroccan communities in Europe. If he was to maintain any effective sovereign claim, as opposed to merely formal, legal ties, to this community of growing resources (human, economic, political and cultural) something would have to change. In this speech he promised that by the following summer (1986) the *amicales* would be reorganized on a more representative and democratic basis.

A ministry for MREs

The *amicales*, which, depending upon community, continued to exercise influence with the *makhzen*, were clearly not structured or oriented to serve as broadly credible mechanisms for maintaining Moroccans' sense of attachment to the homeland. The increasingly family-based communities in Europe were striking roots, the socio-economic profile of the communities was gradually changing, and a third generation was appearing on the horizon. In addition to these transformations, beginning in the mid–late 1980s, the kingdom itself began to undergo a process of domestic political liberalization, which involved, most notably initially, a gradual retreat of the state from its heavy-handed repression, and greater possibilities for freer expression. While the changes were incremental, they were significant, and marked a clear departure from what had been "business as usual."

---

[110] *Al-ʿAlam*, 26 December 1985.
[111] Belguendouz, *Les marocains à l'étranger*, p. 260. Nevertheless, by 1999, the *amicales* were still in existence; even the same *amicale* members of the FHII (see below) board were in place: p. 261.

Finally, at the end of April 1990, a full-fledged ministry charged with the affairs of the Moroccan community resident abroad was created. Previously, MRE affairs had concerned numerous government ministries or bureaus, but two had held primary responsibility: the Ministry of Labor, which had related to the communities as exported workers; and the Ministry of Foreign Affairs, which had a special bureau devoted to MREs, but which also had a natural interest, given the role of embassies and consulates, in the affairs of expatriates. The naming of a minister-delegate to the prime minister charged with the affairs of the MREs signified a recognition by the king and his advisors that both ministries' roles had been overtaken by the increasingly multidimensional nature of the concerns of the communities: housing, education, social security, customs, personal status, investment and the law.

According to the initial decree (no. 2–91–89), the Ministry of the Moroccan Community Abroad (MMCA) was to act in four domains: promoting action (social, economic and cultural) aimed at nationals living abroad; following the migratory movements of Moroccans; participating in relations and international negotiations of all types relative to emigration and to the living conditions of Moroccans abroad; and developing programs to facilitate the reintegration of the emigrants upon their final return. An office to receive complaints, part of the Legal, International Affairs and Documentation division, was opened in 1992 to advise Moroccans residing abroad of their rights.[112]

On 31 July 1989, addressing himself to Rafiq Haddaoui, the newly designated minister, Hassan II gave the following rationale for establishing the ministry:

the representatives of the Moroccan community asked Us to put in place a governmental organ that would be charged with dealing with their affairs outside the realm of employment. Given that the problems of our Moroccan communities have nothing to do with the Ministry of Labor, that We are linked by the act of allegiance (*bay'ah*) to Our subjects abroad in the same way as We are to their brothers in Morocco, that We have a paternal, religious and a moral responsibility to them, Our citizens abroad deserve more concern than their fellow citizens living in Morocco, whose needs are looked into day and night. We charge you with the interests of these sons who are Ours . . . The objective of the mission is to safeguard these ties and the act of allegiance.[113]

According to Haddaoui, the communities themselves had indeed expressed their desire for such a ministry to the king. Up to that point, their problems had been treated in only a very general way by the Ministry

---

[112] Fellat, "Le Maroc et son émigration," in *L'annuaire de l'Afrique du Nord*, p. 987.
[113] Belguendouz, *Les marocains à l'étranger*, pp. 56–57.

of Foreign Affairs, and the MFA was not in a position to respond to all community needs with its limited resources. In order to do its job, such an institution needed to have an intimate knowledge and understanding of the range of MRE concerns related to their stay, their relations with Morocco, and with the possibility of a definitive return. He added that the essential task of the ministry was to defend the interests of the MREs, both in Morocco and abroad. Finally, this ministry was to facilitate MRE contact with various administrative services: it was in daily contact with the MFA, just as it coordinated with other concerned ministries. It also placed social attachés in embassies and consulates. The idea, therefore, was not that it be the only interlocutor for the MREs, but, rather, a privileged one specialized in their situation and problems.[114] The gradual transformation of the Moroccan away from subject and toward citizen could now be read in the ministry's dealings with its nationals abroad.

A proposed structure for the ministry, which envisioned two parts, was adopted by the cabinet in February 1991. The first was to be a division of emigration, intended to follow immigration policy in each of the host countries, at least in part better to determine the possibilities of further emigration into those countries. The second division was to be charged with legal questions, studies, statistics and international relations, both bilateral and multilateral. Among the objectives of the second was to be media coverage as well as the transmission of information on Morocco, because it was felt that MREs did not receive enough information on life in the kingdom.[115]

Indeed, communications and information were an emphasis of the new ministry. In 1994, the first *Annuaire de l'Emigration Marocaine* was published. This was a large volume, with short informational studies on the most important Moroccan communities abroad. As the name indicates, it was supposed to be the first in a series, although it was suspended before a second volume was issued. Two other publications were also initiated, one internal to the ministry and the other aimed at the community abroad. The ministry newsletter, "Lettre d'Information," provided updates primarily on the minister's activities, visits to various communities, and meetings with European government counterparts to discuss MRE-related issues. There were also sections on what various associations were doing, on youth, on religion, sports, preparations for the transit (the summer return), on seminars, conferences and colloquia. It was published in French and Arabic, with exactly the same articles in each.

---

[114] *Interviews de M. le Ministre Rafiq Haddaoui, 1991–1993*, Ministère des Affaires de la Communauté Marocaine à l'étranger, pp. 1–3, 11.
[115] Ibid., p. 14.

It also included segments of interviews given by Haddaoui. Finally, there was *La Tribune du Maroc*, which was a press review available at the embassies and consulates.

Rivages, on the other hand, was a four-color, handsome, and more externally directed magazine that appeared from January 1993, until winter 1994/95, published with the support of the Fondation Hassan II (see below). Articles in both French and Arabic addressed culture, science, new books on Morocco, and Moroccan life and relations with Europe, including problems related to the young, integration, the return, and investment. The articles are well done, and for a researcher or social scientist, this would have been a fascinating magazine. Unfortunately, however, for the vast majority of MREs, it appears misdirected. First, many of the first-generation workers would likely have been only basically literate, and many, as native Berber speakers, would have found the classical Arabic text largely inaccessible. Second, workers were unlikely to have the time to devote to such a magazine, which also appears to have been extremely expensive to produce. So although a quality product, it indicates an administration that was out of touch with the needs of its primary constituency. On other fronts, the ministry began to put in place structures to encourage investment, and was preparing volumes on business creation and enterprise finance in Morocco. It also had among its structures a "reinsertion" service aimed at those emigrants returning definitively to assist them with social and economic issues as well as the education of their children.[116]

The ambitious plans and the changed discourse regarding the MREs make the next chapter of the ministry's history all the more lamentable. For, despite the king's clear, initial support for the ministry, and the ambitious program laid out for it, MMCA activities never fully developed to meet its goals, and its existence was ultimately terminated. Once there was no longer pressure from the MRE parliamentary deputies mentioned above, regarding having a ministry (and this pressure dissipated with the end of the parliamentary term in which they served, in 1992), the decline began.

Yet the problem was larger than the mere absence of parliamentary pressure. The MFA had considered MREs' affairs as part of its turf. Hence, some MFA officials had objected to the establishment of the MMCA from the beginning. The official justification for the objections was the need to have a coherent foreign policy, which could be achieved only if a single bureau were responsible for MRE affairs. In practice, however, some Moroccan ambassadors were irritated by the authority

---

[116] Ibid., pp. 95, 99.

MMCA ministry officials had over aspects of the dossier with which diplomats (MFA employees) theoretically were charged. They were especially annoyed by the fact that another member of the government would make decisions in a realm they considered part of their responsibilities, or make statements in public judging the situation of MREs. Many consuls took exception to the fact that the MMCA received complaints from MREs regarding the functioning of the consular services or the behavior of MFA employees. In the eyes of these diplomats, such actions were either personally embarrassing or could prejudice the high politics with which they were charged.[117] These problems were clearly at least in the back of Haddaoui's mind when he stated that the ministry was not the *sole* MRE interlocutor (suggesting a plurality, or perhaps a cacophony, of voices),[118] although he also indirectly criticized the MFA, saying that the embassies and consulates needed to be sufficiently equipped to be able to respond to all questions and provide the MREs with all the information they needed.[119]

Another source of problems was the *amicales*. In answering questions about this network, Haddaoui responded that there was a need to find serious interlocutors in the MRE communities, especially in the associative / civil society realm. The ministry was looking for groups that were creative and imaginative, concerned about working for their compatriots in a non-self-serving way. He felt such support could come from *amicales* or from other associations; what was important was that they be serious about their work, fully representative, and led by people of intelligence and integrity. More pointedly, Haddaoui contended that while some *amicales* had done excellent work, their numbers were limited.[120]

Taking on the MFA and the *amicales* was a prescription for slow institutional death.[121] The first step came in March 1994 when Haddaoui was replaced by Ahmad al-Ouardi, and the MMCA was downgraded to a sub-ministry (*sous-ministère*). Then at the end of February 1995, as part of a cabinet shuffle, the title of the head of the MMCA was downgraded to "undersecretary of state attached to the MFA," and all of the MMCA's activities were in effect frozen. This period also marked the arrival of Lahcene Gaboune, described by a close observer of Moroccan MRE policy as a man who had no clear policy, to head the

---

[117] Belguendouz, *Les marocains à l'étranger*, pp. 57–58.
[118] *Interviews de M. le Ministre Rafiq Haddaoui*, p. 2.   [119] Ibid., p. 15.
[120] Ibid., pp. 7, 114–15.
[121] Omar Azziman, who was appointed to head the FHII in 1997, apparently also reported that the ministry had undertaken a lot of unnecessary, wasteful projects under Haddaoui, another reason perhaps for the move against the MMCA: off-the-record interview with Moroccan MFA employee.

sous-ministère.[122] The MFA authorities apparently hoped this weakening of the MMCA would give the impression that its structures were useless and that it should be dissolved.[123] At the same time it appears that financial considerations may have played a role as well. The government's budgetary situation led to cutbacks in other ministries, and the support for the associated Fondation Hassan II (see below) declined precipitously.[124]

Finally, as part of a 13 August 1997 cabinet shake-up, the prime minister, at the suggestion of the MFA, ordered the transfer of all MMCA responsibilities to the MFA, thereby effectively abolishing the ministry. This was carried out by a decree that was never published in the *Bulletin Officiel*.[125] Some of the functions of the ministry were subsequently integrated into the office at the MFA concerned with MREs, just as many MMCA employees were absorbed by the MFA, including the researchers and many of the middle-level cadres.

To evaluate this experience one must take a number of factors into consideration: the changing emigration horizons of the Moroccans abroad, domestic political evolution, and domestic bureaucratic infighting. The initial impetus to establish such a ministry is officially attributed to appeals from the communities themselves for a body more responsive and attuned to their needs. That said, the failure of the *amicales*, acknowledged by Hassan II in the speech noted above, in the context of developments in Europe (particularly in France) that offered increasing opportunities for Moroccan integration, made clear that a new framework was essential if the *makhzen* was to maintain any sovereign control in the communities. The gradual liberalization of the political system that began in the mid–late 1980s suggests the king realized that a rethinking of the long-standing monarch–subject relationship was required as well. Thus, the establishment of this ministry both indicated that the incipient process of humanization of the Moroccan subject was being extended to include the communities abroad and served the state's need to maintain some claim on the communities' energies and resources.

The demise of the ministry owes more to bureaucratic infighting and limited state capacity – an indication in this case of compromised state sovereignty as a result of the stage of state-building – than to a lack of interest in or recognition of the importance of the MRE portfolio, which is

---

[122] "Takhsis 'Adad Mahdud min al-Dawa'ir ..." Intervention by Abdelkrim Belguendouz, published in *Al-'Alam*, 18 June 2002.

[123] Belguendouz, *Les marocains à l'étranger*, p. 58.

[124] Interview with Djelal Messaouden of the FHII, Rabat, 30 June 2000.

[125] Belguendouz, *Les marocains à l'étranger*, p. 59.

a common complaint. There was certainly a recognition that more focused, but also more diversified, attention needed to be devoted to the MREs. Nevertheless, turf wars initiated by the MFA and the *amicales,* both of which represented powerful entrenched interests, combined to freeze MMCA activity and ultimately to return primary responsibility for the MRE portfolio to the MFA.

La Fondation Hassan II (FHII)

At virtually the same time as the establishment of the MMCA, a second institution was initiated as a kind of adjunct to it, the Fondation Hassan II pour les marocains résidant à l'étranger (The Hassan II Foundation for Moroccans Resident Abroad). Established by royal decree on 13 July 1990, it is a "non-profit institution with a social vocation, endowed with a moral personality and financial autonomy." Its main mission is the promotion and protection of the Moroccan community abroad and its founding document (Law no. 19–89) listed the following as its principal tasks: to participate in teaching Arabic, national culture, and religion to the children of Moroccans abroad; to contribute to vacation camps for MRE children during the summer; to provide financial assistance to needy MREs; and to organize and finance cultural, associative and sports activities to benefit MREs. There is no mention of a direct political (lobbying) or an economic beneficiary role (i.e., remittance channeling) for the state.

The FHII was to be administered by a board of directors composed of twenty-seven members designated by the MMCA minister in accordance with the suggestions of the thirteen concerned government ministries, each of which was to have a representative. In addition, there was to be a representative of the Professional Association of Moroccan Banks (Groupement Professionnel des Banques du Maroc) and thirteen members chosen from the members of the offices of the Fédération des *Amicales.*[126]

According to its informational material the Foundation:

wishes to be a bridge between Moroccan citizens living abroad and their home country, Morocco. It is a link between cultures and civilizations par excellence. It aims at cultivating a sense of communication with and for the Moroccan community abroad. It is in charge of promoting social, economic, cultural and educational relationships with countries concerned with immigration issues ... It ensures and facilitates their [emigrants'] reintegration once they return to

---

[126] Loi no. 19–89 portant création de la Fondation Hassan II pour les Marocains résidant à l'étranger.

Morocco. The Foundation seeks to be a federation that gathers all the Moroccans residing abroad around their country and its institutions. It defends their rights and interests. It is open to all forms of cooperation with private and public institutions in the countries of residence.[127]

Whence the impetus for founding the FHII at the same time as a new ministry? It has been argued that the same forces – the voices of the representatives of the communities abroad – that pushed for the establishment of the ministry may well have played a major role. It is possible that the evolving political liberalization in Algeria beginning in 1988 and the prominent role played in it by the FIS may have raised Moroccan government concerns about contagion, thus increasing the imperative to influence the MREs more thoroughly, especially in religio-cultural matters, in order to "vaccinate" Moroccans abroad against militant Islam. One source argues that the establishment of both the FHII and the MMCA was a response to the importance of remittances which, in 1990, represented 48 percent of total exports,[128] although the lack of any mention of financial considerations in the founding legislation of the FHII calls this conclusion into question.

The particularity of FHII is that it is not a ministry, but has its orientations set by the government. In an interview, the Director-General of the FHII contended that a foundation was preferable to a ministry, because if it intervened on behalf of immigrants it would not affect the same sensibilities as a ministry (although it seems one could also make the case that it would fail to carry the same weight).[129] At the same time, since it is not simply an association or an NGO, it has a stronger voice with host governments. When it was created it was intended to complement the MMCA. Indeed, interestingly, the two institutions were run by the same person, with the Minister of the MMCA delegated to the foundation. This kind of dualism led, apparently, to a financial dualism as well, summed up by an FHII employee in the phrase, "Le ministère pense, la fondation dépense,"[130] suggesting that the foundation became the cash cow of the ministry. While some of the Foundation's budget came from the state, the FHII also received a certain percentage of the profits from several banks which channeled the lion's share of expatriate remittances

---

[127] Informational brochure of the Fondation Hassan II.
[128] Bernabé Lopez-García and Angeles Ramirez, "Las remesas de los marroquíes en España: los giros internacionales," in Bernabé Lopez-García et al., Atlas de la inmigración magrebí en España. Taller de Estudios Internacionales Mediterraneos. (Madrid: Ministerio de Asuntos Sociales, Dirección General de Migraciones. Observatorio Permanente de la Inmigración, 1996), p. 198.
[129] Interview with Director-General of the FHII Abderrahman Zahi, Rabat, 21 June 2000.
[130] Messaouden interview.

back to the kingdom. The rationale was that since these banks made a great deal of money from the MREs they should, in turn, give something back by contributing to the FHII.

The FHII's mission has largely been understood in the kingdom as limited to providing assistance to the emigrants during their return to Morocco for summer vacation (although it is really the Moroccan Army that is responsible for the bulk of the work and logistical support for this massive movement known as "opération transit").[131] While this is perhaps understandable given the high profile of the summer return, it is not an accurate reflection of the institution's activities, most of which have been in the cultural/educational realm. For example, in 1994–95, as part of its educational program, 484 teachers of language and Moroccan culture taught 70,600 MRE children, of whom 41,500 were in France. In the religious domain, 63 preachers were sent for Ramadan. Finally, among the youth sector, nearly 900 MRE children were received in 1994 in vacation camps, as compared with 1,200 in 1993.[132]

Given the close relationship between the MMCA and FHII, it should not be surprising that the gradual demise of the former had implications for the latter. As we have seen, in February 1995 the MMCA became a sub-ministry, although, even as early as 1994, al-Ouardi had demanded an audit owing to serious weaknesses in management and hiring up to that point.[133] At about the same time, there was a severe drop in contributions from the banks that were paying a part of the foundation's budget. The FHII-subsidized publications, *Rivages* and *La Tribune du Maroc*, ceased to appear, there was a cutback in cultural activities, and employees were dismissed. What followed was a retrenchment of FHII activities in the context of the downgrading and freezing of the MMCA's work. Ultimately, it was decided that the existing arrangement between the foundation and the sub-ministry was not working and that the two should be separated. However, the malaise continued until 1997, when the MMCA was completely abolished and there was a complete reorganization of the Foundation.

In a 7 May 1996 speech addressing the problems of the Foundation, Hassan II announced that he had decided to entrust its presidency to his elder daughter, Lalla Meryem: "Thus our ties will not only be those of allegiance, but also ties of kinship, since you will be like my sons and daughters." The language, the traditional references to loyalty, but also the reference to the MREs not only as a people but as a kind of extended patriarchal family, is significant, as it represents a continuing evolution of

---

[131] *La Vie Economique*, "SMAP 99" supplement, p. 40.
[132] Fellat, p. 989.   [133] Belguendouz, *Les marocains à l'étranger*, p. 256.

the *makhzen*'s approach to Moroccan expatriates, who had long been simply "workers."

The king followed this appointment with the designation of a respected human rights activist and Minister of Justice, Omar Azziman, as the new President-Designate of the foundation. The choice of Azziman sent a clear message about the king's intentions for this institution. The reorganization that followed brought major changes, and the following quote from Azziman highlights a key development in the state's discourse regarding MREs:

At the Foundation we are not at all seeking to hinder the integration of Moroccans abroad. To the contrary, we know that their integration into the host country affects their success. We want our compatriots abroad to live in harmony with their host society and to feel equally at ease inside and outside of Morocco.

This is how they can avoid being torn apart by exile, and escape the distress caused by losing one's points of reference. This is how our community abroad can become a source of wealth capable of contributing to the development and modernization of Morocco.[134]

This view stands in stark contrast to the language used by Hassan II in his speech to the community in France twelve years earlier. Here, while there is certainly an emphasis on maintaining links to Morocco, and on Morocco's implicit claims to the emigrants, there is also a clear recognition and apparent acceptance that MREs will integrate to varying degrees in the host states. The Moroccan state's goal is no longer to block a degree of integration that may serve the needs of its expatriates, but rather to find ways of continuing to preserve ties of loyalty and affection *given* that they are, increasingly, permanently settled abroad. It may appear to be little more than a change in emphasis, but it in fact represents an evolution in policy, the acceptance of a limited form of sovereignty over the expatriates in order not to lose them entirely by joining what would certainly be a losing battle against the reality of growing integration.[135]

The reorganization undertaken in 1997 involved a number of changes in administrative responsibility and financial oversight. Further, a new internal structure for FHII work was also introduced which comprises six operational divisions: education, cultural exchange, sports and youth

---

[134] As quoted in ibid., p. 280.

[135] That said, it will be remembered that the 2000–4 plan discussed above talked about the importance of avoiding Moroccans' opting for integration. Such language may represent divisions in the bureaucracy, different audiences (with the plan aimed at those inside while Azziman's statements are clearly directed to the CME), or different understandings of "integration" in which that of the planning document implies losing the MRE to the host state, whereas that of Azziman implies acceptance of a certain degree of integration to facilitate the emigrant's life abroad.

(which is in charge of educational and cultural programming); social assistance, which offers support and protection to the Moroccan community; communication, which deals with information and documentation issues; legal studies and assistance, which is charged with the defense of rights and interests of the Moroccans residing abroad; cooperation and partnership, which works with public bodies, private corporations and NGOs; and economic promotion, which is in charge of providing information and assistance to Moroccan investors living abroad.

The FHII also has a structure devoted to studies and analysis. This is associated with what is called the Observatoire of the Moroccan Community Abroad, which is intended to make regular, reliable and objective studies of developments among MREs. Work began at the Salon Marocain à Paris (SMAP) and Contact 98 in Brussels[136] in May 1998 with several surveys aimed at gathering information to construct an accurate picture of the communities abroad. Teams of researchers were used to administer questionnaires to the thousands of visitors at these two exhibitions. Azziman also expressed a desire to put in place a scientific council composed of Moroccans and others known for their knowledge of emigration. The hope was that, by using both such a council and the Observatoire, sound strategies for the various MRE communities and their needs could be formulated.[137]

The post-reorganization priorities were outlined by the FHII Director-General Abderrahman Zahi as the following. First, to reinforce the ties between the emigrant and his/her country, both for those who want to return and for those who do not: for those who will return, so that they will not feel marginalized, and for those who will not so that they can maintain their culture, religion, and the like. Second, to aid the Moroccan in his "projet immigratoire," whatever that may be. Third, to work on programs detailed in the original statute as well as others that have subsequently been added.[138]

In fact, much of the restructured foundation's work involves developing activities initiated in the early 1990s. The program of summer youth camps is one example. In 2000, the FHII expected about 1,000 children

---

[136] These are both annual exhibitions intended to attract Moroccans resident in France and Belgium as well as those (French or others) interested in expanding their business in Morocco. Although conceived with largely business/financial goals in mind, both large, multi-day meetings feature a variety of cultural events and displays as well. SMAP was first held in 1997.

[137] "Rencontre avec M. Omar Azziman," *Maghreb Resources Humaines* 19/20 June/July 1998: p. 36.

[138] Zahi interview. He did draw a stark contrast with their Tunisian counterpart, saying that the FHII has much more modest activities.

in two camps each of fifteen days, one at Agadir and the other at Bouznika.[139] Another major program is during Ramadan. As one part of this initiative the FHII sends boxes of traditional sweets to Moroccans who are in prison abroad. The Ramadan program also involves sending preachers to oversee and lead special religious services and functions. (This is in addition to some thirteen preachers permanently based in Europe as of summer 2000.) They are all graduates of facilities in the large universities of Morocco, and hence are approved by the Moroccan government to teach responsibility to God, Islam, family, children, and home.[140]

In the foundation's view, the cultural element is decisive in maintaining the homeland's relationship with the MREs. Those abroad need to be conscious of their identity and their origins, and here Arabic language and Moroccan culture instruction is critical. After the restructuring, the FHII sent experts to Europe to evaluate the oft-criticized Arabic language instruction program. It also launched a study in France and Belgium to establish the broad lines of an integrated program of reform, taking into consideration the education system of the host country. This study pointed out numerous, clear weaknesses, the most important of which was the gap between the content of the instruction and the education system in the host country on the one hand, and the needs of the Moroccan community on the other.[141] As a result the FHII began working with the Ministry of National Education so that new language and culture programs could be designed with a new philosophy and precise objectives.[142]

Investment is another focus, although not part of the original statute. Azziman held a meeting with the principal groups concerned with MRE investment on 15 December 1997 as part of the early steps toward reorganization. It had become clear that when people returned definitively, they discovered a very different Morocco from the one they had left, and if they did not receive proper assistance and information, their investments could easily fail. The FHII thus determined that work was

---

[139] How is participation determined? Director-General Zahi said that the consulates propose the children. They then mix children of different host country communities. In addition, there are summer camp programs other than those of FHII, and they try to arrange for the children from their programs to meet with children in others: Zahi interview.

[140] Zahi stated that those who are chosen are those who are truly able to "passer le message" by which he seemed to be saying that they were better and more capable than preachers from the communities themselves: Zahi interview.

[141] "La Fondation Hassan II au service des MRE," Les Nouvelles du Nord, 7 July 2000.

[142] "Le secretariat d'état à l'habitat lance sa seconde campagne MRE," Les Nouvelles du Nord, 7 July 2000.

needed to change the impressions that those abroad have of the bureau-cracy, based on past experiences.[143] To that end, it now publishes a guide (one of several it produces) to investment, with nine different versions according to sector, and in the languages of all significant host countries.[144]

The FHII also provides administrative and legal counsel and assis-tance. Over the years many MREs have complained of having to spend their entire "vacation" trying to address some administrative, legal or investment problem. In 1999, the FHII looked into some 7,000 files of such problems. Further, in 1998 in collaboration with the Customs administration the FHII edited a "Guide Douanier des Marocains rési-dant à l'étranger" which explains clearly in several languages all the categories of emigrants, the procedures to follow, and the customs regime for each case.

The first real survey of MREs, conducted by the Institut National de Statistique et d'Economie Appliquée (INSEA) in the summer of 1998 among Moroccans returning home for the summer through the port of Tangier, revealed some interesting information regarding the FHII. It should be noted that this was not a random survey of MREs, only those returning by boat to Tangier. Nonetheless, its results are worth consider-ing. First, they expressed a very high level of discontent regarding their children's knowledge of both Moroccan colloquial Arabic and classical Arabic, so the language issue is of importance to the parents (if differen-tially, depending upon length of migration, age and educational level).[145] The same survey also inquired as to people's satisfaction regarding Moroccan institutions; 76.6% stated that they were very satisfied with the operation of banks, 63.4% with the consulates and 50.1% with customs. The percentage drops when it comes to the government admin-istration and local authorities (39.5%).[146] Again, it should be borne in mind that while this survey was conducted following the beginning of the *alternance* government (1998),[147] one should view the satisfaction figures with some skepticism, since many people would have been afraid to

---

[143] "La touche Azziman," *Maroc Hebdo*, 20–26 December 1997. www.maroc-hebdo.press. Ma/MHinternet/Archives302/Azziman.

[144] *La Vie Economique*, "SMAP 1999" supplement, p. 40.

[145] Royaume du Maroc, Premier Ministre, Ministère de la Prévision Economique et du Plan et L'Institut National de Statistique et d'Economie Appliquée (INSEA), *Les marocains résidant à l'étranger: Une enquête socio-économique* (Rabat: El-Maarif al-Jadidah, 2000), pp. 130–31.

[146] Ibid., p. 152.

[147] This was the first government to have been led by a prime minister from an opposition party. In the past, prime ministers had all been chosen from parties close to the palace. Thus it was indicative of the political opening underway in the country.

criticize the government openly in such a survey. As for the FHII, 68.5% stated that they were familiar with it, but only 17.4% had had any real dealings with it.[148] As for their critiques or suggestions for improvement (presumably only from those who said they were familiar with it), nearly half had none; one quarter said it should expand its activity both to Moroccan towns and within the countries of immigration; nearly 10% wanted a more welcoming atmosphere.[149]

Worse, a 2000 evaluation of the FHII was very critical. It claimed that whatever the initial objectives had been, they had been quickly forgotten. With the passage of time, the mission of the foundation had been reduced to support for MREs at the time of the summer return, and even this was undertaken with the support of the OSFAR (social work branch of the Moroccan Army, of which, perhaps not coincidentally, Lalla Meryem is also the president). The article attributes the problems to a number of factors. One is the absence of a clearly defined mission:

Like many "*administrations publiques*" even though that is not its statute, it seems to have no visibility, and each year it undertakes the same activities, with the same brochures, the same communiqués sent to the press. No action of any breadth is organized, there is no involvement of MREs, and to top it all no measures are adopted to improve the conditions of its personnel, who have no work, but also no statute.[150]

A 1999 *La Vie Economique* article criticized two other weaknesses of the FHII. The first was that it was not sufficiently open to those who represented the diversity of Moroccan emigration. Second was that its legal assistance to Moroccans abroad was weak. Why does 75–80% of the budget go to cultural and language education, it asked? This should be handled by the Ministry of Education or the Ministry of Foreign Affairs.[151] Another article included an interview with a young Moroccan abroad involved in youth activities. Among other criticisms, he contended that the foundation made great use, if not abuse, of its association with Lalla Meryam. The foundation served only a few people, while ignoring the rights of its personnel and the proposals of Moroccans abroad. He and many other Moroccans had sent letters, he contended, but had never received responses. Instead of treating MREs as people with agency, the FHII had turned MREs into objects of study.[152]

Azziman was apparently promised another revision of the FHII statute by the Youssoufi government, but it never materialized. An article in *Al-Ittihad al-Ishtiraki* claims that part of what was behind this desire of

[148] Ibid., p. 153.   [149] Ibid., p. 157.   [150] *La Vie Economique*, 2 June 2000, p. 58.
[151] *La Vie Economique*, 5 February 1999.   [152] *La Vie Economique*, 2 June 2000, p. 58.

Azziman's was to be rid of the representatives of the *amicales*, who continue to sit on the governing board.[153] With the end of the Youssoufi government in October 2002, Azziman lost his post as Minister of Justice, but continues in his post with the FHII.

Conclusions

The fact that all three of the institutions examined here – the *amicales*, the MMCA and the FHII – fell short of achieving their goals might lead some to conclude that they were, therefore, unimportant. It is not uncommon to hear in Morocco that the state does not really take the concerns of its expatriates seriously, for, if it did, it would do more and it would do it better. The *amicales* certainly succeeded in intimidating many Moroccans as part of their security function, but their heavy-handed approach also meant that they could not penetrate the communities, nor help provide the state with an accurate picture of the expatriate groupings. Many developed into personal or family fiefdoms that were obedient to the *makhzen*, but, in so doing, served it poorly. In the case of the MMCA, the bureaucratic infighting that quickly paralyzed it was another example of personal or turf battles overwhelming its appropriate and rather lofty goals. Finally, the example of the FHII demonstrated that even efforts by the king and a prominent human rights activist and minister to put a sound expatriate-oriented set of programs in place was hampered by institutional inertia, and personal ambition. In considering institutional development, whether in a first- or third-world context, the issue of capacity must be borne in mind. Intentions do not necessarily translate into effective policy instruments or accomplishments. Nonetheless, this reality does not lessen the importance of exploring the sources of state initiatives. Regardless of success or failure, an understanding of the origins and activities of these institutions is central to explaining state intent toward expatriates.

This chapter's discussion has demonstrated that a number of factors played key roles in the *makhzen*'s decision to establish institutions for or among Moroccan expatriates. The first such institutions, the *amicales*, while modeled on the Algerian experience, nonetheless derived from a confluence of European business and Moroccan security interests. Their purpose was reflective of the character of the MRE communities of the 1960s and early 1970s: largely composed of single or unaccompanied males, some of whom were labor union or student activists seeking radical

---

[153] *Al-Ittihad al-Ishtiraki*, 10 November 2001.

change of the regime back home. To protect the stability of the kingdom as well as the continued flow of workers to Europe, worker and student agitation had to be monitored and minimized. In this regard, the Moroccan regime was extending its function of protecting domestic sovereignty through increased involvement in extra-territorially based communities.

The subsequent institutional forms that were developed indicate a desire to move beyond the *amicale* structure and style, although, given the clientelistic relationships upon which the *makhzen* has depended, the *amicale* leaderships reappear in the second-generation institutions. In the meantime, the communities themselves had undergone important transitions: not only were they larger, they were also family-oriented which, coupled with the effective closing of the borders of most Western European states to new immigration, meant that many MREs were deciding to stay longer. Children would now be born and raised abroad, and that raised a new set of expatriate needs along with Moroccan state concerns. No longer could Rabat assume that these Moroccans would all eventually return home to retire, bringing with them their accumulated savings and expertise. Nor could it simply expect or assume that they would maintain their ties of loyalty to family, culture, religion or, most importantly, king.

This development may be placed in the category of the macro-historical factors referred to in chapter 1. The communities' sizes and their family composition gave them a weight and diversity that they had not had prior to the closing of Europe to new immigration. This alone may have been sufficient to lead the Moroccan state to act, but it seems rather that it was the possibility of greater integration that Western European states were offering in the form of a variety of governmental and civil society opportunities for social and political participation, including, in some cases, citizenship, and the threat to Hassan's claim on his subjects that this represented, that was the primary trigger to act. European policy and the emergence of the Beur movement raised the possibility that the Moroccan state could actually effectively lose parts of these communities – their political loyalty, their economic contribution, their actual sense of belonging – to the host states. In the course of a ten-year period, the kingdom's approach to the affiliation of its citizens abroad was transformed, from one which insisted upon the rejection of assimilation as key to its maintaining its hold on its subjects to one which acknowledged that only by accepting that these MREs were gradually integrating into European host states did it have a chance of preserving (reconstructed, if compromised) ties of sovereignty with people whom it was – ironically – increasingly seeking to treat as real citizens, rather than mere royal subjects.

Also key to understanding the shift in the *makhzen*'s relationship with the expatriates was the process of gradual political opening initiated by the king, which falls under the category of domestic politics noted in chapter 1. This initiative derived from an apparent realization that changes in the regime's *modus operandi* were needed to stave off both political and economic crises and criticisms regarding domestic repression from a Europe into which Hassan wanted to see his kingdom more fully integrated. The liberalization gradually opened the way for discussion and activity in defense of human rights, as the language of "citizen" increasingly took its place next to the more subject-oriented language of allegiance to the monarchy. In such an atmosphere, the effective extension of state concern for its nationals to cover those abroad, therefore, seems natural.

The transnationalism literature stresses the economic goals of many expatriate-oriented institutions, and it is true that both the MMCA and the FHII did include programs intended to facilitate remittance transfer. Yet, it would be a misreading of the origins and histories of these two institutions to argue that their primary concern was hard currency. Certainly they offered programs and services in the financial/investment realm, but had remittances been the primary focus, one would have expected much more emphasis on attracting monies. Perhaps this is simply another manifestation of lack of state capacity or, perhaps, given that, except for during a few years, remittance levels have continued to grow, there has been less of a sense of urgency regarding changing instruments and offerings. One may also conclude, as the evidence here suggests, that such institutional instruments are not always easily reduced to purely economic concerns – domestic or bilateral/international – as much of the discussion of international migration might lead us to believe.

It is worth noting, before concluding, that in the government formed by Prime Minister Driss Jettou in early October 2002, a scaled-down version of the MMCA experience was resurrected, as Neziha Chekrouni was named Minister delegated to the Ministry of Foreign Affairs and Cooperation charged with Moroccans Resident Abroad. The creation of this new department indicated a desire for more active involvement in the affairs of the CME than the FHII alone could provide. In its new form it has been charged with working to consolidate the rights of Moroccans abroad, put in place a global approach in order to modernize emigration policy, encourage integration in the host countries while preserving national identity, mobilize the expatriate community to become an important force nationally and internationally, defend national causes but also to participate in Moroccan public life, and involve the community in the running of its own affairs. In Morocco it intends to work to improve the reception of the community, especially during the summer season of massive return, and to promote direct investment and remittances as well as tourism. In addition, a new communications strategy, using the national media, but also websites, is being developed to assist in creating more permanent ties with the migrants. (Indeed, in summer 2004 a satellite channel, al-Maghrıbıyah, was launched by the Ministry of Communication, aimed at the Moroccan diaspora.) And, according to the king's instructions, 10 August (which coincides with Throne Day) was designated in 2003 as the National Day of the Migrant.[154] The holiday is intended to renew ties with the migrants, learn of their problems and inform them of development projects.

All of these activities are key to a state policy which is concerned with maintaining close links with its communities abroad, but which implicitly acknowledges that full sovereign control will probably never be reasserted over them. Given the current stage of economic and political development in the country, Morocco is keen to reinforce multifaceted ties of affiliation as it probes the boundaries of the evolving identity of Moroccans and their descendants in Europe. In conclusion, while not denying the importance of the remittance factor, the contention here is that language, religion, and cultural identity preservation as foci of these institutional experiments cannot be reduced to mere byproducts of what is really only an interest in foreign exchange. Such a unidimensional analysis overlooks the strong emphasis placed by the state on identity preservation as well as the clear desire of many emigrants, regardless of whether they intend to settle permanently abroad or not, to remain to some extent or in some ways affiliated to the sending country. It also obscures the multidimensional character of sovereignty, which certainly requires national wealth generation, but also claims a much broader range of resources as central to its mission and survival.

---

[154] Ministère des Affaires Etrangères et de la Coopération, Direction des Affaires Consulaires et Sociales, Division des Etudes et des Conventions Administratives, "Migration internationale marocaine: Bilan et perspectives," a paper presented by His Excellency Min. Abderrahim Sassi, at the conference "State–Diaspora Relations," sponsored by El Instituto de los Mexicanos en el Exterior, Mexico City, 18–22 October, 2004, pp. 10–16.

4   Tunisia's expatriates: an integral part of the national community?

A former French protectorate that came to independence in 1956, unlike its often imposing Algerian and Libyan neighbors, Tunisia is both geographically and economically of modest size, although offshore oil discoveries have made important contributions to what was otherwise a largely agriculturally based economy. Whether because of the unpredictability of Libya, which has on occasion expelled Tunisian workers, or the potential spillover of civil war from Algeria, Tunis has pursued policies aimed at insulating itself from the vagaries of regional politics and economics. From independence until the 1980s, a single party, the Parti socialiste destourien (PSD), and the state were led by the country's most prominent independence figure, Habib Bourguiba, a French-trained lawyer who had ideas not unlike those of Turkey's Atatürk regarding modernization and state-building.

In terms of population movement, until the end of the First World War, Tunisia was a region of *im*migration, attracting those seeking wealth, welcome or asylum from other parts of the Mediterranean basin. It began to export labor to France about the same time Morocco did, but the flows did not become important until several years after independence, when unemployment levels began to rise. Unlike Rabat, Tunis took a more interventionist approach from the beginning, in keeping with the developmentalist leanings of its leadership. While not always meeting targets or expectations, the Tunisian state did establish offices to address placement and programs to provide training. It also sought to secure the reach of the state into the expatriate communities through its use of *amicales*, which were all-but-official extensions of the PSD.

Emigration, both legal and illegal, continued apace until the decisions by Western European states to close their doors to foreign labor. As a result, as we saw in the case of Morocco, the change in European policies led to transformations in the composition and work horizons of the Maghrebi emigrants. However, domestic political malaise delayed the Tunisian government in responding institutionally to the new realities. When the state did decide upon a course of action, it embraced the expatriate communities in an unprecedented way, extolling their potential, encouraging their success abroad, but also reasserting their attachment and responsibilities to the homeland: "the Tunisian community abroad constitutes an inseparable part of Tunisian society. Wherever a Tunisian may be, in terms of identity, he is always Tunisian."[1]

Tunisian state policy toward emigration

Tunisian emigration to Europe began with the First World War, when France requested North African labor to replace workers who had joined the military. However, at war's end, unlike the Moroccans and Algerians, who generally remained, Tunisians tended to return home. A larger out-migration to France did not begin until after independence, and even then migration possibilities within Tunisia itself, from the south to the north, and from rural to urban areas, dampened the appeal of a move abroad.[2]

Substantial population growth, the slow development of industry, and a decline in foreign aid contributed to the government's turn toward a form of étatism in the realm of economic policy. Decolonization and the departure of much of the European population also created a new set of circumstances that influenced emigration following independence.[3] Just as important in shaping outmovement were developments in the French labor market, as, during the immediate post-independence period, the traditional European sources of immigrant labor in France were gradually supplanted by new sources from North Africa and Turkey. Shortly after independence the Tunisian government began to use its Emigration Bureau in the Ministry of Social Affairs to fill orders from abroad for qualified labor. The government then went a step further by sending abroad representatives charged with contacting potential employers and soliciting requests for Tunisian workers.[4]

Emigration policy as read through development plans

As in the case of Morocco, Tunisia's development plans over the years offer useful insights into the evolution of regime policy toward

---

[1] *Al-Hurriyyah*, 7 August 1999.

[2] Simon Gildas, *L'espace des travailleurs tunisiens en France: structures et fonctionnement d'un champ migratoire international* (Poitiers: l'Université de Poitiers, 1979), pp. 49, 51.

[3] Ibid., p. 57.

[4] Laurence Michalak, "A Comparison of Morocco and Tunisian Labor Migration Policies in the New Global Economy," presented at the annual meeting of the Middle East Studies Association, Phoenix, Arizona, 19–22 November 1994, p. 5.

emigration. The First Development Plan (1962–64) noted that there had been 125,000 unemployed at the time of independence, but that this figure had dropped to 100,000 in 1961 (out of a total Tunisian population of just under 4.3 million), presumably owing to the departure of the Europeans.[5] Employment policy was to aim at promoting investment in key social and economic sectors and fighting unemployment through work programs.[6] However, the 1960s' experiment with agricultural cooperatives provoked additional, profound disruptions that triggered, among other things, an increase in the ranks of the unemployed from the rural areas.

In response, international migration emerged as a key part of Tunisia's employment policy during this First Plan period.[7] The PSD had initially opposed emigration, out of a desire both to retain skilled laborers and professionals at a critical period in the state-building process and to stem the outflow of capital that had accompanied the departure of the French and of many Tunisian Jews. A realization of the severity of the unemployment situation and the recommendations of experts that emigration abroad could relieve some of the pressure seems to have led to the about-face. Nevertheless, Tunisian officials made clear that emigration was only a temporary measure, and that the ultimate solution needed to come through domestic job creation.[8]

The Second Plan (1965–68), which estimated the unemployed at 120,000,[9] stressed the oversight and organizational role of the employment offices, the number of which was to be increased by ten. More careful monitoring of departures was also called for to rein in clandestine migration – a source of problems for Tunisia with the host countries and for the migrants in the new host society. Until such time as sufficient jobs were created at home, the emigration of a certain portion of Tunisian labor was termed "temporary," to be considered *equivalent to domestic employment* – an intriguing formulation, suggesting either a strong sense on the part of the state that those abroad were clearly considered part of the polity, or a form of denial that their presence abroad represented a failure of regime policy. If such emigration were properly overseen, the plan argued, emigrant youth could receive excellent training in

---

[5] *Al-Mukhattat al-Thulathi, 1962–1964* (Tunis: Kitabat al-Dawlah l-il-Tasmim w-al-Maliyyah, n.d.), p. 311.

[6] Tawfic Baccar and Ali Sanaa, "La genèse des politiques d'emploi et d'émigration en Tunisie," in *Emploi, émigration, éducation & population* (Tunis: Ministère du Plan et du Développement, 1990), p. 65.

[7] López-García, *Atlas de la inmigración magrebí*, p. 248.   [8] Gildas, p. 67.

[9] *Al-Mukhattat al-Ruba'i, 1965–1968* (Tunis: Kitabat al-Dawlah l-il-Takhtit w-al-Iqtisad al-Watani, n.d.), p. 28.

specialized fields which could then benefit the country upon their return.[10] In the Third Plan, 1967–72, unemployment was again singled out as a serious problem. Emigrants were included in the statistics, and their numbers, estimated at 3,000 per year, were taken into account in projections of future domestic job creation needs.[11] Nevertheless, the text was frank in admitting the unreliability of its statistics, a problem which rendered effective planning difficult.

It was in 1967, at the beginning of this Third Plan period, that the Office de la Formation Professionnelle et de l'Emploi (OFPE, the "Office of Professional Training and Employment") was created as part of the Secretariat of State for Youth, Sports and Social Affairs. Until this point there had been little Tunisian administrative control over the departure of workers, the efforts of the recruitment bureaus mentioned above notwithstanding. In the field of emigration (only one of ten areas of responsibility) the OFPE was charged with, in the first place, determining the needs of countries likely to be interested in excess Tunisian labor power. Social attachés at consulates and embassies and special missions of short duration sent directly by the OFPE were to explore such interest. It was to be responsible for selecting those who would go abroad, based on medical and professional criteria, and it was to prepare workers by instructing them in the customs and practices of the receiving country in order to facilitate their adaptation. Finally, it was to keep track of the worker through the network of social attachés, to make sure that he (this was overwhelmingly male emigration) was contributing to the improvement of his family's situation. Upon his definitive return a *service d'accueil* ("reception assistance") was to simplify the procedures of re-entry and of finding employment.[12]

Two years later, in June 1969, a delegation of the French Office National d'Immigration (ONI) was opened in Tunis in order to solicit workers for the French market more directly. Once recruited, and after a stay of several days in the Centre de Préparation des Travailleurs Migrants (the Center for Migrant Worker Preparation) in Carthage, the workers were transferred by the ONI to the French companies that had requested them. The cost of transport was paid by the ONI, which was then in effect reimbursed through a tax on employers.[13]

---

[10] Ibid., pp. 33, 145.

[11] République Tunisienne, *Plan de développement économique et social, 1967–1972, rapport de synthèse*, Volume I (Tunis, n.d.), pp. 47–48.

[12] L'Office de la Formation Professionnelle et de l'Emploi, *L'Office de la Formation Professionnelle et de l'Emploi*, brochure (n.d, n.p), pp. 17, 23.

[13] Gildas, p. 139.

One of the goals of carefully monitored emigration was to give state planners a better understanding of the volume, structure and distribution of the immigration. In fact, however, many emigrants were clandestine, as networks established by the migrants themselves since 1957 continued to operate. Usually, this meant first arriving in France with a tourist visa. Then, with the help of relatives and friends, the new migrant found lodging and ultimately work. Indeed, until 1969, controlled immigration constituted less than a fourth of the worker placements in France,[14] although by 1972 it had risen to 77 percent. Many Tunisians were discouraged by the long, bureaucratic OFPE process, and, for their part, French employers preferred the regularization of illegal emigrants already working for them to what was, in effect, blind recruitment.[15]

The combination of the establishment of the OFPE and the ONI modified the characteristics of the migratory flow and replaced the sporadic or anarchic movement with a more selected emigration. Although the percentage dropped soon thereafter, by 1973 some 80 percent of those who left were part of this controlled emigration.[16] It is important to note here that the Tunisian government's view of emigration continued to be that of a temporary solution to unemployment. Hence, state services were provided with the understanding that the emigrants would all eventually return to Tunisia, and therefore had to be properly equipped – in order to reintegrate with minimum dislocation.[17]

The 1970s, which began toward the end of the Third Plan, marked a second stage in employment policy, one in which the promotion of domestic employment in the government administration was part of a broader economic expansionist thrust.[18] Around this same time, the government passed a number of laws aimed at industrial development and employment creation. For example, Law 72-38 sought to attract foreign investment and encourage export-oriented manufacturing; Law 74-74 offered advantages for employment creation; and Decree 74-793 provided for the organization and operation of the Fund for Industrial Promotion and Decentralization. In addition the Investment Promotion Agency (l'Agence de Promotion des Investissements, API) was created in

---

[14] Khemais Taamallah, *Les travailleurs tunisiens en France: aspects socio-démographiques économiques et problèmes de retour* (Tunis: Imprimerie Officielle de la République Tunisienne, 1980), p. 253.

[15] Gildas, pp. 141–3.   [16] Taamallah, pp. 254, 257.

[17] Interview with Abd al-'Aziz Bouzaidi, responsible for TREs, Rassemblement constitutionel démocratique, 9 August 2002, Tunis.

[18] Baccar and Sanaa, p. 65.

Table 4.1. *Impact of emigration on employment in Tunisia*

	1962–71	1972–81	1982–91
Excess demand before emigration	357,000	469,000	664,000
Emigration	140,000	97,000	50,000
Excess demand after Emigration	217,000	372,000	614,000

January 1973 as was the Agence Foncière, in November 1973, which was charged with managing the development of industrial zones.[19]

Nevertheless, state development policies were also creating additional strains on the job market. While Tunisia was a leader in working to reduce population growth through awareness campaigns and promoting family planning, at the same time Bourguiba's policies on women – particularly on access to education and the workforce – meant that more Tunisian women were seeking employment outside the home. In this atmosphere, the 1973 change in name of the OFPE to l'Office des Travailleurs Tunisiens à l'Etranger de l'Emploi et de la Formation Professionnelle (OTTEEFP – the "Office for Tunisian Workers Abroad and for Employment and Professional Training") signaled a renewed state focus on emigration as a means of solving the country's labor market problems. The emigration section of this office was charged with: studying the foreign markets and promoting Tunisian labor; undertaking the selection of candidates for emigration; and stemming the exodus of skilled labor needed for the development of the national economy. From a population of 52,159 in 1965, by the end of 1973 registered Tunisians in France numbered 149,274, and the total number was probably closer to 161,000.[20]

However, shortly after the beginning of the period of the Fourth Plan, the closing of the doors to immigration in Western Europe meant that emigration would no longer be able to play the same role of attenuating the domestic disequilibrium between labor supply and demand. Table 4.1 gives an idea of what this role was over the first three decades following independence.[21]

In addition to the reduction of future emigration, Tunisia had to face the possibility of expatriates' return as part of French policy to reduce the

---

[19] CERES (Centre d'études et de Recherches Economiques et Sociales) and Communauté Economique Européenne (CEE), *Analyse des mouvements migratoires dans le sud et le sud-est du basin méditerranéen en direction de la CEE: le cas de la Tunisie* (Tunis: CERES, 1992), p. 31.
[20] Gildas, pp. 82, 133, 138.   [21] Baccar and Sanaa, p. 68.

numbers of foreign workers it hosted. It is difficult to estimate the numbers of those who left France, for no bureau was charged with tracking such numbers until 1975; however, Gildas estimates that between 1966 and 1973, about 29,000 returned out of what would have been a population of about 190,000.[22] Understandably, the government was not eager to promote a massive return, for among the difficulties it posed was economic reinsertion: in 1974, the Tunisian government confirmed that all workers abroad had the right to recoup their place in the Tunisian economy, and a special service to address this problem was created in the OTTEEFP. Moreover, from the perspective of the workers themselves, even those who were *un*employed abroad had little interest in returning home, where the unemployment rate was three times as high and where there was no system of social security. Tunisian businesses were also concerned about the salaries former TTEs (*travailleurs tunisiens à l'étranger*) would seek, just as there was a certain distrust of workers who had become used to the climate of labor activism in France.[23]

The closing of Western Europe to any substantial additional immigration (and a change in Tunisian nationality law, discussed below) are the context in which, as we saw in the Moroccan case, the composition of the Tunisian community abroad began to change. For those who did not accept European financial offers to subsidize definitive returns, the new demographic and social reality was that of gradual family reunification and an increase in the projected length of stay abroad. Although it was not until nearly ten years later that concrete steps (beyond allowing dual nationality) were taken, the government did begin to take account of the changing context. For example, rather than preparing workers for an ultimate return, the focus shifted to guaranteeing the rights of Tunisians already abroad,[24] an interesting change in the state's conception of political community as well as a recognition of the changes in responsibilities that implied. Tunis continued its efforts to place laborers outside the country – at this stage, looking increasingly to Libya and the Gulf – but gradually the meaning of "managing emigration" came to mean working with increasingly stable and settled communities abroad.

In the Fifth Plan (1977–81) there is again an admission that, despite employment promotion, rural development, a revision of the investment code, and a good agricultural season, unemployment remained a problem. The plan attributed the continuing disequilibrium to the increasing numbers of youth and women seeking work, the decrease in the

---

[22] Gildas, p. 85.   [23] Ibid., pp. 370, 372.   [24] Bouzaidi interview.

placement of Tunisians abroad, and the accelerated return of migrants.[25] It anticipated that some 20,000 workers would return from abroad during the planning period, but argued that this return could be accommodated without major additional disruption owing to two factors: (1) some workers would return to *retire*, not to find places in the Tunisian workforce; and (2) the majority of those who were still active would likely return and establish their own businesses.[26] In the event, during this period, emigration was higher than projected, with 60,000 net exits. In addition, between 1972 and 1981, the economy created some 400,000 new jobs. Thus the country was able to absorb most new entrants into the labor market, keeping unemployment at 12.8 percent in 1975 and 11.4 percent in 1980.[27]

It is worth noting that none of the planning documents up to this point included a serious discussion of TTE remittances: the state was focused on the workers' employment safety valve role. Not until the Sixth Plan (1982–86) is there a discussion of change on the horizon. This document acknowledges that during the 1970s, the country had lived beyond its means. Aggregate consumption had increased more than production, imports had surpassed exports, and wages had risen faster than labor productivity. This situation had been sustained by favorable terms of trade, largely thanks to oil revenues. However, with no reason to expect a new boom in the price of either oil or phosphates, the country's main natural resources, it was projected that the years of the Sixth Plan would witness a 2 percent annual contraction, rather than the 5 percent annual growth that characterized the period of the Fifth Plan.[28] In fact, the 1980s was a difficult decade for Tunisia: worker strikes, student revolts, a military uprising in the town of Gafsa, and economic protests owing to the downturns noted above all revealed the fragile nature of the political system and the economic inequalities that the development path followed to date had produced.[29]

The Sixth Plan argued for greater efforts to place Tunisians in the Arab world, especially in Libya and the Gulf. Moreover, since the Gulf states had specific labor needs (teachers, health care workers, hotel workers, post office employees, bank workers, etc.) the plan advocated emphasizing

[25] République Tunisienne, *Plan de développement économique et social, 1977–1981* (Tunis, n.d.), pp. 154–55.
[26] Ibid., pp. 159–60.
[27] République Tunisienne, *Septième plan de développement économique et social, 1987–91* (Tunis, n.d.), pp. 69–70.
[28] Republic of Tunisia, *Plan for Economic and Social Development, 1982–1986*, Volume I (Tunis, n.d.), pp. 119–20.
[29] CERES and CEE, p. 42.

training in these areas.[30] In this way, Tunisian needs would be filled and cooperation with Arab states would be expanded.[31] Some measures had already been taken, among them employment missions, constituted jointly by representatives of the National Agency for Technical Cooperation and representatives of the OTTEEFP, which had been set up in the embassies in Saudi Arabia, Kuwait, the Emirates, Qatar and Iraq. The plan also made an interesting distinction between emigration to Arab states and European states: emigration to European states was, by its nature, supposed to end, whereas emigration to Arab states could build upon existing ties with Arab countries, it asserted. It noted that Arab countries were contributing to Tunisia's development through their investments; Tunisia, therefore, had a responsibility to contribute in turn to their development through providing human capital.[32]

The initiation of the implementation of a structural adjustment program (SAP) in 1986 marked the beginning of a new stage in employment policy.[33] The broad lines of SAPs have been the same for all countries: opening domestic markets to imports through the reduction in trade barriers, focusing on export promotion, rationalizing prices, dampening domestic consumption demand, and reducing social spending, including subsidies. Therefore, the Seventh Plan (1987–91), produced just a few months before the coup that retired Bourguiba, advocated a program of structural reforms that targeted the promotion of exports, the rationalization of investments, and an improvement in competitiveness (reduction of tariffs, relaxation of investment restrictions, change in exchange rate policy, etc.). The plan mentions the role of the Technical Cooperation Agency in placing cadres abroad and discusses simplifying recruitment procedures, reducing transportation costs, organizing language training sessions – all of which were intended to facilitate worker placement. The plan, like its predecessors, also continued to emphasize investment

---

[30] At the same time, part of what Tunisia was experiencing during this period was a brain drain. A 19 May 1987 article in *Le Temps* discussed a then-recent examination of this problem in/from Tunisia. It discerned four major reasons behind the brain drain in addition to the desire for a better wage, which apparently was not the most important one: better professional conditions overseas, proper facilities so that one could exercise one's profession well (equipment, laboratories, etc.); limited opportunities in Tunisia to demonstrate one's creative spirit, as well as uncertainty about the future; feelings of marginalization or alienation, especially among those who had studied abroad; and the inability to find work owing to the lack of fit between the curriculum offered by Tunisian schools and the demands present in the labor market. The specific example mentioned was that Tunisia was producing too many engineers and not enough specialized workers.

[31] This was the period of Mohammed Mzali's prime ministership during which there was a greater opening to the Arab states, and greater influence from the Gulf on Tunisia, especially in the form of greater religious influence.

[32] Republic of Tunisia, Volume I, p. 128.   [33] Baccar and Sanaa, p. 65.

and family planning as key to addressing the employment issue.[34] Nonetheless, during this period, unemployment rose from 13.1 percent to 16.1 percent, and would have been worse had it not been for emigration to the Gulf states, to Libya and to Italy.[35]

On 7 November 1987, Prime Minister Zayn al-'Abdin Ben 'Ali led what has been called a "Constitutional Coup" which removed the ageing and increasingly detached Bourguiba from power. Ben 'Ali's move put an end to a period of economic and political malaise and launched an era of state institutional renewal. In a speech given to the cabinet only two weeks after what came to be called the *changement*, the new president made special reference in his remarks on youth to the need to devote greater attention to the problems of the second generation of emigrants.[36] While the tenor and content of this speech seem normal today, given the changes that his regime has implemented regarding its expatriates (to be explored in detail below), at the time it marked a significant change in the state's articulation of its relationship to Tunisians abroad. For the first time, the second generation of emigration was included in a program aimed at the youth of the country, thus putting those living outside Tunisia's borders on a par with those living within. It viewed them as deserving of the same consideration as those at home, while at the same time recognizing their special status.[37] This same interest was manifested in the ninth point of Ben 'Ali's program for the future which stressed the need "to continue to kindle the feelings of belonging to Tunis and to its culture and civilization among the second generation."[38]

In 1984 the OTTEEFP had been divided into two offices, the Office de la Promotion de l'Emploi et des Travailleurs Tunisiens à l'Etranger (OPETTE) and the Office de la Formation Professionnelle. Now, in the aftermath of the coup a real reorganization of the offices dealing with the communities abroad took place and the Office des Tunisiens à l'Etranger (OTE, see below) was established. Job placement was no longer included in the charge of this bureau, which was thenceforth to focus exclusively on Tunisians already resident abroad. It is important to

---

[34] République Tunisienne, *Septième plan de développement économique et social, 1987–91*, p. 196.

[35] CERES and CEE, p. 33.

[36] At the time of the *changement*, 47 percent of the émigré population (122,000) was fifteen years of age or younger, and almost all who were fourteen or younger had been born in the host country (*l'Action*, 16 December 1987).

[37] Youssef Alouane, *Droits de l'homme et émigrés tunisiens en Europe* (Tunis: SAGEP, 1992), p. 123.

[38] Office des Tunisiens à l'Etranger, "Nadwah Wataniyyah l-il-Tunisiyyin f-il-Kharij, Waraqat 'Amal Lajnah: al-Ajyal al-Jadidah l-il-Hijrah bayna al-Muhafizah 'ala al-Hawiyyah w-al-Indimaj fi-Buldan al-Iqamah" (7 August 2002).

note the time lag here. The family and longer-term nature of the community presence abroad had already become clear by the late 1970s, but there was no real institutional acknowledgement of this (except the first reorganization of the OFPE–OTTEEFP in 1973) until after the *changement*. This can probably be explained by the general malaise that characterized Tunisian politics with Bourguiba's health failing and his party, the PSD, increasingly sclerotic.

In both the president's and the prime minister's speeches introducing the Eighth Plan (1992–96), the first drafted after the *changement*, unemployment is clearly mentioned. Both emphasized the need for greater opening to foreign investment, but there is nothing on the TREs (*Tunisiens résidant à l'étranger* as they were increasingly called). Nor does the section on employment mention emigration as part of the strategy of job creation. That said, this is the first plan with a special section on what was called the CTE (*communauté tunisienne à l'étranger*, "Tunisian community abroad"). During the course of the plan, as part of a program clearly aimed at asserting more forcefully the state's claims to the loyalty of its expatriates, efforts were to be intensified to deepen Tunisian national identity among emigrants and to consolidate their ties with the home country. The plan also stated that government activity would be oriented toward encouraging the CTE to contribute still more to the task of developing the country,[39] thus also making this the first plan in which there is the enunciation of a two-way relationship between state and community, rather than simply between local job market and potential labor exports. This is a serious, qualitative change. The discourse is no longer just about how enabling people to emigrate will affect the local labor market; it is now about communities abroad, what the state will do to preserve and reinforce their ties to the homeland, *and* what the members of these communities abroad can do to contribute to the state's development. As the plan insists, North African states needed to defend the rights of the emigrant communities. This presupposed a reinforcement of the *encadrement*[40] of the expatriate communities and an intensification of the activity of associations, *amicales* (see below) and other organizations.

---

[39] République Tunisienne, *Huitième plan de développement, 1992–1996* (Tunis, 1992), p. 235.

[40] *Encadrement* does not translate easily into English. It has the sense of "framing" or "surrounding," thus implying a kind of support, it also suggests a (political) surveillance or organizing. Such state involvement is in keeping with the nature of the essentially one-party Tunisian state. It is a term which one does not find, for example, in Moroccan discourse.

The Eighth Plan was also clearly concerned with cultural attachment and values. Specifically, greater attention was to be devoted to developing appropriate methods to teach Arabic (see below).[41] More broadly, the authors realized the impact that exposure and access to other cultures might have on the emigrants. In response, they called for a kind of intervention that would furnish the community with cultural tools to reinforce their feelings of pride and belonging to the homeland. The goal of such an approach should not be misunderstood, however, for, since the *changement*, Tunisia has promoted the integration of its nationals into the host countries, while insisting that such integration does not require the relinquishment of their own language, culture or religion. On the contrary, official discourse has promoted full rights in both countries, and has stressed that the better the expatriate knows his/her own culture, the better equipped s/he will be to play an essential role in the dialogue between cultures, another important theme of the Ben 'Ali period. By demonstrating that Tunisia is an example of tolerance, TREs can serve as vehicles of cultural rapprochement, while making an economic and social contribution where they are.[42]

In 1993, during the period of the Eighth Plan, in a speech to the Tribune of the European parliament, Ben 'Ali was the first to call for a Euro-Maghrebi charter, intended to define the rights and obligations of the North African communities in Europe. Subsequently, as the first Southern Mediterranean littoral state to sign a partnership accord with Europe (1995), Tunisia insisted upon inserting in this document a social component consolidating the rights of Tunisians in Europe and affirming the principle of non-discrimination between Tunisians legally resident in Europe and EU nationals, on the level of employment, salaries, work termination, and social protection.[43] In this way, the state not only manifested concern for the welfare of its citizens abroad, but also insisted that they be treated on a par with host country nationals in key areas. Tunis thus projected both moral authority as well as sovereign concern, while at the same time accepting a significant degree of effective integration of its nationals abroad.

---

[41] République Tunisienne, *Huitième plan de développement, 1992–1996*, p. 239.

[42] Interview with 'Abdelmajid Baouab, Director-General of Consular Affairs, Ministry of Foreign Affairs, 10 August 2002.

[43] Office des Tunisiens à l'Etranger, "Nadwah Wataniyyah l-il-Tunisiyyin f-il-Kharij, Waraqat 'Amal Lajnah: Ta'thirat Ahdath 11/9/2001 'ala Wad' al-Muhajirin bi-Buldan al-Iqamah" (7 August 2002). Tunisia currently has twelve social security conventions, eight of them with EU countries: France (1965), Belgium(1975), Holland (1978), Luxembourg (1980), Germany (1984), Italy (1984), Austria (1989) and Spain (2001).

While the Ninth Plan (1997–2001) did not include a separate chapter on the CTE – they instead figured in the section entitled "Human Resources and Social and Cultural Development" – it did mark the first time that the CTE was *consulted* in the discussions leading to the drafting of the plan, thus treating these extraterritorial residents as full members of the political community.[44] To adapt and modernize the existing *amicale* and associational work to respond to changing conditions, special emphasis was to be placed on building/maintaining ties with the second and third generations.[45] The plan specified a budget of 6 million TDs annually for social action among TREs, as well as 4 million TDs for Arabic language instruction. It further reported the enlargement of the consular network, an increase in radio and TV broadcasts, the opening of additional Agence Tunisienne pour la Communication Extérieure (ATCE)[46] offices abroad, and the diffusion of new journals and informational documents.[47]

The new plan period was also to pay special attention to the Tunisian family to enable it to confront such challenges as delinquency, unemployment, and family conflicts. In general, greater efforts were to be directed toward women and youth, who represent 40 percent and 45 percent of the CTE in France, respectively. In addition, studies were to be undertaken aimed at encouraging greater participation of TREs in Tunisia's development. Finally, the plan expressed concern about the future of the first generation of TREs, who were facing retirement and possible definitive return. Given the reduced opportunities, especially in the European host countries, a large return influx could not be ruled out.[48]

Emigration policy as read through the law

Before examining the institutions that Tunis has established to deal with its expatriates, it is worth discussing briefly several legal changes that have affected expatriates. Perhaps the most significant change of the Bourguiba period came in November 1973, when the Tunisian nationality code of 1963 was amended to allow for dual citizenship. A French law of 1923 had assimilated Tunisian territory to France and hence, during the pre-independence period, when Tunisians had had the

---

[44] République Tunisienne, *Neuvième plan de développement, 1997–2001*, Volume II, *Continue sectoriel* (Tunis, 1997), p. 313.

[45] Ibid., p. 240.

[46] The Agence Tunisienne de la Communication Extérieure is the primary informational arm of the Tunisian government abroad.

[47] République Tunisienne, *Neuvième plan*, Volume II, *Continue sectoriel*, p. 311.

[48] Ibid., pp. 313–14.

possibility of obtaining French nationality, to do so was seen as treasonous. This same emotional response was present in the nationality codes of 1956 and 1963, according to which anyone who took a new nationality not only lost his/her Tunisian nationality, but also was obliged to leave the territory. The timing suggests that the change in Tunisian law, which permitted the acquisition of a second nationality, came in response to France's 1973 abrogation of the 1923 law.[49] Gildas further argues that the change came in recognition of the fact that, given the unemployment situation in the home country, those who had gone abroad were part of a generation that had been in effect "sacrificed," and whose situation needed to be improved.[50] Allowing those abroad who would not return to take a second nationality seemed a reasonable response and a partial solution. An alternative reading would be that, if policymakers realized that increasing numbers of citizens were likely to stay abroad, the state had two choices: to risk losing any sovereign claim to the TREs by forcing them to renounce their Tunisian nationality; or to allow them to preserve their Tunisian citizenship (and as a by-product, hopefully, their ties and goodwill) while still enjoying the benefits of citizenship in the host country. Such a relaxation of the notion of the exclusivity of membership in the political community traditionally associated with sovereignty offered the Tunisian state a better chance of maintaining relations with its nationals than would have a rigid insistence upon singular allegiance.

Other significant legal changes have been overwhelmingly in the area of the economy. As part of the broader liberalization of the economy, the state exempted equipment for investment projects from customs upon émigrés' definitive return, offered them preferential interest rates, and permitted them to open bank accounts in convertible dinars. Indeed, encouraging CTE investment in Tunisia has been a key goal since 1987. In what appears to be the first acknowledgment of their financial contribution, at least in such a document, the Eighth Plan noted that during the period 1982–88, TRE investments of 74 million TD had created some 40,000 jobs.[51] In recognition of this potential, during the plan period, new economic facilities were to be offered upon an expatriate's definitive return: additional customs privileges if one imported materials for an investment project; the suppression of the VAT for local equipment purchases for such projects; and permission for

---

[49] Intervention by Mohammed Charfi, Institut de Recherche sur le Maghreb Contemporain, in *L'Etranger: Actes des Journées d'études organisées dans le cadre du séminaire annuel de l'IRMC, "Identités et territoires: les catégorisations du social,"* Tunis, 16–17 February 2002 (Tunis: IRMC, 2002), pp. 39–40.

[50] Gildas, p. 370.

[51] République Tunisienne, *Huitième plan de développement, 1992–1996*, p. 239.

non-resident Tunisians to benefit from resident status to facilitate a variety of measures, especially in the fields of banking and finance.[52]

The 1993 Investment Code also offers numerous fiscal and financial advantages to non-resident Tunisians as well as to those who return to live in the country. In addition, investment information centers, which host investment briefings coordinated by the embassy, have been set up in Tunisian consulates and embassies in European cities with concentrations of Tunisian immigrant entrepreneurship.[53] In official discussions of investment, the catchphrase is the *mis à niveau*, or comprehensive upgrading, that the state has placed at the center of its development strategy. As part of this strategy the government argues that it is a patriotic duty of Tunisians, in particular businessmen abroad, to make a proper contribution to national development.[54] Among the various institutions that the Tunisian state has put in place to facilitate such investment are the *guichet unique* (meaning "one-stop investing") rather than forcing TREs to deal with many different government offices, the API mentioned earlier, regional investment companies/societies, assistance cells for launching new projects created within the customs administration, and clubs of Tunisian businessmen abroad.[55]

In terms of social concerns, children of returnees are now permitted to enroll at the educational level in the Tunisian system corresponding to their level abroad. They may also take advantage of remedial classes in Arabic, and register for degrees in both French and Arabic. To facilitate home purchases, the Housing Bank offers special savings accounts free of taxes for a period of at least four years, and there are special credit arrangements for those who want to buy houses, with loans available up to 20,000 TD at an interest rate of 8.25 percent. In addition, the Société Nationale Immobilière sets aside for TREs 10 percent of the number of residences constructed in any given project.[56]

---

[52] République Tunisienne, *Neuvième plan de développement, 1997–2001*, Volume II, *Continue sectoriel*, p. 312.

[53] Jean-Pierre Cassarino, *Tunisian New Entrepreneurs and Their Past Experiences of Migration in Europe: Resource mobilization, networks, and hidden disaffection* (Burlington, VT: Ashgate, 2000), p. 5, and p. 9, note 10.

[54] *Le Renouveau*, 4 April 1996.

[55] *Le Renouveau*, 30 March 1997. The number of industrial projects initiated by TREs and agreed to by the API from 1975 to 1993 was more than 3,000 (TD 158 million), and allowed for the creation of 34,389 jobs. This was one-tenth of all the projects agreed to by the API. More than three-quarters of these projects were initiated by Tunisians living in Europe. In agriculture, from 1983 to 1995, 302 projects (TD 20 million) permitted the creation of 875 jobs (*Parfum du Pays*, 1 November 1996, pp. 6–7).

[56] *Le Temps*, 7 January 1996.

Thus, the number and type of privileges that the government has put in place to benefit TREs are extensive. The state assumes a continuing allegiance to the homeland on the part of its expatriates, but has also initiated a range of measures that further strengthen its claim to emigrant loyalty and resources. The authoritarian content of the political system may lead some Tunisians to continue to be wary of interaction with it, but its commitment to maintaining ties to TREs and to attracting expatriate investment cannot be disputed.

The role of remittances

Before concluding this section on government policy toward emigration, a brief consideration of the role of remittances is in order. (See Table 4.2.) During the 1960s and early 1970s, the period of expansion in the numbers of TREs and of economic growth in Tunisia itself, remittance levels also rose. Through the mid-1970s, more than two-thirds of Tunisian workers transferred the major part of their savings to families back home. In 1975, official statistics put remittances in third place behind tourism and petroleum exports in terms of hard currency contributions to the economy.[57]

Through the mid-1970s the post office remained the most important channel for sending money home.[58] Only post-1970 did Tunisian banks begin to realize the importance of worker transfers, as the flows were quite small in comparison with their major interest: international commercial exchanges. The TREs also had their reservations, as the state character of Tunisian banks, especially the Société Tunisienne de Banque (STB), generated mistrust. Beginning in 1970 the banks undertook a number of initiatives, including sending informational missions to the communities in France and establishing savings accounts for emigrants. The STB also opened a number of new branches to serve expatriates. Finally, there was the French banking system, which had direct relations with the large Tunisian banks, many of which were former branches from the colonial period.[59]

The drop in remittance levels from 1982 to 1985 can be explained by such domestic developments as: the Bourguiba succession struggles, the stagnation of the state, increasing social tensions, problems with Libya, the drop in oil and phosphate prices, decline in employment creation

---

[57] Moustafa Kharoufi, "Les effets de l'émigration sur les sociétés de départ au Maghreb: nouvelles données, nouvelles approches," an article from *Correspondances, Bulletin Scientifique de l'IRMC*, from the website of l'Institut de Recherche sur le Maghreb Contemporain, p. 4: www.irmcmaghreb.org/corres/textes/karoufi.htm.
[58] Gildas, p. 226.   [59] Ibid., p. 228.

Table 4.2. *Tunisian expatriate remittances (millions of dinars)*

Year	Amount	Percentage change
1963	2.4	
1964	4.7	95.8
1965	5.0	6.4
1966	4.0	−20.0
1967	5.8	45.0
1968	7.7	32.8
1969	11.4	48.1
1970	15.2	33.3
1971	22.7	49.3
1972	29.5	30.0
1973	41.2	39.7
1974	51.6	25.2
1975	58.7	13.8
1976	61.9	5.5
1977	72.2	16.6
1978	91.7	27.0
1979	115.4	25.8
1980	153.0	32.6
1981	178.3	16.5
1982	219.6	23.2
1983	243.8	11.0
1984	245.9	0.9
1985	225.8	−8.1
1986	287.1	27.1
1987	403.0	40.4
1988	466.6	15.8
1989	463.0	−0.8
1990	526.0	13.6
1991	527.0	0.2
1992	508.0	−3.6
1993	599.5	18.0
1994	695.7	16.1
1995	711.8	2.3
1996	798.3	12.2
1997	845.9	6.0
1998	901.9	6.6
1999	1,019.7	13.1
2000	1,091.1	7.0
2001	1,234.2	13.1

Source: Banque Centrale de Tunisie.

Table 4.3. *Tunisian expatriate numbers*

Year	Expatriates in France	Total worldwide
1994	344,488	607,848
1995	350,000	603,300
1996	384,716	646,365
1997	385,523	629,735
1998	411,863	660,259
1999	411,863	660,272
2000	436,461	698,108
2001	470,549	763,980

Source: Tunisie, Ministère des Affaires Etrangères.

(−12%), a commercial deficit growing at 2% per year, and debt representing 60% of GDP.[60] The notable resurgence of remittances in 1986 and 1987 is explained first by the devaluation of the dinar as part of the SAP, and then by the peaceful regime change and the restoration of confidence it engendered.[61] This growth has continued almost unabated, encouraged in part by the rising standard of living of the expatriates themselves.[62] For the period 1962–90, transfers represented more than 4% of GDP and 10% of receipts in the current account, equivalent to more than half of the debt service or of tourism receipts, and more than three-fifths of petroleum exports. With the continuing debt burden and the decline in the importance of oil, these transfers – and hence the CTE in general – have acquired a tremendous importance for the macroeconomic stability of the country.[63] (See Table 4.3.)

Summary

In terms of economic policy, state interest in emigration was guided for the first decades following independence by the "employment effect," the impact that outmigration had on dampening excess demand for jobs domestically, and hence in reducing the potential for social unrest. Perhaps as a way of trying to deflect criticism that the state could not provide sufficient employment for its nationals, the planning documents considered employment abroad as equivalent to employment at home, an interesting twist on the notion of insiders and outsiders to the polity. In any case, there was no question during this period of the affiliation of

[60] CERES and CEE, pp. 77–8.   [61] Alouane, p. 113.
[62] *Jeune Afrique* 2172, 26 August – 1 September 2002.   [63] CERES and CEE, p. 78.

these workers. They could only be viewed as belonging to, and hence the responsibility of, Tunis, although the need to export them raises the issue of the Tunisian state's failure to meet the sovereign's responsibility to provide for its citizens/subjects.

The closing of Western Europe to additional, substantial emigration, and the impact on Tunisia of the domestic and international economic developments examined above, gradually led the state to re-evaluate its approach. The post-coup regime introduced a discourse about the expatriates which emphasized that they were considered an integral part of Tunisia, while not seeking to undermine their degree of integration into the host states. The discourse implies the inseparability of the expatriate community from the homeland, as symbolized by the phrase which has now become common: "al-Tunisiyyun f-il-kharij fi qalb al-watan" ("Tunisians abroad are in the heart of the homeland"), in which "heart" can refer either to ties of affection or to locational centrality. According to such a view, their residence outside the territorial boundaries of the state in no way diminishes either their Tunisianness or the state authorities' claim to their loyalty and what may proceed from it. Thus, a new or invigorated sovereign claim was being laid to these communities and their resources, mediated by the state's pragmatic acceptance that a certain degree of integration/acculturation abroad not only was inevitable, but could in fact be put to work to Tunisia's advantage. Those who were abroad and successful not only were in a better position to contribute to development back home, they also helped to cement strong bilateral ties between the homeland and the country of residence.

As we saw in the case of Morocco, while planning documents reveal some elements of state policy, their focus is limited. We now turn to examine chronologically the evolution of state institutional involvement in the Tunisian emigrant communities. Parallels in terms of broad historical developments are notable, but the content and practice of Tunisian state institutions evolve in a way that differs markedly from that of their Moroccan counterparts.

State institutions during the Bourguiba era: independence–1987[64]

Although a small state with limited resources and relatively small numbers of nationals abroad, Tunisia established one of the most extensive

---

[64] One of the results of the 1987 coup has been the subsequent gradual removal of or difficulty of access to materials dealing with the Bourguiba period. This includes a general unwillingness (fear) among most people to discuss specifics or even mention

consular networks in France, with one office for every 11,000 Tunisians. Consulates in Paris, Lyon and Marseille were opened between 1956 and 1964, while second-tier establishments developed largely between 1970 and 1975, with the real consolidation of the Tunisian community in France. An evaluation written at the end of the 1970s summed up consular activity in the following terms:

Although the consuls are charged equally with representing the government administratively, commercially and culturally, the majority of their time is devoted to management and contacts with the migrant workers and their families ... Thus, the consulate is an important social space for the migrants, because it plays for them a double role of intermediary and mediator, as much with French institutions as with the Tunisian administration.[65]

Beyond the expanding network of establishments belonging to the Ministry of Foreign Affairs, the first set of institutions opened to deal with expatriates were the Amicales des Travailleurs Tunisiens en France. On their premises, nationals could consult the Tunisian press and participate in meetings on politics back home or immigration in France. The *amicales* also played an important socio-cultural role: they sponsored folk groups from Tunisia, sports teams, the celebration of certain religious occasions, and Arabic language instruction. Thus, they were meeting places where the Tunisian community could gather for events that helped preserve ties with the homeland.[66]

While there is very little written about the Tunisian *amicales*, it appears that their unofficial, yet perhaps most important, function was to monitor the community abroad as an extension and in the service of the authoritarian state at home. The first ones were opened between 1956 and 1960, in Paris, Lyon, Marseille and Nice.[67] Given that their establishment came immediately on the heels of independence when Tunisian numbers abroad were quite small, the Tunisian state's interest in penetrating the communities abroad through such structures suggests that they were seen as natural or necessary extensions of the state apparatus, and that the communities were regarded as extensions of the homeland. Indeed, although theoretically independent of the consular networks, in practice they often had their headquarters inside the consulates themselves and were in fact offshoots of the regime, barely veiled cells of the PSD, the only legal political party in Tunisia at the time. The person responsible for

Bourguiba's name. Hence, the written/published materials I was able to find on this period during my research stint were few (and, in any case, were no less characterized by the *langue de bois* [political cant] than those of the current period), and interviewees generally avoided questions or answers that might shed light on the record of Bourguiba's regime.

[65] Gildas, p. 235.   [66] Ibid., p. 237.   [67] Ibid., pp. 236–7.

the PSD cell was usually an official or unofficial employee of the consulate, and the directors were chosen or preselected by the consul, who
presided over the congress of cells. As a result, the *amicales* were viewed
warily by those members of the expatriate communities who were not
sympathetic to the PSD.[68]

As time went on, the *encadrement* of Tunisians by the *amicales* was
intended to reduce the risks of the same political and social "contamina-
tion" about which the Morocco regime was later to worry. Tunisians
often participated in demonstrations and protests, and such involvement
irritated their home government. In March 1973, the Tunisian Council of
Ministers published a statement in which it condemned "the irresponsi-
ble behavior" of these workers, "whose plotting risks to damage the
prestige of the country and in any case, upsets the French authorities to
whom we are linked by accords regulating the entry of Tunisian labor into
France."[69] Probably pressured by the French, at a late summer 1973
"Regional Seminar for the Emigrés of the South," Tunisia's Minister of
the Interior stated: "Your role is to preserve this outstanding image [of
TREs] and to fight with us against these intruders who are generally as
useless at home as they are abroad."[70] In such a climate, the role of the
amicales, in the official discourse of the government, was to create among
Tunisian workers abroad a climate of "security and unity" which would
protect them from any bad habits or ideologies that were hostile to their
country and its reputation.[71]

In addition to this work abroad, beginning in 1966 the state began to
hold annual expatriate conferences in Tunisia as part of the policy of
encadrement. Key party and government officials presided at these events
in which emigrants were reminded of the principles of national politics,
their rights and their obligations, as well as their role in the development
of the country. They were also an important forum for workers, for the
concerns expressed in these meetings often subsequently served as the
bases for discussions between Tunisian and French officials. In 1974, the
government also launched a journal (*Billedi*) with the goal of maintaining
ties with the homeland. Printed in Arabic, it provided information on life
and politics in Tunisia and on the life of emigrants. Emigrants themselves
sent in articles, and *Billedi* was distributed in Tunisia as well as through
the consulates and *amicales*.[72]

Nevertheless, despite the state's efforts, its policies and institutions
were clearly out of touch with important developments in the CTE.

---

[68] Michalak, p. 15.   [69] *La Presse*, 17 March 1973, cited in Gildas, p. 144.
[70] *La Presse*, 14 August 1973, cited in Gildas, p. 144.   [71] Gildas, p. 133.
[72] Ibid., p. 237.

A 1 August 1987 article mentioned the dual cultural attachment of the second generation abroad, and the problems this raised regarding the relationship between citizenship (*muwatanah*, meaning "attachment to the homeland") and nationality (*jinsiyyah*, referring merely to having a passport). This was during the heyday of the Beur movement, and the article was no doubt correct in arguing that there was a crisis of identity among the second generation which was leading it to reject both the host and the home society and their respective lifestyles. Indeed, the young were searching for new forms or models to assert their presence and uniqueness, and to establish pressure groups inside France or other host societies.[73]

However, in 1980, prior to the emergence of the Beur movement, and as a harbinger of subsequent developments on the religious, political and identity fronts, an important Tunisian oppositional group, the Groupement Islamique en France (GIF) was established. Its work in organizing summer camps and conferences paralleled some Tunisian state activities, although it was best-known for its publications.[74] The GIF was the forerunner of the Mouvement de la Tendance Islamique (MTI), which was ultimately institutionalized in the form of al-Nahdah, an Islamist political party which emerged as the strongest competitor to the PSD – and about which, more below.

The *changement*

Political stagnation, economic malaise if not crisis, and a growing Islamist movement ultimately triggered the coup of 7 November 1987. Bourguiba's forced retirement and replacement by his prime minister and former minister of the interior Zayn al-'Abdin Ben 'Ali marked the end of an era. Ben 'Ali moved quickly to reinvigorate and restructure a host of state institutions, including the PSD, ultimately renaming it the Rassemblement constitutionnel démocratique (RCD). The new government also began to change the state discourse to one that emphasized *citoyenneté* ("citizenship") and *partenariat* ("partnership" or "cooperation") between the state and civil society. At least initially, it appeared that Tunisia was on a new path leading to a less authoritarian future.

A presidential decision in April 1988, only a few months after the *changement*, gave Tunisians abroad the right to vote in presidential elections, and, as noted in the previous section, it was under Ben 'Ali that, for the first time, the CTE figured into and subsequently was actively

---

[73] *Al-'Amal*, 1 August 1987.   [74] Nielsen, *Muslims in Europe*, p. 17.

involved in discussions of the development plans. Once termed "le moindre mal" ("the lesser evil") by Prime Minister Hedi Nouira under Bourguiba, emigration was now seen as an opportunity, as long as the affective and economic ties with the homeland were not broken.[75]

In France, shortly after the coup, the Tunisian government established a Council of the Tunisian Communities in France (CTCF), a framework for a broad range of associations. In the initial post-*changement* period, Tunisians of all political stripes, from communists to moderate Islamists, were represented, all of whom were convinced that significant changes were underway at home. However, members of the RCD then used the newly created CTCF to found the Rassemblement Tunisien (the "Tunisian Grouping") en France, which was charged with controlling or managing the community there. What followed was a proliferation of associations serving a wide variety of TRE sectors and interests, but led by people with close ties to the regime. The decentralized nature and official NGO status of these organizations provided the regime with a greater capacity both to monitor the expatriate communities and to raise funds from French sources.[76] "Pluralism" remained a centerpiece of official discourse just as a proliferation of associations gave it institutional form, but the conduct of the state continued to be that of an authoritarian system based in a single party with mass mobilizational pretensions and little use for associational independence.

In the meantime, the more secular orientation of the Tunisian state was also being challenged, both at home and abroad. By the end of the 1980s, and particularly owing to its role in the 1989 controversy over schoolgirls' wearing of the veil in Creuil, the French-based Union of Islamic Organizations (UOI), a Muslim Brotherhood-inspired group led by Tunisian Rachid al-Ghannouchi, a founder of MTI, had come to dominate the Muslim associative movement in France: "Its success was principally due to the professionalism of its organization, which deployed many young, university-educated, bilingual Arabic-French officers to implement a coherent strategy."[77] Most UOI founders were Tunisian students who had been initiated into activism through MTI, which had been repressed in the latter days of Bourguiba's rule. However, after a brief respite under Ben 'Ali, by 1989, as its European offshoot was asserting its influence in France, MTI's political party heir, al-Nahdah,

---

[75] *Jeune Afrique* 2130, 6–12 November 2001.
[76] Nicolas Beau and Jean-Pierre Tuquoi, *Notre ami Ben Ali* (Paris: Editions de la Découverte, 1999), pp. 191–92. The authors detail numerous examples of often vicious Tunisian state harassment and persecution of exiles: pp. 189–98.
[77] Kepel, *Allah in the West*, p. 195.

also began to be suppressed at home. Indeed, the early promise of greater pluralism in Tunisia gradually gave way to a full-scale assault against al-Nahdah and the Islamists (1989–91), brutally ending the nascent political opening.[78] Little wonder, then, that the Tunisian state extended its persecution of al-Nahdah's members across the Mediterranean.

Although tolerance was a focus of official discourse, the regime's definition of it implied combating "obscurantism," a code word for political Islam.[79] From Ben 'Ali's perspective, al-Nahdah supporters in the communities abroad threatened Tunisian domestic security as well as his regime's plans to transform Tunisians abroad into the kind of strategic assets with European states implied by the following quote:

We are working to make emigration one of the junctions of economic cooperation and civilizational exchange between the North and the South. In this we are relying on our conviction that partial and temporary solutions, like measures and administrative formalities, cannot constitute a solution to the problem of immigration. The most effective means to contain it consists of joint action toward the promotion of sustainable development in the country of origin and the establishment of relations based on balanced cooperation between the northern and southern shores of the Mediterranean.[80]

For its part, Paris was deeply concerned with what an Islamist victory in Algeria, which seemed just a matter of time in the early stages of the civil war, would mean for France's large, resident North African population. Given European concerns about the unrest in Algeria and the role of Islamists in it, the early years of anti-Islamist repression in Tunisia saw regular and often high-level coordination between the Tunisian and French security services, and little sympathy was shown applications for refugee status filed by members of al-Nahdah.[81] As time passed, however, although coordination between French and Tunisian security services has continued, it has diminished in intensity. Tunis's relentless pursuit of opposition figures of *any* political stripe, even absent a serious Islamist threat, has wearied its French partners, and in some cases has even led them to afford a certain protection to regime opponents. For example, Ghannouchi, who resides in London, nonetheless makes periodic low-profile visits to France to which the French police simply close their eyes.

---

[78] A number of subsequent laws, such as the 1992 organic law on associations, largely directed against Tunisia's human rights organization the Ligue Tunisienne des Droits de l'Homme, should also be understood as part of a broader state effort to rein in what had promised to be a vibrant and independent NGO sector: Cassarino, p. 109.

[79] This concern with the rise of a certain kind of political Islam continued even after Tunisia crushed its domestic Islamist movement, as the ongoing bloody civil war in Algeria continued to cast its shadow over political developments in Tunisia.

[80] *Le Renouveau*, 8 August 1999.   [81] Beau and Tuquoi, p. 187.

Moreover, thanks, on the one hand, to the various forms of intimidation the Tunisian state has been willing to use against them and, on the other, to the penetration of the communities that has been possible through the institutions that will be further discussed below, by the mid–late 1990s the Tunisian communities in Europe were largely depoliticized and quiescent. As one French official stated, "The Tunisians are a dream for the police. If only all the foreign communities were that peaceful."[82]

Government institutions: L'Office des Tunisiens à l'Etranger (OTE)

Of the Tunisian state institutions involved in expatriate affairs since the *changement*, the Office des Tunisiens à l'Etranger (*Diwan al-Tunisiyyin b-il-Kharij*) in the Ministry of Social Affairs deserves first mention. The product of a June 1988 restructuring of what was then called the Direction de l'Emigration,[83] the OTE was charged with: developing and implementing programs overseeing TREs; establishing a program of assistance for them, and for their families in their country of residence or in Tunisia; carrying out cultural programs intended to develop and reinforce the attachment of their children to the homeland; facilitating the reinsertion of Tunisian emigrants returning to Tunis into the national economy; and instituting a system regularly providing information to TREs about the homeland.[84] This reorganization represented an institutional expression of the fact that the possibility for extensive worker placement abroad had ended: henceforth, this bureau would have responsibility for matters concerning the communities already established abroad. The realms of professional training and placement were subsequently dealt with by the Office de la Formation Professionnelle (for those who were lesser-skilled or unskilled workers) and the Agence Tunisienne pour de la Coopération Technique (in existence since 1972) for skilled cadres.[85]

The new focus was also intended to enable the OTE to respond better to the changed nature of the problems the CTE faced. In this regard, the

---

[82] Ibid., p. 188.

[83] The OTE traces its origins to the OPETTE, which, it will be remembered, had been separated from the OTTEEFP in 1984. Thus, the establishment of the OTE was in fact simply a new stage in state interest, focused on the changing realities of Tunisian emigration and life in the CTE.

[84] Article 14 of Law 60–88 of 2 June 1988. République Tunisienne, Ministère des Affaires Sociales, *Office des tunisiens à l'étranger* (a brochure) (Tunis, 1995), p. 3.

[85] Interview with 'Adel Snoussi, Agence Tunisienne pour la Coopération Technique, 12 August 2002, Tunis.

Director-General of the OTE mentioned five major challenges. The first was the children, the new generation. OTE activities encourage them to integrate into the host country, while maintaining their ties to their roots. This has at times put the Tunisian government at odds with the host countries, some of which seek integration in the form of assimilation, which the Tunisian government rejects. The second challenge concerns women. Since it is they who are, according to society's understanding, principally involved in transmitting societal values and traditions, they need special attention. It is also they who, because of level of education, language ability or employment possibilities, are more likely to suffer from isolation and alienation abroad. The third challenge involves the development of institutional responses to the increasing numbers of the skilled and well-educated in the communities. These people have something to contribute to Tunisia's development, and the state is seeking ways to involve them. Related to this is the fourth challenge: the presence of growing numbers of businessmen, who are potential investors. The state needs to find ways to tap into them as a source of both finance and information. Finally, there are the traditional problems of the first-generation emigrants, sometimes with their work, but also at times with their families who may not want to return definitively to Tunisia.[86]

The OTE depends upon a central administration and a decentralized network in Tunisia and abroad. It has in-country offices in Ariana, Ben Arous, Binzerte, Nabeul, Kasserine, Sousse, Sfax, Medenine, Gafsa, Tatouine and Kebili. These regional delegations are charged with organizing and coordinating all the activities set out in the office's mission as well as with putting in place programs at the level of the territorial entity that they cover.[87] In keeping with the challenges outlined above, the OTE sponsors activities in several different realms.[88]

In terms of the economy, the OTE's task is to marshal the support of Tunisian emigrants for the development of the country. As part of this function, the OTE organizes special development support days (*journées d'appui au développement*) for Tunisian businessmen resident abroad, to familiarize them with the country's investment needs. One of the primary objectives is to orient investment away from the large cities and to create a dynamic of contact between TREs and their regions of origin. Tabarka, Kairouan and Douz have recently hosted such meetings.

---

[86] Interview with Beshir El-Jema'i, Director-General, Office des Tunisiens à l'Etranger, 9 August 2002, Tunis.
[87] République Tunisienne, *Office des tunisiens à l'étranger* (brochure), pp. 4, 7.
[88] What follows is taken from ibid., except where noted otherwise.

In the social realm, the OTE is charged with assisting TREs and their families abroad, aiding those who have returned, and supporting families of non-resident Tunisians who have stayed behind in Tunisia. On the cultural front, the OTE is engaged in developing the community life of Tunisians abroad, and in deepening the sense of belonging to Tunisia among the young generation of emigrants. The OTE's community development strategy is directed at two primary target populations: the first generation of emigrants, composed essentially of workers and their wives, and the new generation, made up of the young who were born abroad or who have joined their parents at an early age. Here, not surprisingly, the goal is the creation and enrichment of ties between non-resident citizens, and between these same citizens and their country. To that end, beyond its network of social attachés, the OTE organizes informational campaigns and specialized seminars abroad. It has also created a network of offices called *espaces femme*, the objective of which is to strengthen the cohesion of the community and of the family. These offices target primarily young women of the second generation whose cultural referents are, naturally, no longer those of their mothers. As of late 1998, four of these offices were already functional in France – in Paris, Lyon, Marseille and Grenoble – and others were soon to be opened in Nice and Nanterre, as well as in five other major European cities – Düsseldorf, Rome, Palermo, Brussels and Hamburg.[89]

The OTE has also continued and expanded the program of Arabic language instruction intended for the young generation of emigrants. In Tunisia, summer programs were initiated in 1994, with the largest concentration of students hosted by the Bourguiba Institute in the capital. In 1998, 3,686 students benefited from classes in 126 centers around the country.[90] In the same vein, the OTE sponsors excursions, study trips, and vacation camps in Tunisia for the younger generation. The first such visits were in early 1988, and had as their objective dispelling prejudices about the home country among second-generation youth and reminding them of what the state has termed their "Arabo-Islamic" identity.[91] Its other activities include programs of religious supervision and cultural awareness, as well as the sports activities of numerous *amicales* (which, under the RCD, continue to be extensions of the party) and associations abroad.

As a different means of reaching out to the CTE, in November 1995 the OTE published the first edition of a magazine entitled *Parfum du*

---

[89] *Jeune Afrique* 1973, 3–9 November 1998: p. 79.
[90] *Jeune Afrique* 1965, 8–14 September 1998, and République Tunisienne, *Office des Tunisiens à l'étranger* (brochure), p. 8.
[91] *La Presse Soir*, 25 February 1988.

Pays / *Rihat al-Bilad* ("Scent of the Homeland") about and for the TREs. Over the next three years eight issues appeared. This four-color, glossy magazine had articles in both Arabic and French, but not simply translations of each other, with the exception of some speeches by the president, which were always prominently featured. Stories provided useful information for TREs on changes in European laws or accords with Tunisia, improvements in the summer return process, changes in Tunisian law of interest to TREs, the communities abroad, and Tunisian culture. Most of the articles, however, were about government measures and activities, either specifically targeting TREs and their *encadrement* abroad (especially women and youth) or promoting social and economic development. TREs were regularly reminded in these articles of the range of services the state provided, and were repeatedly encouraged to play an appropriate role in the development of the country.[92]

The collection of information has also been viewed as critical to OTE work. Hence, as in the case of the FHII's Observatoire, the OTE has established a Center for Specialized Documentation charged with assembling statistics on Tunisian emigration, determining the impact of emigration on economic and social development, and devising programs appropriate for assistance and training.[93] However, at the time of the fieldwork for this project it did not appear that this center was much farther along in its development than its FHII counterpart.

A final piece of OTE work relates to "the return." As is the case for Moroccans, for many Tunisians this means the annual pilgrimage home during the summer. For others it is the permanent return. Whichever is the case, the OTE has established a series of posts to orient the returnees and to provide travel assistance. Its regional offices facilitate the academic reintegration of returning children as well as the professional reinsertion of parents, and, like their counterparts overseas, the OTE's domestic offices are in place to inform and orient Tunisian emigrants interested in launching investment projects. For that purpose, it has permanent offices conveniently located at the major airports and ports.

Each summer thousands of Tunisians return home, especially by ferry from Marseille, with literally carloads of presents and merchandise. The Tunisian government has taken a growing interest in ensuring that this migration proceeds as smoothly as possible. To supplement the facilities mentioned above, special summer season OTE offices are provided at a number of secondary airports, ports and border crossings.[94] In addition,

---

[92] *Parfum du Pays*, various issues.
[93] République Tunisienne, *Office des Tunisiens à l'étranger* (brochure), p. 13.
[94] Ibid., p. 11.

the OTE has sought to enable Tunisians to make reservations for sea returns more than six months in advance, just as it has coordinated with maritime companies to ensure an increase in the number of trips available.[95] The OTE has also worked with the national airline, Tunisair, to upgrade service, reduce prices and increase the number of flights.[96]

Last, but certainly not least, is the annual émigré conference, the continuation of a practice that began in the 1960s. From the journalistic coverage of the first such meetings following the *changement*, it seems clear that, under Bourguiba, these meetings had been closed affairs bringing together representatives of the *amicales* and the PSD, not gatherings in which voices of independent Tunisian associations were welcome. In 1988, less than a year after the *changement* and with many developments indicating that Tunisia was set on a new, pluralist path, the attendance and content of the meeting changed dramatically. Many representatives from independent associations came, as did a significant number of youth. All were vocal in expressing their concerns and problems, primary among which was the continuing fusion of the consulates, the party cells and the *amicales*. Another was that consulates needed to give the same attention to civil society associations that they gave to the *amicales*. The message was clear: TREs wanted NGOs to have the same chance to receive support as the *amicales* as part of a truly pluralist opening. The young in particular expressed their desire to be accorded a more significant role. It was at this meeting that the youth complained about the appellation TTE (*Travailleur tunisien à l'étranger*, which had been commonly used in the press up to that point), and expressed their preference for TE (*Tunisien à l'étranger*) or TRE (*Tunisien résidant à l'étranger*).[97]

Ben 'Ali was present at the opening ceremony of this meeting and the prime minister at the closing, both indications of the attention the new regime intended to devote to the communities abroad. The president noted in his address that migration needed to be seen as a social and cultural, not just an economic, phenomenon; and the prime minister issued a call for the meeting to become truly a meeting of all TREs, not just workers. It was also at this meeting that a proposal was made that a Higher Council for Tunisians Abroad, an expatriate consultative body, be established. Hence, on a variety of fronts, this gathering appeared to represent a real break with the past.[98]

---

[95] *Le Temps*, 8 May 1996.   [96] *Al-Hurriyyah*, 12 April 1996.

[97] L'Office des Tunisiens à l'Etranger, a compilation of press articles on the "Seminaire Nationale des Travailleurs Tunisiens à l'Etranger," 1988.

[98] Ibid. The suggested Higher Council was subsequently deemed unworkable and the idea was discarded.

A mere year later, however, the gradual retreat from political opening occurring on the national level was reflected in this annual meeting. While some reports note that the discussions were still more open than in the pre-*changement* period, and businessmen were included for the first time as a significant sector, the exchanges were not as free and the discussion was not of the same quality. For some reason the final plenary session was not held, and people went away, as one journalist described it, "thirsty." The previous year the debate had been long and stormy, and the participation of the young had been particularly notable. Some wondered aloud whether the government had in fact achieved its stated goal of reconciling itself to the existence of independent Tunisian civil society associations abroad.[99]

Regardless of the criticisms and the subsequent political closing, these annual expatriate meetings have continued, and they have coincided with the National Day for Tunisians Abroad, designated in 1995 by the president as 7 August. Each year there is a different theme, but in general they focus on the TRE role in promoting Tunisia's development, in serving as ambassadors abroad, or on the experiences and needs of CTE women and the second generation. The government uses the opportunity of the conference to in effect reassert its claim over them, to remind the expatriates of what it has done for them, of its continuing interest in them, and of what it expects of them. For example, in 1997 the focus was on investment, encouraging TRE transfers and reminding the expatriates of their responsibilities, indeed, their patriotic duty, to make external investors aware of the business opportunities in Tunisia. Nonetheless, economics was not all that was on the organizers' minds, as a report on the 1997 event ended with a statement about what emigrants could do so that "the bright image of Tunisia not be altered by pernicious allegations from individuals who had renounced their homeland and who upset the climate of concord, security and stability that prevails."[100] Here, the *encadrement* aspect of the conference is obvious. Through it the government communicates with the CTE about activities and positions that are acceptable and those that are not, just as it registers that it is watching and listening to what transpires in the CTE.

In the absence of any other representative body, this annual meeting is the closest thing the TREs have to an elected body that discusses concerns specific to them in the presence of state officials. To prepare for this

---

[99] *Tunis Hebdo*, 12 August 1989, from L'Office des Tunisiens à l'Etranger, compilation of press articles on the "Seminaire Nationale des Travailleurs Tunisiens à l'Etranger," 1989.

[100] *Le Renouveau*, 3 August 1997.

meeting each year, conferences are organized with OTE / Tunisian state assistance in all the major host countries, and representatives are elected, although participation in such conferences is limited to *amicale* members, and thus there is the continuing problem of a lack of voice for non-RCD-linked people. A total of 600 people attend, sent by their peers, but at their own expense. (The only thing the government provides is lunch on the day of the meeting.) Ministers participate to hear problems and help formulate solutions. In this way, in the government's words, this annual meeting represents a "trait d'union" (*hamzat wasl* – "hyphen" or "link") between it and the TREs.

This section has detailed a large set of responsibilities that constitute the realm of OTE activity. Such a broad mandate would be impossible for a single government bureau to carry out without substantial support. To assist it, the OTE has established direct relations of cooperation with the *amicales* and other TRE associations. However, the most important institution through which the OTE works, both at home and abroad, is the RCD.

The RCD

Just as the PSD and its extension through the *amicales* was the primary means of penetrating the community abroad under Bourguiba, so the post-*changement* regime has sought to use the renewed PSD-turned-RCD to carry out similar, if more expanded or ambitious, functions. In his speech on the occasion of the 1999 National Day of Tunisians Abroad, Ben 'Ali noted the central role of the RCD in supporting various associations and *amicales* (many of which the RCD in essence created): "We were convinced of the importance of these structures and hence we got to work to promote the associative fabric to aid and supervise Tunisian émigrés. Thus we have overseen a generalization of these structures and a diversification of their domains so that they will be in harmony with the social, demographic and professional evolution of the Tunisian communities." As of summer 1999 there were 395 RCD associations and cells abroad.[101]

Summer activities

The RCD, with its constituent women's, youth, student and other organizations, has special responsibility for the organization of and follow-up to the extensive program of activities held each summer for returnees.

---

[101] *Le Renouveau*, 8 August 1999.

The event that launches the summer season is the RCD's annual meeting for its cadres from abroad. In 1996, for example, the sixth annual conference had three themes: the contribution of the TRE communities to the development effort; Tunisian associations abroad and their ties with the RCD structures; and the role of the community in making known the orientations of this "new era."[102] There is a national meeting for the party's students studying abroad,[103] just as there is the annual Journée de la Jeunesse Tunisienne à l'Etranger (1 August), a meeting devoted to the participation of an elite of young TREs.[104] There are also annual meetings of the social attachés, of innovators (*mubdi'in*) and artists, businessmen and investors, of leaders from associations in support of students, and of expatriate women.[105] There are also regional TRE conferences in the governorates.[106]

The annual programs for women focus, not surprisingly, on women or the family. For example, in 1996 the RCD women organized the fourth such event under the title, "The Tunisian Émigré Family: Continuous Concern and Comprehensive *Encadrement*."[107] At the 1999 conference, again, the special responsibility of Tunisian emigrant women for imbuing their children with attachment to the homeland was stressed. For, "nothing is more dangerous for our children abroad than the phenomena of acculturation, marginalization, and becoming rootless (*déracinement*). We salute the efforts of the Tunisian woman to this end. She will find from us, always, support and encouragement."[108]

The RCD abroad

Like its predecessor the PSD, the RCD is inseparable from the state, and hence its presence in the embassies and consulates as well as in official party cells abroad gives it a looming presence in the expatriate communities. For example, in the lead up to presidential elections in 1999, party cadres abroad were assigned special responsibility for mobilizing the vote and making it a success.[109] The party also holds periodic meetings with TREs of all categories (students, businessmen, women, etc.), to learn their concerns but also to convey whatever the regime's message of the day is and elicit statements or manifestations of support.[110] Celebrations of aspects of Tunisian culture are also used as occasions for speeches to

[102] *Le Renouveau*, 21 July 1996.   [103] *Al-Hurriyyah*, 31 August 1997.
[104] *Le Renouveau*, 2 August 1996.   [105] *Al-Hurriyyah*, 9 May 1996.
[106] *La Presse*, 24 July 2000.   [107] *Al-Hurriyyah*, 18 July 1996.
[108] *Le Renouveau*, 30 July 1999.   [109] *Le Renouveau*, 27 April 1999.
[110] *Le Renouveau*, 6 August 1999.

remind TREs of the president's frequently proclaimed special interest in them. Such occasions may also be used to inform them of any recent changes in laws or practices that serve or privilege the community abroad and to reinforce the message regarding the community's responsibility to maintain its ties with the homeland.[111]

Embassy, consular or RCD grounds also house the *espaces femme* run by the OTE. These *espaces* include classrooms for Arabic language instruction, computer and music clubs, and workshops for various art activities. A 1999 article in the party's newspaper attributed the state's interest in these *espaces* to its desire to expand the possibilities for citizenship: through them new types of political, associative and cultural practices may emerge.[112] While this may be true, it is also the case that, as in the past, most Tunisians who have and want no RCD affiliation stay away from such places, and there is little in the past or current history of the party to suggest an interest in developing independent citizen associations. For youth as well, a large part of the *encadrement* is expected to take place through RCD cells. In a summer meeting in Tunis, the general secretary of the party noted the role of the RCD cadres in consolidating Tunisia's reputation abroad and emphasized the concern of the RCD that its cadres receive a solid political education to enable them to accomplish their mission, while being omnipresent in the regions where they live.[113]

Arabic language instruction

Since 1974 Tunis has sponsored a program to teach Arabic to its citizens abroad. In the beginning, based at least in part upon concerns voiced by parents at the expatriate conferences, the instruction aimed at paving the way for the reintegration of those TREs who faced the possibility of return from Europe.[114] Initially, the Ministry of Social Affairs and the Ministry of Education were charged with supervising the effort in cooperation with the *amicales* and consulates. In France, which hosts the largest CTE, the teaching of Arabic is governed by a memo of 9 April 1975 and a subsequent accord of 12 March 1986 which advocated integrating Arabic instruction into the primary school curriculum. According to these agreements, the Tunisian government would appoint and pay teachers, while the French government would put classrooms at their disposal. Arabic was to be considered a regular part of the curriculum.[115] When the

---

[111] *Le Renouveau,* 11 May 1996.   [112] *Le Renouveau,* 7 August 1999.
[113] *Le Renouveau,* 21 July 1996.   [114] *La Presse,* 15 October 1996.
[115] *Al-Wahdah,* 21 May 1999.

program was initiated, both Tunisia and France, each for its own reasons, had an interest in strengthening the bonds between young Tunisians and their homeland: both had an expectation that the TREs would ultimately return to Tunisia.

In Germany, the community, numbering about 200,000, enjoys relative freedom in Arabic instruction. There is a certain competition with some of the Gulf states' Arabic programs, but about 7,000 take Arabic classes and some teachers are recruited by the German authorities. In Belgium, in 1996 the number of Tunisian children under the age of sixteen was only about 2,000, and only about one quarter took Arabic classes. Despite an accord signed in 1983, there are still difficulties in recruiting teachers from Tunisia. In Italy, there are even smaller numbers, although in 1996 the Tunisian government opened two primary schools with a capacity of 180 in Sicily.[116] As for other European countries, the language program is part of associational activities, not part of a bilateral agreement.

A revised set of goals for the Arabic instruction programs was issued in 1989 following the *changement*: preserving Arabo-Islamic-Tunisian identity; contributing to achieving psychological stability, supporting the personality and preserving the special characteristics of the young Tunisian and ensuring his/her development; and securing his/her ability to acclimate to the environment while maintaining ties with the homeland. In 1974 there were only 470 students and 9 teachers at 6 centers;[117] in 1987–88, there were 10,500 students and 113 teachers. By the end of the first year following the *changement*, the numbers were 143 teachers and 14,000 students.[118] Since the mid-1990s, however, the numbers have been relatively stable, with 14,696 students in 772 centers with 199 teachers in 1994–95[119] and 14,000 students, 814 schools and 190 instructors for 1996–97.[120] Of Tunisians who benefit from these classes, 88 percent are in France, a number only slightly higher than the total estimated percentage of TREs in France.

The organization of Arabic language instruction depends upon the efforts of the consulates. It is they who obtain permission from local officials for the use of rooms, and it is they who are charged with liaising with the local Tunisian community. Moreover, oversight of the program is the responsibility of an inspector working directly with the ambassador and cultural attachés.[121] The RCD helps to provide Arabic-language

---

[116] *Le Renouveau*, 9 October 1996; *La Presse*, 15 October 1996.
[117] *La Presse*, 15 October 1996.   [118] *Billedi*, 26 September 1989.
[119] *Al-Wahdah*, 21 May 1999.   [120] *La Presse*, 15 October 1996.
[121] *Le Renouveau*, 9 April 1989.

instructional materials free of charge to TRE students[122] just as it has cooperated with the OTE to build new lecture facilities.[123]

Nevertheless, only about 13 percent of all CTE children participate in such programs. One reason for the low percentage of participation is the dispersed nature of the community, especially outside France, which renders problematic the provision of affordable language instruction to small numbers of children, by either the Tunisian or host state. Second are parental attitudes. Parents' positions on language instruction seem to be a function of whether they plan to return soon to Tunisia. Those planning a short stay tend to want Arabic for their children, whereas, if a long stay is planned, they are more interested in their children's learning the language of the host state. However, if they are not growing up in a francophone (or Italian-speaking) environment, there appears to be a stronger desire for the children to learn Arabic, since if they speak only Dutch or German, for example, they will be unable to communicate back home. Beyond this issue is the quality of the instruction offered and the attitudes of the children, who are not always enthusiastic about such language study.[124] Today's generation in no way resembles the previous one, from a cultural, social or economic point of view. Fathers and sons, products of emigration, often do not share the same objectives, especially regarding definitive return. The result can be a negative perception of the culture of origin, of religion, and a near or total ignorance of reading and writing Arabic.[125]

There have also been numerous critiques of the goals and the methods of these classes. First, it appears that learning Arabic is a goal in and of itself, unrelated to circumstances or context. The curriculum has not changed since it was instituted, despite the transformations in the immigrant community, perhaps the most important of which is the fact that many of these children will never return to Tunisia to live. Moreover, in Europe there is a high drop-out rate among Tunisian children, and teachers in these programs do not receive special training for the difficulties they will encounter. Worse, teachers' postings are short-term, so that just about the time that they have come to understand the community and its problems, they leave.[126] Thus, even with the increased attention and funding the program has received since the *changement*, it appears still to be in serious need of rethinking and reform.

---

[122] *Al-Hurriyyah*, 12 April 1996.   [123] *Al-Hurriyyah*, 6 November 1996.
[124] Alouane, pp. 90–1.   [125] *Le Renouveau*, 9 April 1989.
[126] *Al-Wahdah*, 21 May 1999.

Expatriate-directed information and media

In keeping with its approach of comprehensive *encadrement*, the Tunisian state has long targeted expatriates with its media. Programming in the 1980s was primarily of a seasonal type, with programs for TREs only just before and during the summer return. However, since the *changement*, there has been a marked development and expansion of state informational efforts aimed at the CTE. Video and audio cassettes are regularly sent to the consulates, *amicales*, and related associations to keep people abreast of developments in different sectors. Businessmen receive informational materials directly, as do more than 5,000 children in Europe who receive the review *Yasmine*, a monthly magazine for children published by the OTE. Its cartoons, games and stories are aimed at children six to fourteen years of age, "these future 'acteurs de développement' of Tunisia." In addition, twenty regional reviews are sent three times a year to more than 5,000 addresses in Europe.[127]

As for national radio, all programs are now available on the web (www.radiotunis.com). In 1990, a program entitled *Huna Tunis* ("This is Tunis") began with some segments devoted to TRE communities. Broadcast on Sunday evenings, it has largely a social function in keeping families in touch, but there are also segments that address travel, social security, investment, and the like. This is not a special broadcast for TREs, but there is a great deal of information for them available through it.[128]

In the realm of television, in 1992 a program *Sabah al-Khayr, Tunis* ("Good Morning, Tunis") was initiated and continued for three years. A subsequent program, *Fi Khidmatikum* ("At Your Service") followed, with some segments devoted to topics of interest to TREs, but it was really with the launching of the satellite TV Channel 7 that the goal of strengthening ties between the community resident abroad and their homeland through the visual media was seriously tackled. Obviously, TV7 is available not just to Tunisians, but to all those with access to a satellite dish. In 1996, the program *Hamzat wasl* ("Hyphen," meaning the connection between Tunisia and the CTE) was launched to broadcast year-round, although it has an expanded format during the summer, given all the TRE meetings that take place and the issues that are raised by the summer return. Everything from transport possibilities during the summer to questions about social security, housing, investment, and the

---

[127] Alouane, p. 108.
[128] Interview with Khaled Ben Feguir, Directeur-Adjoint, Tunisian National Radio, Tunis, 12 August 2002.

law are covered during the course of the year. The program is broadcast each Saturday and Sunday around mid-day.[129]

Conclusions

Tunisian state institutional involvement in the CTE has passed through several stages, related to the same historical periods we saw in the Moroccan case. The first was during the period of open emigration to Europe, prior to 1973. During this time frame, when the Tunisian abroad was viewed as simply a worker whose departure relieved pressures on the domestic labor market, the institutional interest took two forms. The first was in Tunisia itself, through the successive iterations of state bureaus that dealt with labor recruitment and placement abroad. In this respect Tunisia's experience parallels that of Morocco, although Tunis's efforts appear to have been more developed and certainly placed greater emphasis on training and preparation.

However, much earlier in the emigration experience than we saw in the Moroccan case, the Tunisian state also put in place a second set of structures whose charge was to monitor the communities abroad, largely for political/security reasons. Through the embassies and consulates, the PSD created its own cells for political education and mobilization as well as *amicales* to give the state a presence in the social and associative realm. Through this involvement the regime clearly sought to inculcate its version of political correctness and to marginalize or repress voices that were out of step with the philosophy of Bourguiba's developmentalist, single-party state. Just as the regime's economic philosophy regarded employment abroad at this point as equivalent to domestic employment, apparently the state also viewed its expatriates as part of the domestic body politic: they were subject to the same surveillance and harassment regarding political opinions and activities as were their compatriots back home. A small country facing substantial challenges to its sovereignty during these early post-independence years, domestically as well as from its powerful neighbors, Tunis seemed intent upon cultivating solidarity and insisting upon unity. Although the statement had not yet entered official discourse, even in this period "Tunisians were Tunisians" regardless of where they resided, and maintaining their loyalty through close involvement (and, when needed, coercion) was one component and gauge of state sovereignty.

---

[129] Interview with Mondher Kala'i, director of programs, Channel 7 (Tunisia's satellite channel), Tunis 12 August 2002.

The crude *devisard* or milk-cow image that observers of Morocco claim characterized the kingdom's approach to TMEs was not central to the Tunisian approach in the early period. While statistics make clear that remittances from TREs (or TTEs as they were still generally referred to at the time) have long constituted a significant contribution to the Tunisian economy, it is not until economic crisis loomed large in the early 1980s that greater attention was accorded this aspect of the CTE contribution. Even then, largely due to the political malaise of the last years of Bourguiba's rule, there was little institutional change in response either to their growing importance, or to the fact that the composition of the CTE, as well as the time horizon of their *projets immigratoires*, had substantially changed.

It was not until the 1987 coup that broad institutional and discourse reconstruction appears in the state's approach to the CTEs, as their contributions came to figure more centrally into the definition of who was Tunisian and what the sovereign state could expect from its people living outside its borders. In the case of Morocco, Hassan's subjects were linked to him through their oath of allegiance, a feudal type of tie in keeping with the nature of his regime. In Tunisia, under Bourguiba, but then in a more focused or insistent way under Ben 'Ali, state discourse practice is a completely different matter – has drawn upon a republican notion of citizenship as the link between state and TRE. Indeed, one notes a transformation in the construction of the relationship from that of one between emigrant worker and domestic labor market, to that of one between national abroad and the state. Emigrants were no longer faceless exported laborers whom the state monitored in order to keep them in line politically; instead they were members of a social and political community that was an extension of the homeland. Tunis accepted and even celebrated the integration (if not the assimilation) of its nationals abroad, while insisting upon their tie to their country of origin or, constructed differently, upon the state's claim upon them. The multi-faceted nature and needs of these communities were acknowledged through new programs addressing the special concerns of expatriate women, youth and businessmen, just as members of the CTE were invited to participate in the socio-economic planning process. All of these elements shared in reformulating the link, both institutional and discursive, between the state and its citizens abroad, as the CTE and its resources became more central to the needs and stability of the Tunisian state. The 1973 change in the citizenship law had laid the formal basis for such an approach, but it took several decades – including a change in the composition of the communities, an economic crisis and regime change at home – before its institutional underpinnings were more fully developed.

The real innovation of the post-1987 period has been the articulation of the obligations of both sides to this citizen–state relationship. Shortly after the coup, Ben 'Ali began to include in his speeches references to the CTE and its centrality to the country: *al-Tunisiyyun f-il-kharij fi qalb al-watan* – "Tunisians abroad are in the heart of the homeland." Tunisia is a small country, part of whose wealth is its human resources (a theme we will see repeated in the Lebanese and Jordanian cases). Thus the TREs represent a critical form of scarce capital which should be oriented toward the interests of the homeland. Migrants are no longer viewed as income bearers who return home after a certain period of time but, above all, as potential contributors and investors.[130] In exchange for the president's "solicitude sans cesse" ("unceasing concern") TREs are expected to fulfill their patriotic/civic duty by playing an active role in their country's development and by serving as political, economic and cultural ambassadors for Tunis. By developing close ties and integrating, but not assimilating, the expatriates can be in a position to advocate for policies from the European side that will be favorable to Tunisia and its development. TREs are therefore responsible for presenting a positive image of themselves and their country abroad.[131] This is one reason why the state has not hesitated to repress activities that could be construed as critical of the Ben 'Ali regime.

This highly securitized approach to the community abroad, a near replica of the approach used at home, may well be a strong indication of the state's struggle to reinforce domestic sovereignty at home as well as project its sovereign reach abroad. At the same time the regime's discourse of partnership and citizenship appears aimed at reinforcing its "moral" authority and hence its claim to the loyalty and resources of its expatriates. The fact that the pluralist content of this imagined political community is more superficial than real has led to a bifurcation among Tunisians into those who, out of conviction or opportunism, work with the state, and those who, out of fear or alienation, have withdrawn or have been coopted into a minimal level of cooperation. A third category, active opponents, has been largely driven underground or destroyed, within the country as well as in the communities abroad, through high levels of harassment and coercion.

Given Tunisia's size and resources, the extent of the programs and activities it sponsors abroad is impressive. That said, the preeminence of their security function has often meant that they have fallen short of achieving their formal social, associative and even *encadrement* goals.

---

[130] Cassarino, p. 5.   [131] Baouab interview.

A sympathetic, but nonetheless strong, critique of many of the state's programs and actions appeared in August 2000. The Tunisian press rarely prints critical material when discussing the state, thus rendering this article particularly noteworthy.[132] One target of the critique was the social attachés based at the embassies. Despite the resources at their disposal, it argued, they have neither the experience nor the multidisci plinary training to understand and address the community's problems in a European context. In some cases, the article argues, discontent, especially among the young, has led them to give up on Tunisian services altogether.

Regarding the *espaces femme*, the author contends that, despite the tremendous financial resources at their disposal, they have barely met the president's expectations. They are frequented by a number of youth, and visited irregularly by others, but most belong to RCD families. The thousands of other CTE members are not affected or involved, and little has been done to attract the youth of the *banlieue*s to these well-equipped places. The author claims that the *intégristes* (Islamists) have attracted to their schools (for which one has to pay) hundreds of Tunisian students to be "brainwashed," while the lesser-attended classes offered by the Tunisian state at the *espaces femme* are free.[133] At some point, apparently, the provision of "security" begins to have negative marginal returns.

Finally, regarding associations, the author argues that they continue to proliferate without real means or impact. Their discourse is that of *langue de bois* and their programs, if they have activities, are quite weak. In the French context, where there is such a vibrant associative life among Maghrebi expatriates, the Tunisian state-affiliated associations distinguish themselves by their inertia. Their lists of members may be long, but the author questions whether they are real or fictitious. As for the football teams that attract hundreds of youth of all ages, they seriously lack funds, despite the fact that the role that such associations (whose financial needs are modest) can play in integrating and supervising youth has already been clearly demonstrated.[134]

The results on the investment front are also less successful than they may at first appear. Cassarino shows that, regardless of the various formal Tunisian institutions that operate abroad to promote investment, such institutions played little or no role in the investment decisions of return migrants. Without exception, his interviewees pointed to their own

---

[132] Chraiet, "La Communauté tunisienne en France au quotidien," *Réalités*, no. 764, 17–23 July 2000.
[133] Ibid.   [134] Ibid.

personal networks as key to helping them develop market opportunities.[135] Most in fact were very critical of the activities of the formal institutions.

A final critique is that, despite the clear importance of expatriates' contributions to the country's development, there is no effective, central bureau that conducts studies about migration or coordinates gathering the information that is produced by a variety of Tunisian bureaus on the topic.[136] Academics puzzle over the absence of interest on the part of government officials in participating in their meetings on subjects related to emigration. Is this an example of institutional underdevelopment, insufficient capacity? Or is it rather another manifestation of a top-down approach which proceeds from the belief that, without the burden of concrete information and statistics on CTE realities, the state knows what it wants and will inform the people of it and mobilize them around it? For information on the conditions of TRE life, reliance seems to be almost totally on party cadres abroad in diplomatic missions, *amicales*, RCD cells or related associations.

Thus, while the government is engaged in ongoing efforts to assert or maintain its political, economic and cultural claim to Tunisian expatriates (and, increasingly, their descendants), problems related to state capacity and the political system interfere. As we will see in the case of Lebanon, there are limits to what small, lower-to-middle-income states can invest in consular and other networks abroad. However, in this case, state intent appears to be more important than capacity. A transformation in the discourse regarding state concern with TREs has been accompanied, not by a true opening of the political system, but by an authoritarianism that empties real citizenship of its content and drives away many TREs who are not interested in being a part of what remains a largely one-party system. The participation that does occur, then, derives largely from coercion or patrimonialism. While superficial expressions of attachment from both regime and citizenry abound, the state's authoritarian practices in fact impede the development of effective, rather than merely discursive, sovereign claims on emigrants and their resources. As a consequence, resources, both human and material, that might otherwise have been channeled to the state's benefit, instead may lie dormant. Worse, they may eventually seek other, less regime-friendly, outlets.

---

[135] See Cassarino, ch. 3.

[136] Jamal Bourchachen, *Statistiques sur la migration internationale dans les pays mediterranéens: rapport de mission Algérie, Maroc, Tunisie*. Eurostate Working papers, Population et conditions sociales 3/1999/E/n*11 (n.p.: European Commission, 1999), p. 36.

5   Lebanon and its expatriates: a bird with two wings

Of the cases covered in this book, Lebanon's migration is the oldest and its communities the most widespread. Beginning with waves directed principally toward the Western Hemisphere in the late nineteenth and early twentieth centuries, significant diaspora communities subsequently developed in Africa and then in the oil states of the Persian Gulf. With the outbreak of civil war in 1975, new groups left; some changed the confessional composition of existing communities, while others began to shape the development of largely new groupings in Canada, Europe and Australia. The long and varied Lebanese emigrant experience has also given rise to more diverse terminology for those who have left than one finds in other cases. In Lebanese discussions of the topic, the most common term for those abroad is *mughtarib* ("expatriate"), although in recent years *al-intishar* (a word akin to diaspora) has gained increasing currency, just as one finds the terms *mutahaddir* ("descendant," referring to the second, third and fourth generations) and *muhajir* ("one who has emigrated/fled").[1]

Like Morocco and Tunisia, Lebanon witnessed the beginnings of significant emigration during the pre-independence period. However, unlike the Maghrebi cases, Lebanese emigration was undertaken on individual initiative, not on a colonial government-organized work-contract basis.[2] At the beginning of the migration, the territory was part of the Ottoman Empire, and what was finally delineated as the Lebanese state did not coincide with the historical boundaries of Mt. Lebanon. Just as important, the type of state that ultimately evolved following two decades of post-First World War French control, was of a minimalist nature,

---

[1] This list is far from exhaustive. In the writings on Lebanese expatriates one often sees reference to the two wings (*jinahayn*) or two parts (*shaqqayn*) of Lebanon, *al-muqim* (resident), and *al-mughtarib* (expatriate). Some authors also refer to the diaspora as Lebanon's "colonial empire": Joseph Saouda, "Importance de notre émigration, services rendus à la mère-patrie," *Cahiers de l'Est* 1 1945: p. 163.

[2] I am grateful to both Salim Nasr and Farid el-Khazen for pointing this out and discussing its implications.

certainly by regional standards. Such a framework meant a different relationship between emigrants and the subsequently established state, one which
explains at least in part Lebanon's laissez-faire approach to outmigration.

A second factor distinguishing the Lebanese case is that, although
perhaps a third of those who left for the Americas ultimately did return
home,[3] the sheer distance between Lebanon and this part of the *mahjar*[4]
was so great as to render the Lebanese experience of exile and subsequent
relationship with the homeland quite different than that of Maghrebi
emigrants and their home countries or of Jordanian/Palestinian expatriates and the Persian Gulf states to which they migrated. Indeed, one of
the striking features of the Lebanese case is that, depending upon
how one counts or defines "Lebanese," a majority of Lebanese-cum-
descendants are no longer citizens. Some are dual nationals, but many
have never been to Lebanon, do not speak Arabic, and have even changed
their family names to integrate more easily into their host societies.

Another difference deriving from history and political development is
that emigrants have long been an important theme in Lebanese political,
economic and cultural life. Writers, publishers and politicians in the *mahjar*
have had a significant impact; émigrés continue to send remittances back to
their home villages for building or to support relatives; Lebanese political
and religious leaders often visit the diaspora; and representatives from
communities of Lebanese origin frequently travel to Lebanon. Nevertheless, despite a clear recognition of the emigrants' real and potential
contributions, the Lebanese *state* has largely failed in marshalling their
energies. The limited political and economic reach of the state has not
deterred expatriates from transferring home substantial levels of remittances – indeed, it may well have been a key factor in encouraging such
activity. However, as a result, these monies and other energies have been
overwhelmingly directed to more particularistic rather than public interests.

Thus, the relationship between the Lebanese state and Lebanese emigrants is quite different from what we have seen in the Moroccan and
Tunisian cases. Certainly there has been a similar state interest in
encouraging emigrant investment, especially in the period immediately
after independence and certainly following the fifteen-year civil war as a
way of shoring up the resources of the floundering state. However, unlike
in the Maghrebi cases, emigration has long been a central theme in the

---

[3] See Akram Fouad Khater, *Inventing Home: Emigration, Gender, and the Middle Class in
Lebanon, 1870–1920* (Berkeley: University of California Press, 2001).
[4] This is a particularly Lebanese term, and it refers to the place to which one migrates. It
became the common word used to refer particularly to the diaspora communities in the
Western Hemisphere.

Lebanese narrative, with emigration romanticized as a path to success for the entrepreneurial and adaptable Lebanese. Moreover, numbers of Lebanese abroad have far surpassed those of the Maghrebi communities. Most important, however, emigrants have been much more central to the highly contested definition of Lebanese identity and to national political struggles than in the other cases examined here.

Surprising to those unfamiliar with the history, Lebanese abroad were counted in the only census conducted to date (1932), and were included in the calculations that underpinned the delicate balance of power established among the country's numerous confession-based communities. As a result, their potential role in politics in Lebanon has been among the most sensitive of domestic issues. The subtitle of this chapter, "a bird with two wings" (meaning resident and expatriate), is just one of a number of phrases used in writings about Lebanon's relationship with its diaspora communities which suggests that they are not viewed merely as an adjunct or an extension, but as an integral part of the body (politic). While such a formulation would lead one to expect state attempts to extend the realm of sovereignty to embrace communities abroad similar to those undertaken by the Moroccan or Tunisian states, in fact, as we shall see below, the confessional balance within the country and the emigrants' potential role in it have played critical roles in shaping the *extremely limited* sovereignty the Lebanese state has exercised over its territory and population over the years.

Official concern with emigration

Emigration out of Mt. Lebanon, the area to the northeast, east and south of Beirut, was initially triggered in the 1860s by overpopulation, unemployment, and changing socio-economic conditions related to developments in the silk trade. Ottoman authorities at the time were aware that economic development was needed to stem the tide of this emigration, which had already reached what they viewed as alarming levels by 1885–87, climbing to an average of 15,000 departures a year by the beginning of the First World War. In addition to poor economic conditions, including famine, as well as in some cases persecution by the Ottomans, outmovement was encouraged by a network of agents working in transport who enticed the poor of the mountains to leave and assisted emigrants in avoiding government officials.[5] An examination

---

[5] Engin Deniz Akarli, "Ottoman Attitudes Toward Lebanese Emigration, 1885–1910," in Albert Hourani and Nadim Shehadi (eds.), *The Lebanese in the World: A Century of Emigration* (London: I. B. Tauris, 1992), pp. 110 and 112.

of the lists of villages and the numbers of people who migrated abroad reveals staggering percentages for many, with the average 15% in some areas and 18% in others.[6] Some 80% of those who emigrated were Christians, overwhelmingly Maronites, the largest Christian group in the country.

The Maronite church tried to intervene with France, then the "protector" of the Maronites, to call on the international community to send these people back to Lebanon; *fatwas* were also issued by some of the Muslim religious authorities forbidding emigration;[7] and various official attempts were made to restrict travel abroad. Nonetheless, the Ottomans realized the difficulties of trying to rein in the maritime companies and their agents who offered services the emigrants wanted. Moreover, when the authorities tried to bar people from leaving, prospective emigrants either sought exit through smuggling networks, or used their Ottoman travel papers to go elsewhere in the empire and then from there left for Europe, Africa or the Americas.[8]

The second stage of emigration came during the inter-war period and the French mandate. During this period, many of the same factors that had triggered emigration under the Ottomans continued to drive departures, but overall numbers of emigrants declined, largely because of poor economic conditions in Europe and the Americas. In fact, countries like Canada, the USA, Australia and some countries of Latin America temporarily halted immigration in the wake of the First World War. As a result, the emigration was directed largely toward the areas of French colonial administration in Africa.

With the 1920 imposition by the French of borders creating a Lebanon Mandate territory that extended well beyond the limits of Mt. Lebanon, and as emigration moved into the second and in some cases the third generation, the question of establishing who was Lebanese became increasingly important. With the end of the Ottoman Empire, the Treaty of Lausanne entrusted the successor states with the responsibility of conferring citizenship upon their residents. Those who had migrated could, in the Lebanese case, opt for Lebanese citizenship, or retain Ottoman/Turkish citizenship. However, by 1930, the total number of families that had applied for Lebanese citizenship was only 23,463 out of a total number of Lebanese abroad estimated at the time to be 500,000. Apparently, the majority of emigrants had already acquired citizenship

---

[6] See Jihad Nasri al-'Aql, *Al-Hijrah al-Hadithah min Lubnan wa-Ta'ati al-Mu'assasat al-Rasmiyyah w-al-Ahliyyah ma'aha 1860–2000* (Beirut: Dar wa-Maktabat al-Turath al-Adabi, 2002), pp. 80–83.

[7] Ibid., pp. 87 and 91.   [8] Akarli in Hourani and Shehadi, pp. 115–23.

in their new host countries, most of them the settler-colonial states of the Americas, and hence did not feel a need to apply for Lebanese nationality.[9]

The question of Lebanese citizenship remained sensitive and topical during the late Mandate and early independence period, largely because the emigrants up to this point were still largely from the Maronite community. While the Maronites formed a majority in the smaller Mt. Lebanon area, the establishment in 1920 of a Greater Lebanon that included much more territory but also many more Muslims meant that the Christian majority in the larger entity was tenuous at best. The emphasis on maintaining or restoring Lebanese citizenship to emigrants, therefore, had everything to do with the confessional/political balance in Lebanon as it moved toward and then beyond independence.

With independence, according to a law promulgated at the end of 1946, anyone of Lebanese origin living abroad who had not yet chosen Lebanese citizenship had the right to reclaim it upon his/her definitive return to Lebanon. Nonetheless, whether because of the weakness of consular representation or the lack of initiative in making Lebanese abroad aware of the benefits of home-country citizenship, very few people ever exercised this option.[10] Examples abound of memoranda and articles published calling for the extension of the Treaty of Lausanne's deadline for applying for citizenship and for better facilities abroad so that Lebanese could take advantage of the possibility of acquiring or maintaining their nationality.[11]

Following independence, emigration continued along lines similar to those described above, largely for economic reasons. It was the civil war, which began in 1975, that triggered several new trends. The first involved greater family emigration. The second was toward a diversification of the economic status of emigrants. The third was the movement to a broader, multi-sectarian emigration,[12] thus transforming the politics of the numbers and composition of the communities abroad.

The number of Lebanese abroad remains a highly political issue. As with the domestic population (for which the 1932 census registered

---

[9] Hashimoto, "Lebanese Population Movement 1920–1939: Towards a Study," in Hourani and Shchadeh, pp. 75–76.

[10] Al-'Aql, p. 158.

[11] See, for example, Pierre Gemayel, "Libanais de l'étranger: le Congrès des Emigrés," *Cahiers de l'Est* 2 1945: pp. 171–73; and Georges Moannack, "Libanais de l'étranger: point de vue d'un émigré," *Cahiers de l'Est* 4 1946: pp. 176–86.

[12] Boutros Labaki, "Lebanese Emigration during the War (1975–1989)," in Hourani and Shehadi, p. 621.

793,396 resident citizens and 254,987 emigrants),[13] there are no reliable statistics on the communities abroad. Instead, one finds widely (or wildly) ranging numbers. In the course of this research the guesstimates ranged from 3 million to 14 million, although most serious analysts lean toward the lower figures.[14] It is worth noting here that the basis of citizenship in Lebanon, as in the rest of the Arab world, is *jus sanguinis*: whoever is born of a Lebanese *father*, no matter where s/he is born, is Lebanese, even if s/he acquires the nationality of the country of residence. Lebanese women do not have the same right to transfer their citizenship to their children. Hence those who accept the high figures are implicitly suspending the application of this key, discriminatory element of nationality law, at least when it comes to the population abroad: one could entertain higher figures only if all the children of Lebanese women, whether married to Lebanese or not, are included.

The Lebanese political system and the role of emigrants

As it has evolved, an integral part of the Lebanese political system has been the formalization of institutional representation based on confessional or sectarian affiliation. In 1943, General Catroux, who had been designated by de Gaulle in 1941 as the délégué-général of the Free French in Syria and Lebanon, began, in consultation with the principal local political personalities, to prepare for the restoration of constitutional life in Lebanon and Syria. In Lebanon, Catroux called upon Ayoub Tabet, a Protestant who had played a political role during the Mandate, to take charge of some preparations. Tabet proceeded to attempt to include the (overwhelmingly Christian) Lebanese abroad in calculations for apportioning seats among the different communities, thus causing an uproar, and leading to his replacement. Ultimately it was General Spears, the head of the British mission, who mediated the problem and succeeded in securing a Christian–Muslim compromise which took on the form of a convention: the formula of six Christian seats to five Muslim seats in the parliament.[15]

---

[13] Rania Maktabi, "State Formation and Citizenship in Lebanon: The Politics of Membership and Exclusion in a Sectarian State," in Nils A. Butenschon, Uri Davis and Manuel Hassassian (eds.), *Citizenship and the State in the Middle East: Approaches and Applications* (Syracuse: Syracuse University Press, 2000), p. 161.

[14] Questions over numbers and who to count are not accidents, but highly political issues. As Labaki has written: "comme tout ce qui a trait à la démographie au Liban, ces chiffres sont des instruments dans la compétition politique multiforme": Boutros Labaki, "L'émigration depuis la fin des guerres à l'intérieure du Liban (1990–1998)," *Travaux et Jours* 61 spring 1998: p. 83.

[15] Edmond Rabbath, *La formation politique du Liban politique et constitutionnel* (Beirut: Librairie Orientale, 1986), pp. 474–76.

Nonetheless, a precedent for including emigrants in the calculations had been raised, if not confirmed; and, although the formula did not include expatriate representation, the large numbers of expatriates continued to figure into political calculations on both sides of the 6–5 divide.

The National Pact of 1943 then reinforced this formula as intrinsic to the post-independence period. The Pact was the product of a combination of factors relating to the wartime regional environment, the desire for independence, and the confessional composition of the country. This informal agreement between Maronite politician Bishara al-Khoury, Lebanon's first post-independence president, and Sunni leader Riyad al-Solh, the country's first post-independence prime minister, was an attempt to close the gap between the Maronite and Sunni elites' understandings of the identity and role of the entity of Greater Lebanon, and of the need to end the French Mandate.[16] In brief, Lebanon was to be independent, sovereign and neutral. This meant a Muslim resignation to no unification with Syria or any other Arab state and a Christian commitment not to seek special ties with any Western power (at this point, France in particular).[17] This principle was to serve as a basis for foreign policy, but was also reflected in domestic governing structures. Based on the results of the 1932 census, which, as noted above, found a slight Christian majority in the country, the 6–5, Christian–Muslim formula for the parliament was reinforced. In addition, each of the top governmental offices – president, prime minister and speaker of parliament – became the domain of a particular confessional group (Maronite, Sunni, Shi'i, etc.), just as cabinet posts were distributed to ensure representation of the major confessional groups (although there were seventeen formally recognized groups in all). The 6–5 distribution was also to be adhered to throughout the civil service and government, although this was changed to 6–6 after the 1958 civil war. In this way the National Pact served to underpin a political and economic system in which the Maronite elite enjoyed preeminence.

In addition, at independence, important parts of the Lebanese political and economic elite, regardless of confessional affiliation, felt their interests lay in maintaining a state with what Krasner would call limited domestic and interdependence sovereignty: a weak state could not

---

[16] It should be emphasized that the elites' positions did not necessarily represent a consensus view within their respective communities, just as there was a certain diversity within the elites of any given community.

[17] For a thorough discussion of the background to the conclusion of the National Pact as well as its role in subsequent Lebanese political development, see Farid el-Khazen, *The Communal Pact of National Identities: The Making and Politics of the 1943 National Pact* (Oxford: Centre for Lebanese Studies, 1991).

challenge the Pact's commitment to neutrality; nor would it obstruct the freewheeling financial interests of the Lebanese bourgeoisie. Hence, Lebanon's economy began as, and remained throughout the decades following independence, one characterized by so-called "economic liberalism." A limited bureaucracy underpinning a weak state and a strong commercial class kept government involvement in or control over economic activity minimal, something which increasingly came to distinguish Lebanon from its neighbors, as many of the states in the region embraced state socialist or state capitalist economic forms. It also meant, however, that Lebanon was more susceptible to foreign influence in both the economic and political realms from a variety of quarters, both Arab and Western. In this way, although intended to provide for independence, sovereignty and neutrality, the National Pact in fact laid the basis for one of the most highly penetrated, least sovereign entities in the region.

Interest in the emigrants

Formal state concern with the large Lebanese expatriate (LE) presence was manifested in a number of institutional developments, beginning in the pre-independence period. For example, the government of December 1941 through July 1942 included a Ministry of Foreign Affairs and *Interests of the Lebanese Abroad* (under Hamid Franjiyyah). However, on 16 May 1942, a legislative decree was promulgated delineating the responsibilities of the Ministry of Foreign Affairs, and the reference to the communities abroad was removed from the title of the Ministry with the cabinet change in July 1942. That said, at this point all the ministries were in an embryonic state, and it was not until complete independence was achieved that the institutions of state really began to function.[18]

During this period, interest in expatriates was most consistently expressed by two prominent political parties. The Syrian Social Nationalist Party (SSNP) of Antun Sa'adeh (who had himself lived in the Americas from 1921 to 1930 and again from 1938 to 1947) had repeatedly expressed its concern over the loss to the homeland of those who went abroad. The SSNP's interest was constucted not in confessional terms (although many of its members were Greek Orthodox Christians), but rather in terms of its belief in the expatriates' ability to support "national causes" back in Lebanon.[19] However, it was the

---

[18] Rabbath, p. 467, note 10, and p. 497.
[19] See *Zad al-Muhajir* (Beirut: Dar Fikr l-il-Abhath w-al-Nashr, 2002). This book is a collection of articles written by Antun Sa'adeh.

overwhelmingly Maronite Kata'ib or Phalange Party of Pierre Gemayel (who had also lived outside of Lebanon, in Egypt) that called in September 1945 for holding a conference to discuss how Lebanon's relations "avec ses absents" should be structured. This call proceeded from the Phalange's deeply held belief that the participation of these *absents* was indispensable for Lebanon. Gemayel was convinced that half, if not more, of all Lebanese lived abroad. National independence meant that Lebanon needed to call upon its émigrés to invest their wealth and their talents in a national renaissance. To do so, the Phalange's position was that they needed to return to Lebanon, so that the transition to independence would be a success. Gemayel was convinced that if the government was truly to cultivate émigré interest, the creation of a ministry was necessary.[20]

Among the fifteen resolutions of the Phalange's September 1945 Émigré Congress in Zahleh were calls for: creating an émigré ministry; giving Lebanese nationality to every émigré who sought it; facilitating émigrés' participation in national politics, and modifying the electoral laws in order to do so; providing all possible aid to repatriate émigrés; taking all measures necessary to stop the continuation of emigration; adopting measures to encourage émigré investment; holding periodic émigré conferences; and turning over to the service of Emigration and Immigration of the Phalangist Movement, along with the Club des Emigrés (Nadi al-Muhajirin), responsibility for overseeing the implementation of these resolutions.[21]

In a meeting only a few days later, on 6 October 1945, the Lebanese cabinet adopted the following resolutions regarding the émigré question: to create a special section in the Ministry of Foreign Affairs to take care of questions regarding émigrés;[22] to restore Lebanese nationality to any émigré returning definitively to the country, and to secure other accords to safeguard Lebanese nationality among the communities abroad; to extend consular representation; to conclude international agreements to protect émigré rights; and to provide financial assistance to repatriate émigrés. In this way, the state took its first concrete steps toward asserting a claim to its nationals and their descendants abroad. Clearly, however, this governmental response fell short of the Phalange's call for the establishment of a separate ministry, as only an authority/division (*maslaha*) of

[20] Gemayel, pp. 171–73.

[21] "Résolutions du Congrès des Emigrés organisé par les Phalanges Libanaises," *Cahiers de l'Est* 3 1945: pp. 149–50.

[22] The name of the ministry was actually changed to that of the Ministry of Foreign Affairs and Expatriates with the cabinet reshuffle of 14 December 1946, when Henri Phara'on took over the MFA portfolio from Philippe Tacla.

Expatriate Affairs was established as part of the Ministry of Foreign Affairs. Nor did the government entrust the party with any responsibility for the implementation of these resolutions.[23]

It is important to keep in mind that at the time, Lebanon had no real model to look to in terms of either state institutions involved in émigré affairs or the size of its emigration. At independence it also lacked the trained cadres necessary to undertake such work.[24] A number of commentators further mentioned that the government simply was not in a financial position to establish full diplomatic or consular facilities in every country or city where there was a substantial Lebanese émigré population.[25]

Financial constraints alone *may* explain the 1945 decision simply to add an Emigrant Directorate to the MFA, and to change the name to the Ministry of Foreign Affairs and Expatriates (MFAE) rather than establish a separate ministry. However, in discussing this issue at the time, several writers mentioned the more likely explanation: the need to overcome sectarianism (*al-ta'ifiyyah*) or other narrow partisan intrigues if émigré institutions and policy were to succeed.[26] This was a veiled way of expressing concern that the vast majority of Lebanese expatriates were Christians (hence the Phalange preoccupation with the issue) and that the establishment of a separate ministry to deal with them would have fueled Muslim anxieties in the context of the delicate confessional relationship that underpinned Lebanese Westphalian sovereignty. Indeed, a recurrent theme, and one that featured prominently in the Kata'ib's recommendations, was that Lebanese abroad were unjustly excluded from participation in the political system at home. In other words, Lebanese expatriates deserved the right to vote in Lebanon,[27] a demand that would have upset the balance established by the National Pact. As a result, and to avoid a conflict, members of the elite called for solving the problem '*ala al-tariqah al-lubnaniyyah* ("the Lebanese way"): the solution would have to involve compromise and hence fall short of the establishment of a separate ministry.[28]

---

[23] "Résolutions adoptées par le gouvernement libanais en Conseil des Ministres le 6 Octobre 1945," *Cahiers de l'Est* 3 1945: p. 150.

[24] *Al-Kitab al-Abyad: Wizarat al-Mughtaribin – matlab wa-'athirat wa-baramij 'amal* (Beirut: Ministry of Expatriates, 1994), p. 11.

[25] See Moannack, p. 177.   [26] Ibid., p. 177.

[27] Moannack argued that considerations other than those of democracy and fairness had led to opposition to emigrant political participation, considerations that had nothing to do with the general interest or with equity. In addition, while not disagreeing with the Phalange's recommendations regarding the state's facilitating émigré investments, he argued that the best means of attracting the émigrés was to reform existing political practices: pp. 184–85.

[28] That said, over the years the MFAE remained a largely Christian domain.

A state policy toward emigration?

Successive post-independence governments each took steps that suggested concern with, if not a full-fledged policy toward, the diaspora communities. For example, during the presidency of Camille Cham'un (1952 58) the government worked to extend the Lebanese Turkish agreement (proceeding from the Treaty of Lausanne) to give more Lebanese a chance to opt for citizenship. It also organized an 'emigrant summer' in 1954 in recognition of the passage of 100 years since the departure of the first Lebanese emigrant for the Americas. Cham'un also visited Brazil, the first visit by a president of an independent Lebanon to a country with such an important Lebanese emigrant community.[29]

The subsequent period, the presidency of General Fu'ad Chehab (1958–64), saw the convening of the first world conference of émigrés in Beirut. The product of this meeting was the establishment of the World Lebanese Union (WLU or *al-Jami'ah al-Lubnaniyyah f-il-'Alam*) (see below). In his address to this meeting Chehab called upon the participants to set ambitious goals for economic, cultural and social development from which both the mother country and the country of residence would benefit, and to strengthen the ties of friendship between Lebanon and the host countries.

Some have argued that, once the WLU was established, the MFAE lowered its profile in LE affairs. In fact, the MFAE's responsibilities toward the sector were never formally reduced, but in practice, its interventions and initiatives, undertaken by the administration of some of the diplomatic missions, apparently owed more to the efforts of individuals than to centrally planned policy. The MFAE did continue to take care of official administrative matters related to personal status and paperwork/documentation through the Expatriate Authority's two bureaus: expatriates and emigration; and property and registry/documentation. Yet, even there, problems in the area of property and documentation led some emigrants to lose holdings back in Lebanon to fraudulent agencies.

Expatriates seem to have suffered most from the state of personal status documentation/registry. There were periods when events (births, marriages, etc.) were not registered: apparently this was a problem for Christians between 1938 and 1964, while others claim that this was a problem for Muslims during the 1952–58 presidency of Cham'un. Moreover, records were sometimes discarded upon a person's death rather than preserved for future reference by relatives. Al-'Aql insists

---

[29] Al-'Aql, p. 227. The community in Brazil is estimated to be the largest among those of the diaspora.

that the source of this problem was the politicization of the registry process itself, given the demographic/confessional balance at stake. While most parties were interested in asserting greater influence over or mobilizing the resources of Lebanese abroad, any moves that might tip the purported equilibrium threatened domestic power relations. He also claims that the Emigrant Directorate was handicapped from the outset by the fact that it was given neither sufficient authority, nor budget;[30] perhaps the result of weak state capacity, but just as likely the result of a deliberate policy.

Unlike the other country cases examined here, Lebanon did not produce successive economic or development plans through which one might trace state policy toward émigrés. Several studies were conducted in the 1960s which pointed out the positives and negatives of migration, but they spawned little action.[31] The one development plan that was issued, for 1972–77, made few references to émigrés, no mention of their remittances,[32] and, in any case, its implementation was thwarted by the outbreak of civil war in 1975. A less comprehensive document, published in 1978 following the end of the first phase of the civil war, focused on the country's need for help in rebuilding. Such rebuilding, it contended, could form the basis for attracting the money and skills of those who had left because of the war.[33] Unfortunately, the war's resumption dashed any hopes for a mass return of people or capital for another twelve years.

Can one then talk about a Lebanese state policy toward emigration over the years? In interviews, this question elicited different responses. If one means an explicit set of policy principles, then the answer is probably no. As one former ambassador noted, he did not even have explicit instructions for dealing with high-profile foreign policy issues, much less expatriates. That said, there was general agreement that successive governments had been concerned with maintaining or rebuilding ties between the expatriates (or their descendants) and Lebanon, especially with the goals of encouraging tourism and investment, and of lobbying for Lebanon on critical occasions with their host countries. There was also, apparently, a general commitment by the government to promote

---

[30] Ibid., pp. 241–42, 247–48.
[31] Kamal Hamdan, "Lebanon: Emigration Policies, Trends and Mechanisms" (Lubnan: Siyasat al-Hijrah wa-Tayyaratuha wa-Anthimatuha). A paper presented at the ILO/UNDP Seminar on Migration Policies in the Arab Labor-Sending Countries, Cairo, 2–4 May 1992, p. 33.
[32] République Libanaise, Ministère du Plan, *Plan sexennal de développement 1972–1977* (n.p., n.d.).
[33] Majlis al-Inma'w-al-I'mar, *Mashru' al-I'mar* (Beirut: n.p., 1978), pp. 1–4.

co-existence among the members of the different confessional communities in the diaspora, although the civil war period rendered that exceedingly difficult.[34]

In his study of Lebanese migration policy, Hamdan insists that successive governments did realize the importance of the role of the emigrants, both in Lebanon and abroad. His evidence includes several of the elements mentioned above – the establishment of the special directorate for expatriates in the Ministry of Foreign Affairs, the expansion of the country's diplomatic and consular networks – as well as the role of the Ministry of Tourism in increasing ties with the LEs and in providing them services. Nevertheless, after surveying these efforts he concludes that they were superficial and uncoordinated. Successive governments devoted no attention to learning the specifics of the communities, nor to the forms of their integration into host state labor markets with an eye to organizing the labor exodus or signing agreements regarding work conditions with receiving countries.[35] All of these elements suggest a state seeking to benefit from its expatriates, but within the confines of policies that would not challenge the domestic confessional balance of power.

The most common image evoked in discussions of state policy toward LEs is that of the milk cow, the Lebanese expatriate who is valued by the state only for the remittances s/he sends home. Because of the laissez-faire economic system that Lebanon has long had (and because banks are not the sole channels for remittances), money transfer has been easy, but not well tracked. Hence, statistics on remittances tend to be anecdotal rather than comprehensive or consistent. According to Saouda, in 1945 the money sent to the country ensured the survival of thousands of families. Citing only the French West African empire, for 1944–45, he claimed that 160 million francs had been sent.[36] Petran stated that remittances from emigrants rose from 58.5 million lira in 1951 to 112 million in 1966.[37] These remittances were one of the principle factors in the budget surplus that Lebanon had uninterruptedly beginning with the end of the Second World War.[38] (See Table 5.1.)

There is no question that the substantial boost in remittance levels in the 1970s owed in large part to the increasing size of Lebanese emigration to the Gulf oil-producing states following the oil price hikes. The

---

[34] Author's interviews with former ambassadors (from different confessional backgrounds) conducted for this study.
[35] Hamdan, pp. 14–15.   [36] Saouda, p. 162.
[37] Tabitha Petran, *The Struggle Over Lebanon* (New York: Monthly Review Press, 1987), p. 59.
[38] Ambassador Fu'ad al-Turk, as cited in Nabil Harfush, *Al-Hudur al-Lubnani f-il-'Alam*, Volume III (Beirut: Dar al-Funun, n.d.), p. 349.

Table 5.1. *Lebanese expatriate remittances (in millions of US dollars)*

1972	307
1973	361
1974	912
1975	515
1976	27
1977	1114
1978	685
1979	1772
1980	2252
1981	1920
1982	1200
1983	900
1984	700
1985	400
1986	850
1987	2130
1988*	2600

*Preliminary

Source: calculations and estimates of the Association of Banks and the Chambers of Commerce and Industry in Beirut. From Hamdan, p. 26.

value of remittances was $251 million in 1970, whereas it had jumped to $2.252 billion in 1980 and $1.92 billion in 1981.[39] Harfush, citing a 1986 "Study of a Group of Lebanese Banks Operating Abroad," gives $500 million, $881 million and $895 million for the same three years.[40] A Ministry of Expatriates (see below) publication noted that, in 1979, remittances were more than 55 percent of the GDP, exceeding 15 percent of the commercial/trade deficit.[41] Another source in 1982 cited a report that the Lebanese community in Saudi Arabia (150,000 people) was sending home $150 million a month, some $1.8 billion a year.[42] A 1984 report claimed that more than 2 million people in Lebanon were living off the high level of remittances sent by Lebanese émigrés and that, without their contributions, Lebanon would not have survived the war.[43] The director-general of the former Ministry of Expatriates

[39] Wizarat al-Mughtaribin, *Watha'iq min Mahfuzat al-Wizarah* (Beirut: Manshurat Wizarat al-Mughtaribin, 1998), p. 185.
[40] Harfush, Volume III, p. 20.   [41] Wizarat al-Mughtaribin, p. 185.
[42] *Al-Hawadith*, 10 December 1982.
[43] *Daily Star*, 28–29 July 1984, citing a study by the WLCU.

stated in 2002 that, in recent years, expatriate remittances to Lebanon had been $3–4 billion per year.[44]

Whatever the exact figures over the years, it is clear that LE contributions to the economy have been substantial, although there are no special tax or customs privileges for Lebanese expatriates: if one holds Lebanese citizenship one is treated as a Lebanese and if not, one is subject to the laws governing foreigners. Being of Lebanese descent is irrelevant. That said, as noted above, the free market environment in Lebanon has meant that few obstacles are deliberately placed in the way of foreign investment.[45]

In sum, even in the absence of official documents indicating the contours of an explicit policy toward expatriates, the state's refusal or failure to intervene more directly in matters related to citizen departure or remittance channeling constitutes a policy of sorts. As in the other cases examined here, the economic angle – the general desire for remittances and investment to reinforce state capacity – is certainly clear, but it is only a part of the story. Additional evidence of the state's approach to the communities may be found through a careful examination of its institutional responses to the emigrant communities. Indeed, it is here that the larger story concerning the emigrants' identity, ties and role in the complex domestic political balance becomes clear.

The WLCU

The impetus behind and the organizational result of the first serious initiative to establish an expatriate-related institution can be understood only in the context of the political aftermath of the civil war of 1958. The head of the army at the time, General Fu'ad Chehab, viewed the revolt as a factional struggle and therefore sought to keep the army out of the fray. As a result, then-President Cham'un called on the Kata'ib and the SSNP (which were antagonistic toward each other but both of which were opposed to the rebels) to assist the gendarmerie. In July 1958, US marines landed, a cease-fire was arranged, and Chehab, who had kept the army neutral and hence probably kept to a minimum the areas of the conflict, was elected president on 31 July 1958.

Muslim leaders had hoped through this revolt to cut the power of the Maronite Christian presidency and to strengthen their own position in the context of a rising regional tide of pan-Arabism associated with

---

[44] Interview with Haytham Jum'ah, Director General, Ministry of Expatriates, Beirut, 21 October 2002.
[45] Discussion with the legal counsel office of Fu'ad al-Turk, 7 October 2002.

Egyptian President Gamal ʿAbd al-Nasir. However, not only were the returns on this investment minor, they also triggered a Kataʾib revolt (24 September–15 October), after Chehab formed a government that excluded any supporters of former president Chamʿun. Then-prime-minister Rashid Karami (a Sunni) was forced to resign, but shortly thereafter announced the formation of a new government of four leaders: Husayn ʿUwayni (a former prime minister) and himself, both Sunnis, and Pierre Gemayel and Raymond Eddé, both Maronites. According to this formula, the cabinet comprised representatives of the two warring factions (Gemayel and Karami) as well as two who had not been involved (Eddé and ʿUwayni). That same day the Kataʾib ordered an end to the strike it had called, and the crisis was brought to an end.[46] This quadripartite government of reconciliation or "national unity" as it was called, remained in place until 14 May 1960.

The confessional stakes in both the unfolding and the termination of this crisis intersect to explain why it was that within the first year of Chehab's presidency, the government endorsed the Kataʾib's long-standing call for establishing an institution to organize Lebanese expatriates. It was the power of the Phalange in the crisis that had led Chehab, who had no popular power base of his own, to include Pierre Gemayel in this government of national unity in the first place; and it was Gemayel's presence in the cabinet – the first time that the Kataʾib had been in power – that likely explains the decision by this cabinet, on 29 August 1959, to call for the holding of a conference for Lebanese émigrés. This decision, and a series of measures that followed, led to the convening of a government-organized meeting in September 1960 at which the Lebanese World Union, mentioned above, was founded.

The Phalange had long supported a larger role in Lebanon for the Lebanese abroad. Gemayel's idea was to create a worldwide Agence Libanaise, which he clearly stated was to be modeled on the Zionist Jewish Agency. Having seen the successes of the Jewish Agency in promoting the establishment of a Jewish National Home in Palestine, Gemayel felt that the Lebanese presence abroad, well established and with a stronger sense of corporate identity (he believed) than the diverse Jewish communities around the world, could accomplish even greater things for Lebanon. His vision included the recruitment of former presidents and ministers as well as religious leaders and experts in diverse fields. He also envisioned a strong role for the Lebanese state, which was to give such an agency an adequate budget as well as a national, rather

---

[46] Rabbath, p. 569.

than a partisan or confessional, character. In his view, such an organization would constitute the crowning of national reconciliation (so important after 1958), by bringing together the energies of all Lebanese with a view to consolidating the independence and sovereignty of the country.[47]

Members of the diaspora communities were to be contacted through the diplomatic missions to participate in this congress. Another committee, an offspring of the first, was headed by the director-general of the MFAE and was to study how to make the conference a success. A subsequent decree authorized the establishment of a central, standing body, whose task was to prepare for this congress, and three committees were formed – for tourism, culture, and the economy. The first was to prepare the invitations to the conference, the second to put in place studies of Lebanese cultural activity in the *mahjar*, and the third to prepare statistical studies to inform the expatriates about the sectors of the Lebanese economy.[48]

While this committee structure suggests varied interest on the part of the Lebanese state, the greatest efforts in preparation appear to have been put into matters related to the economy. The report of the preparatory meeting of April 1960 clearly stated: "it is well known that the economic and financial aspect needs to be and will be hegemonic in the studies of the conference and its results, because it constitutes the practical and effective means of strengthening existing ties and establishing new ones between all Lebanese." (It was also, perhaps, the least politicized.) The report also recommended the establishment of five branch committees: financial participation and investment of expatriates in Lebanon; financial participation and investment in the host countries; commercial exchange; financial and tax systems; and transport/communications. The report then laid out a detailed schedule for the completion of the various committees' tasks. A follow-up meeting on economic matters was held on 17 June, and its report included a detailed presentation on the Lebanese economy.[49]

The conference was finally held on 15 September 1960 in Beirut, with representatives from thirty-six countries. After various sessions and discussions, the congress decided to establish the World Lebanese Union (al-Jami'ah al-Lubnaniyyah f-il-'Alam). A permanent secretariat was then elected, with the presidency going to the Minister of Foreign Affairs and Expatriates, and with membership comprising some ministers of state, the director-general of the MFAE, the head of the Expatriate Directorate,

---

[47] Elie Safa, *L'émigration libanaise* (Beirut: Université Saint-Joseph, 1960), pp. 259–61; p. 262, note.
[48] Al-'Aql, pp. 345–46.   [49] Harfush, Volume III, pp. 168–71, 173–83.

and heads of the congress committees. Despite the presence of government representatives in top positions, the union was officially established as an independent, not a state, institution. That said, the government provided 150,000 LL (Lebanese lira) each year to cover the expenses of the general secretariat, which was to work in close cooperation with MFAE officials. The WLU was also given an office in the MFAE building, and the WLU secretary-general was to be appointed by the elected president in coordination with the MFAE.[50] Official permission for registering the union according to the Associations Law came from the Ministry of the Interior, but the MFAE continued to exercise a certain tutelage over the union.[51]

Given such a structure, one of the potential problems for WLU members, the possibility of dual loyalty, was addressed early on. Philippe Tacla, then Minister of Foreign Affairs and Expatriates, insisted that joining the union in no way affected matters related to nationality or nationality acquisition by Lebanese. The WLU was meant to include all those who were Lebanese or descendants of Lebanese, whether they had maintained their Lebanese nationality or not. He also stressed that one of the union's goals was to strengthen the ties of loyalty and respect among those of Lebanese origin toward the state whose nationality they had acquired; indeed, it was a WLU goal to encourage those of Lebanese origin to be positive links between the two societies. In this way, he argued, the knowledge of Lebanon around the world would increase as would peoples' affection for and confidence in it. Tacla warned of the corrupting influence of politics, and urged the WLU members not to let the union become a victim of political battles. He also stressed that the union was not meant to replace existing local associations and societies, although such institutions could join the WLU or perhaps become branches of it, if they so desired.[52]

Four years passed between the founding of the Union and its second meeting, which was held in Beirut in August 1964. The primary importance of the second meeting was that it established a constitution and elected the union's first world council. According to the constitution, the WLU was to be a non-governmental, apolitical, non-confessional, and non-labor organization. It was to include Lebanese expatriates as well as resident Lebanese who had spent at least five years abroad and then returned. The goals were: to strengthen the ties of loyalty and respect between its members and the people of the countries in which they were

[50] Nabil Harfush, *Al-Hudur al-Lubnani f-il-'Alam*, Volume I (Juniyah: Dar Kurayyam, 1974), p. 225; Volume II, p. 28.
[51] *Al-Kitab al-Abyad*, p. 15.   [52] Harfush, Volume III, pp. 190–91.

resident, and to participate in the development of these countries; to reinforce the bonds between its members and Lebanese living in Lebanon; to build relationships between its members on the national and international level; to encourage the participation of its members in economic, social, cultural and tourism activity in Lebanon; to strengthen cultural, economic and financial ties between the host countries and Lebanon; and to spread Lebanese culture/heritage throughout the world.[53]

The WLU constitution provided for the establishment of local branches and regional councils; and from the regional councils on the American and African continents, continental committees were to be formed. With its executive headquarters in Beirut, its world council was to be composed of the heads of the continental committees and eight deputies elected for a period of three years at each world meeting, which was to be held in Lebanon. The by-laws also limited the contact of the union with official and public institutions to the channel of the Expatriate Directorate of the MFAE.[54]

Regardless of these accomplishments, the fact that it had taken four years between conferences was indicative of malaise in the union from the beginning. There were financial problems, and difficulties in establishing a presence internationally, the result of local or regional differences and traditions, as well as political battles. A third congress was held in 1968 and a fourth in 1971. At the fourth meeting the goals of the WLU were modified so that it was described as a charitable, *cultural* organization with no profit motive. At this point the word "cultural" (*thiqafiyyah*) was added to the name, so that it became *al-Jami'ah al-Lubnaniyyah al-Thiqafiyyah fi-l 'Alam* (WLCU). This modification came in response to a request from representatives of the large Brazilian community because Brazil did not allow foreign organizations to operate on its soil if they had other than a cultural character.[55]

During this period the union received official licensing from the Ministry of the Interior, and was recognized as an independent civil association, subject to the Ministry of the Interior just like any other Lebanese association. Nevertheless, the MFAE continued its tutelage over the union. According to law, the union was required to send minutes of all WLCU meetings to the MFAE and the director-general of the ministry was empowered to render judgments in any dispute that occurred in the union. The MFAE also provided diplomatic passports to the union's president and secretary-general.[56]

---

[53] Al-'Aql, p. 351.   [54] Ibid., p. 352.   [55] Ibid., p. 353.   [56] Ibid., p. 354.

Whatever institutional reinforcement the WLCU gained from such support, the outbreak of civil war in Lebanon was to have a serious and continuing impact on the organization. It took several years for the problems to manifest themselves institutionally but, once they did, the WLCU found itself in a situation of increasing internal contestation and, as a byproduct, paralysis when it came to its primary functions. The story of its unfolding is extremely complex. An already weakened state, that – in part because of the emigrants' relationship to the issue of Lebanese identity – had never given much more than superficial treatment to its émigrés, was hardly in a better position to implement a coherent policy during a period when its already minimal sovereignty was further undermined as it was paralyzed, riven by factionalism, or captured by one of the militias. While neither the impact nor the response was uniform, the rivalries and violence that began to tear Lebanon apart were reflected in the communities abroad. The exodus of new waves of emigrants, this time by force of arms or intimidation, changed the composition of many of the communities, as increasing numbers of those who left were Muslims, both Sunni and Shi'i.

A full exposition of the exodus or its impact on the communities is beyond the focus of this work. Labaki and Rjeily estimate, based on a variety of sources, that nearly 900,000 Lebanese left the country during the fifteen-year war,[57] probably between one quarter and one fifth of the total population. The Ministry of Information issued figures in 1985 indicating that the total Lebanese population was 5.6 million. Ten years later a UN estimate placed the population at 3 million, while the World Bank estimated 4 million.[58] More precise statistics have been impossible in the absence of a census, which continues to be too sensitive a topic to broach.

Over the course of the fifteen-year civil war the participants and their alliances shifted, in some cases dramatically. The first stage, often referred to as the Two-years' War, pitted Lebanese (largely, but not exclusively Muslim) fighters allied with Palestinian factions against largely Maronite Christian Lebanese. This first stage came to an end in October 1976, with an Arab-imposed settlement that left the Arab Deterrent Force, overwhelmingly composed of Syrian troops, in occupation of large parts of the country. The latter part of the 1970s saw a number of intra-Maronite battles, or Maronite–Syrian battles as well as the first large-scale Israeli invasion of the South in 1978.

---

[57] Boutros Labaki and Khalil Abou Rjeily, *Bilan des guerres du Liban, 1975–1990* (Paris: l'Harmattan, 1993), p. 94 Table 24.
[58] Maktabi in Butenschon *et al.*, p. 155.

The sixth conference of the union was held in 1977, following the end of the Two-years' War. As had some past meetings, this gathering called for the establishment of a separate ministry for Lebanese throughout the world: it would coordinate with the MFA, but the Expatriate Directorate would be attached to it, and it would be called the Ministry of the Lebanese Diaspora.[59] A more controversial call, particularly in light of the union's desire to be independent of the Lebanese state, was for the expatriates to channel some of their financial support away from development projects and instead participate in supporting the Lebanese Army.[60] The seventh meeting was held in 1980 and then, only a year later, the eighth in Montreal. At this congress two presidents and two secretaries-general were elected – they were to split the terms – an early sign of serious problems.[61] The ninth meeting was not held until 1985, and it was at this meeting that the union entered into a period of real division and serious infighting, again largely the reflection of politics back home.

The then-ten years of civil war had produced numerous changes in the balance of forces within Lebanon. While the Amal Movement[62] had its origins in the pre-war period, it began to assert itself gradually after the disappearance of its founder, Musa al-Sadr, in 1978. In the context of the 1982 Israeli invasion of Lebanon, the subsequent expulsion of the PLO, and the continuing Israeli occupation of the southern part of the country, the large Shi'i community, long marginalized socially, economically and politically, developed as a formidable political and military force. The emergence of this new actor had implications for Lebanon's relationship with the diaspora as well, as the Shi'a were the only Lebanese confessional group (beyond the Maronites) with a numerically important presence in the diaspora, a concentration of that presence (on the African continent) and a nascent political organization of strength sufficient to make it a potentially important player in expatriate affairs. Prior to the emergence of Amal, there had been little challenge to the dominance of the Maronite community in the WLCU: the battles over leadership were largely personal, not political or confessional, affairs. However, with continuing civil war and the reconfiguration of socio-economic and political forces, that changed: now, in addition to whatever personal-interest-related quarrels may have affected the union, there were political/confessional ones as well.

---

[59] Al-'Aql, p. 356.   [60] *Al-Nahar*, 7 August 1977.   [61] Al-'Aql, p. 356.
[62] For a discussion of the origins and evolution of "Amal" (an acronym which means "hope," and which stands for *Afwaj al-Muqawimah al-Lubnaniyyah*, "Detachments of the Lebanese Resistance"), see Augustus Richard Norton, *Amal and the Shi'a: Struggle for the Soul of Lebanon* (Austin: University of Texas Press, 1987).

These developments began to be manifested in the lead-up to the WLCU's 1985 congress in Saõ Paolo. A superficial analysis of this might reduce it to one of the largely Christian communities of the Americas versus the Shi'i communities of Africa. However, the reality was far more complex than this: none of these communities was mono-lithic confessionally or politically, nor is any confessional group unified ideologically. That said, in the context of the constellation of political forces in Lebanon at the time, the most important dividing line was that of support for or opposition to the Syrian presence in the country. On this question, regardless of how active they were in the WLCU, most of the old, largely Maronite, communities of the Americas took an anti-Syrian line, while those of Africa, whether sympathetic to Amal or the SSNP, tended to be pro-Syrian. This issue was not the only one of importance in the diaspora, but it was a key and bitterly divisive one.

In terms of Lebanese domestic politics, the period from 1986 until the end of Amin Gemayel's presidential term in 1988 was characterized by paralysis owing to the continuing civil war. An attempt by the Syrians in late 1985 to reach an agreement to end the conflict had come to naught after being rejected by both Gemayel and Samir Geagea of the Lebanese Forces.[63] As the end of his term approached, and the prospects for holding elections to select a successor appeared dim, Gemayel appointed General Michel 'Awn, the head of the army, as interim president. The constitutionality of such a move was questionable, and as a result the legitimacy of the 'Awn cabinet was not recognized outside the Christian areas of the country. In the other areas, the cabinet of Gemayel's prime minister, Salim al-Huss, continued to be regarded as legitimate, even though it had formally resigned, leaving a vacuum of governmental authority. In March 1989, 'Awn launched a "War of Liberation" against the Syrians which backfired and led in fact to an increased presence of Syrian troops in the country. The areas under 'Awn's authority were besieged, devastated, and witnessed major emigration.

At the end of the summer of 1989, after nearly fifteen years of civil war and increasing public as well as regional desire to bring the fighting to an end, the surviving Lebanese deputies from among those who had been elected in 1972 (the time of the last parliamentary elections) – sixty-two out of an original ninety-nine – met in the city of Ta'if, Saudi Arabia, to

---

[63] The Lebanese Forces were a militia that was organized by Bashir Gemayel, and which extended well beyond the initial Kata'ib party base built by his father, Pierre. Bashir was killed in a bombing of the Kata'ib offices in East Beirut in September 1982, shortly after being elected president of Lebanon in the shadow of the Israeli invasion and siege of the Lebanese capital. He was succeeded by his brother Amin, who, nonetheless, never achieved the popularity with the Lebanese Forces that his brother had enjoyed.

discuss national reconciliation. At the end of the three weeks of meetings, the National Accord Document, generally referred to as the Ta'if Agreement, was announced – the outcome of a process of reconciliation between the Lebanese, with the effective participation of the Syrians, other Arabs and the international community.

All of these developments had an impact on the union, but in the direction of continuing paralysis. In addition, personal ambition continued to play a role. As one key example of ambition rather than ideology as a basis of WLCU problems, Niqula Khoury, who had led the Americas faction to victory over the Africa group in the elections at the 1985 congress, gradually shifted his political position away from that of the Americas group. What was apparently of greatest concern to him was that he become minister of a rumored-to-be-created Ministry of Expatriates. Indeed, Khoury bore some personal (rather than political) responsibility for the union's paralysis, apparently believing that, if he could postpone the holding of a WLCU congress long enough and strengthen his position, he could secure a ministerial portfolio. In late 1990, he was finally appointed Minister of State in the first post-Ta'if cabinet, and he appeared to be on his way. Meanwhile, in the WLCU, there was renewed talk about the need to revive the union and fill the void left by the appointment of its president to the cabinet: the by-laws of the union prohibited Khoury from concomitantly holding such a governmental post and a position in the administrative body of the union.[64] However, Khoury was not about to go willingly.

A meeting of the world council (not congress) of the WLCU was held a few months later, in Paris in April 1991. Khoury left this meeting with the agreement of those who had attended to support his taking over an expatriate ministry, and, from Paris, he had only to secure the agreement of Lebanese government circles. Two months later, in June 1991, Khoury continued his campaign as Cairo hosted the WLCU conference for the African continent. However, both Lebanese President Elias Hrawi and Foreign Minister Faris Bouwayz opposed the establishment of a separate Ministry of Expatriates.[65] Hrawi's position was evidently that Khoury should be content being a minister of state, while Khoury continued to make a case for a full ministership.[66] In any case, despite confessional and other differences, a majority had apparently finally come to the conclusion that Khoury needed to go.

---

[64] *Al-Hayat*, 19 March 1991; *Al-Safir*, 10 August 1991.
[65] Bouwayz's power (and probably his position on this issue) derived from the fact that he was Hrawi's son-in-law. Hrawi's opposition to the establishment of such a ministry may have been due to rivalry with Khoury, who was also from Zahleh. I am grateful to Farid el-Khazen for alerting me to these points.
[66] *Al-Hayat*, 5 June 1991.

On 13 August, Bouwayz disbanded the administrative body of the WLCU. He based his right to do so on Article 28 of the union's constitution, which made the MFAE the authority of last resort in the case of conflicts.[67] He then replaced the Khoury group with a transitional committee composed of former presidents of the union and other former officials from or associated with it. However, both sides to the dispute rejected the MFAE move, and the group in the Americas went ahead with its own conference.[68] Khoury also appealed Bouwayz's decision to the state Consultative Council, and on 13 May 1992, one day before the union's conference was to begin in Mexico, the Consultative Council ruled that Bouwayz did not have the authority to disband the body headed by Khoury.[69]

This administrative and political disarray continued as, in addition to the existing infighting, *Anwar* Khoury, the president of the hosting community (Mexico), emerged as a new WLCU presidential contender. Thereafter, MFAE Director of Expatriates Samir Hubayqa met with Anwar Khoury (AK) in Beirut and referred to *him* as the president of the WLCU. He further took AK's side by giving a representative of his group the WLCU office in the MFAE, and by formally recognizing him as the WLCU president in spring 1993.[70]

In the meantime, on 31 October 1992, Dr. Ridha Wahid was appointed Minister of State for Expatriates. (See below.) The WLCU–AK group's response to this development was that if such a ministry would have the right to appoint attachés and have diplomatic immunity to move about freely, the WLCU would support it. If not, then the alternative it proposed was the creation of a ministry of state for émigré affairs within the MFAE which would be given full authority.[71] However, the tone of the AK group quickly changed, as they objected in March 1993 to a new law proposing to give the Ministry of Expatriates (ME) supervisory responsibility over the WLCU. (See below.) This group's concern about what ME supervision would mean was certainly heightened by the fact that Wahid was a Shiʻi, although he had had a long distinguished career in government service and was by no means beholden to Amal's Nabih Berri, whose influence the AK group sought to curb.[72] The AK group contended that such ME

---

[67] *Al-Nahar*, 14 August 1991.   [68] Al-ʻAql, p. 360.   [69] *Al-Diyar*, 30 May 1992.
[70] Al-ʻAql, pp. 362–64.   [71] *Al-Nahar*, 30 December 1992.
[72] Wahid was a medical doctor who had studied in both Lebanon and France and had previously served as the secretary-general of the Ministry of Labor and Social Affairs. He had been a parliamentary deputy, the Minister of Health (1966) and the Director-General of the National Social Security Fund (1965–73). The opposition to Berri was not simply because he headed a Shiʻi organization, but because he was a strong political ally of Syria, which the AK group opposed.

oversight of the WLCU would lead many Lebanese to quit the union, that it would cause problems between the union's branches and the host countries, and that it would undermine Prime Minister Rafiq al-Hariri's call for expatriates to return and to invest in Lebanon:[73] only the union's independence from the Lebanese government, they argued, had enabled the WLCU leadership to sell such an organization to the communities.

In response, on 18 May 1993, Wahid's first decision was to declare the WLCU to be in violation of the law and to withdraw his recognition of the union or of any activity it undertook. Joseph Yunis, the secretary-general of the AK group riposted, condemning the establishment of the ME as contradictory to diplomatic tradition and as interference in the affairs of the WLCU.[74] Only days later, Wahid forbade the WLCU to represent emigrants or to speak in their name. His decision came just one week before the annual meeting of the WLCU world council was to be held in Brazil (21–23 May 1993), and he was backed up by the Minister of the Interior at the time, Bishara Mirhaj.[75]

Formally, Wahid based his action on the WLCU's failure to submit the required documents to put its house in order. The ministry's contention was that the union's style of operation was the opposite of what it was supposed to be: instead of initiatives coming from the base, people were appointed by the WLCU to represent the communities and to establish branches and institutions. Nor did the WLCU program promote unity: many people were uninterested in associative goals and activities; confessionalism played an important role and, with it, theft and extortion, according to the minister's assessment. WLCU positions were sometimes used for political, commercial or investment benefit, and some leaders had been in the same position for twenty years or more.[76]

Wahid repeatedly stressed that the ME's goal was not to put an end to the union, but rather to trigger a positive shock that would reunite it and push its leaders to cooperate to make it successful.[77] He saw the functions of the ME and the WLCU as very much distinct, and from his statements there is no reason to conclude that he sought permanently to close or completely control the WLCU.[78] Nevertheless, the ME's withdrawal of recognition of the WLCU led to a public polemic and a legal battle between the two in which some official parties became involved on the side of those who criticized the ME's move. Wahid insisted that the goal was to have an institution that would be administratively and organizationally independent. This independence was not, however, to lead it to

---

[73] *Al-Nahar*, 19 March 1993.   [74] *Al-Nahar*, 18 March 1993.
[75] *Al-Hayat*, 18 May 1993.   [76] Al-'Aql, p. 313.   [77] *Al-Kitab al-Abyad*, p. 19.
[78] *Al-Minbar*, February 1993.

serve as a political platform (*minbar*) from which to incite sectarian factionalism against the state.[79] The minister contended that that was in fact one thing the WLCU *had* done successfully: it had strengthened confessionalism and sectarianism in expatriate society,[80] in effect serving as one more force that further undermined the already highly circumscribed sovereignty of the Lebanese state. The polemic continued for three years, subsiding only with the departure of Wahid and the appointment of 'Ali Khalil as minister in May 1995.

However, during the first days of the ME it was not even clear that Wahid would remain as minister. He had been promised that he would be consulted before a secretary-general was named to the ministry, and he offered his resignation when the post was filled without his input. In all his statements about the issue, Wahid remained diplomatic, but it was clear that his objection concerned both form and content. He was well aware of the displeasure/skepticism in some Christian diaspora circles at the appointment of a Shi'i to the top ME post. He had insisted that he would be a minister for all expatriates, not just the Shi'a, and his political independence tended to confirm this. Hence, all the more his dismay when he found himself faced with, not just a Shi'i secretary-general, but a top Amal militiaman turned politico. His desire to make the ME a confession-blind ministry appeared thwarted. Wahid stated repeatedly that he had nothing personal against the appointee, Haytham Jum'ah, but that he wanted to avoid even the appearance of confessional favoritism in the ministry. In taking such a stance, Wahid triggered the puzzlement and in some cases the wrath of some parts of the Shi'i community, which did not understand why he had insisted upon having a Christian appointed to the secretary-general post. Wahid might well have insisted upon resigning had the WLCU–AK group not immediately thereafter at its meeting in Brazil issued resolutions calling for the abolition of the ministry and demanding an apology from Wahid. At least officially, he withdrew his resignation in order to defend his actions and the ministry, although others have suggested that Prime Minister Rafiq al-Hariri would not allow him to resign.[81]

The ME then called upon all émigré organizations to get their houses in order or face withdrawal of recognition. In the midst of all this, the head of the Lebanese clubs in Brazil and a number of authorities from the union called for the convening of the tenth congress of the union in the Brazilian capital in September 1994 during which agreement was reached to end the differences in the WLCU. This conference calmed the

[79] *Al-Kitab al-Abyad*, p. 19.   [80] *Al-Kifah al-'Arabi*, 3 May 1993.
[81] *Al-Nahar*, 25 May 1993; *al-Shira'*, 31 May 1993.

atmosphere internally among the various leaderships/poles of the Union, and externally, with the ME.

The WLCU's problems with the ME were finally laid to rest with the departure of Wahid in May 1995. Nevertheless, the union continued to suffer from a split along the same basic political/confessional lines, focusing primarily on the Syrian role in Lebanon. WLCU elections continued to be contested by some parties as illegitimate, and divisiveness among the ranks prevailed, despite successive Lebanese government initiatives to reunify and restructure the union.[82]

Evaluating the WLCU

An examination of WLCU activities over three decades reveals a mixed record. If one tries to catalogue the positives, it held 9 congresses, more than 40 world council meetings, and an equal number of national and regional meetings. It established more than 250 branches around the world, with more than 6,500 members. The union also held 2 world councils for *mutahaddir* youth, one in Montevideo in September 1986, and the second in Denmark in early August 1987. There was also a host of parties, celebrations and cultural activities.[83]

That said, the record briefly chronicled above is, on balance, dismal. The union complained that one problem was state support, which was minimal (400,000 LL, about $130,000 at the time), but community support was also lacking. There were few incentives for expatriates, especially the young, to join Lebanese societies.[84] While one set of 1974 statistics indicated that the union had 150 branches in the world, in fact it had only about 20 active, working branches.[85] By 1999, only 14 countries had branches: the USA, Brazil, Australia, Mexico, Argentina, Canada, South Africa, Ivory Coast, Uruguay, Nigeria, Liberia, Guinea, Egypt and Greece. Even among these branches many were inactive owing to internal political and confessional divisions, leadership struggles and the narrow/exclusivist nature of the representation. The branches were criticized for their verbal clamor, pretentious behavior, and disappointing leaders who seemed to care more about having their pictures in the newspapers and on TV than about engaging in serious associative work.[86]

Four main reasons may be cited for the failures of the union. The first lies in the realm of organization, as the WLCU did not take into account the fact that the means of operation might need to be different from one

---

[82] *Al-Nahar*, 4 October 1999; *Al-Diyar*, 17 November 1999; *al-Nahar*, 15 March 2003.
[83] Al-'Aql, pp. 371–72.   [84] Ibid., p. 385.   [85] Harfush, Volume I, p. 231.
[86] Al-'Aql, pp. 386–87.

diaspora community to another. Another problem in this realm was the lack of clarity in the relations between the world council and the general secretariat and the absence of any principle requiring annual or periodic plans for expatriate work. A second major problem area was individualism on the one hand, and what is described as a "communal mentality" on the other, among some of the expatriates, who thought that this new institution was competing with traditional institutions, and hence put obstacles in its way. Third, the failure had its roots in the Lebanese diplomatic missions, which limited their activities to purely consular and political work, treating expatriate problems as if they were of only secondary importance. Fourth, but probably most critical, was the transfer of political party, tribal/familial and confessional animosities to the *mahjar*, and the impact of the civil war.[87]

Thus, if the union was reasonably active, if not terribly effective, in the first ten years of its existence, the record thereafter is quite sad. An institution conceived of as a means of further binding emigrants to Lebanon instead found itself penetrated, riven and ultimately paralyzed by sectarian concerns that had contributed to the outbreak of armed conflict. Indeed, through this institution (although it was far from alone) the diaspora communities were drawn into the larger process of the reconfiguration of the political landscape underway in a more violent fashion back home. The story of the multi-faceted relationship between the diaspora communities and the various factions involved in the civil war is properly the topic of another book. However, there is no question that, given the long-standing ties between parties in Lebanon (religious, political or otherwise) and these communities in the context of civil strife within an already weak state, the lines between the inside and the outside of the polity blurred even further. What was already relatively circumscribed Westphalian and domestic sovereignty was further eroded, not only by external players from the region (Israel, the PLO, Syria, Iran, etc.) but through the very activities that constituted the relationship with the diaspora as well.

The Ministry of Expatriates (ME)

The previous sections have made clear the numerous shortcomings or failures of the WLCU and the MFAE in putting in place a coherent policy to address expatriate needs. An analysis published by the new ME, which traced the relationship between expatriates and the state over

---

[87] Ibid., pp. 374–5.

time, stated frankly that the basic problem over the years had been lack of governmental interest or concern. Added to that were the institutional and domestic political factors that have been examined above.[88] Nevertheless, the obvious need for reform or for a more effective institution does not fully account for why, in the early 1990s, the step to establish a separate ministry was finally taken.

To explain the establishment of the ME one must add to the contextual factors already discussed a particular set of domestic factors. One element was the marked need by the state for the LEs after the civil war. Fifteen years of fighting had taken a terrible toll, in terms of destruction, loss of human life, and population displacement. To rebuild, the country needed all the human and financial resources it could mobilize. For Lebanon, its strategic reserves – so critical during such a period – lay with its expatriate communities. In order to organize clear and targeted relations between the two wings of Lebanon – resident and expatriate – a new mechanism was needed: an authority that would take over the task of marshaling diaspora contributions.[89]

In addition, however, were domestic, confessional and political considerations related to restructuring the government after Ta'if which were critical in the decision to create several new ministries during the first Hariri government.[90] The Ministry of Expatriates was but one of these; among the others were the ministries of culture, municipalities, technical and vocational training, transport, environment, and social affairs. Those in government circles, close to the prime minister, insisted that the policy of establishing the new ministries responded to a set of tangible needs; certainly from the names, one could make this case. However, others believed the decision owed to the need to create sufficient spoils to satisfy all the political groups who were party to the Ta'if accords. In other words, the implicit charge was that new ministries were part of a post-war settlement that had to divide the existing political pie in additional ways.

The proposal to establish these ministries was part of the government program presented by Prime Minister Hariri for a parliamentary confidence vote in November 1992. In his statement regarding the proposed ME, Hariri, who himself had spent years as an expatriate working and building a fortune in Saudi Arabia, promised that the government would strive to reinforce ties between the homeland and the Lebanese diaspora in a way that both strengthened the Lebanese presence and role in the world and maintained the ties of the expatriates with their homeland, preserved their interests, and organized their institutions. He argued that

---

[88] Wizarat al-Mughtaribin, p. 186.   [89] Al-'Aql, p. 270.   [90] *Al-Diyar*, 9 April 2000.

this required working to create a special ministry for expatriates which would place among its priorities – in addition to concerns regarding the conditions of expatriate life – attracting Lebanese energies from abroad and encouraging the *muhajirin* (presumably especially those who had departed because of the war) to return and participate in the process of rebuilding the country.[91] Ridha Wahid, the first ME minister, also rejected the idea that the establishment of the ministry was a political solution.[92] His assessment was that there was a serious need, since nothing had really been done for expatriates for thirty years: the mere addition of the words "w-al-mughtaribin" ("and expatriates") to the MFA title so many years earlier had accomplished little.[93]

In the deputies' commentaries on the government's program, there was little that could be interpreted as opposition to the establishment of such a ministry. However, a number of deputies did stress the importance of carefully studying any proposal for a new ministry, to avoid overlap or duality of functions. The concern was both for efficiency and for the state of the Lebanese budget, as Lebanon's resources were meager. Indeed, of the deputies who spoke in favor of such a ministry, most mentioned its importance in attracting expatriate energies and monies to help rebuild the country.[94]

Whatever domestic political problems such ministry creation solved, there was no doubt that it concomitantly opened up a range of administrative problems. Budgetary demands and the potential overlap of functions raised by the deputies were both serious issues. For it was not that most of the tasks with which the new ministries were charged had simply been ignored before; rather, they had been handled (if imperfectly) by existing ministries. Thus, separating or removing responsibilities from existing ministries created tensions, and came close to provoking resignations from or refusals to participate in the new Hariri government.[95]

In the case of the ME, according to a law of 2 April 1993 (which was followed by a ministerial decree of 10 May 1994), the MFAE was in effect split, and the responsibility for expatriates was turned over to the ME. At the time of the parliamentary discussion of this law formally creating the

---

[91] Al-Jumhuriyyah al-Lubnaniyyah, Majlis al-Nuwwab, *al-Dawr al-Tashri'i al-Thani 'ashr, al-'Aqd al-'Adi al-Thani, 1992. Mahdar al-Jalsah al-Thalithah*, 9–10 November 1992, p. 492.
[92] *Al-Safir*, 7 March 1993.   [93] *Al-Diyar*, 3 March 1993.
[94] See the deputies' speeches, Majlis Al-Nuwwab, *Mahdar al-Jalsah al-Thalithah*, 9–10 November 1992, pp. 504, 510–11, 527, 534, 547.
[95] *Al-Safir*, 7 March 1993. This article asks why these particular ministries, but not, for example, a ministry of planning, were established. It also asks why more thought was not given to how to pay for them.

ME, new problems were discussed, and the sharp parliamentary exchanges are quite revealing. The primary issue of contention was an amendment that had been introduced by the finance committee intended to give the ME legal supervision (*ishraf qanuni*) over the WLCU. For a number of deputies this was unacceptable. Some objections were dressed in the concern that a Lebanese ministry could not have such authority over branch organizations that were established in other countries. In other words there was a question of host state sovereignty and concern that this would cause problems for the émigrés in the receiving countries. For others the concern was expressed in terms of potential divisions that such WLCU oversight would trigger in the expatriate communities and the damage it could do to them and to their relationship to Lebanon.[96]

Of course, as was noted above, the real issue was the opposition of some communities abroad (or at least the local WLCU leadership) to the new ministry largely because it was being headed by a Shi'i, whose community's two major political parties, Amal and Hizballah, were sympathetic to the Syrian presence in the country. They were also concerned that this amendment from the finance committee was meant to cut the power or independence of the union in the context of the ongoing political battles discussed above. At the time of the parliamentary discussions, a number of deputies were apparently bombarded with statements issued by various branches of the WLCU, either supporting or opposing the new ministry. As speaker of parliament, Nabih Berri (himself a former émigré born in Sierra Leone) intervened forcefully on several occasions during the sessions, once commenting that the possible divisions in the communities about which some deputies expressed concerns in fact already existed, and that the ministry was unlikely to add to them. If there were serious problems with the law, he argued, then the government could withdraw it.[97] In fact, however, Berri wanted this law (or an amended version of it) and this ministry, which he regarded as part of his (Amal's) spoils in the post-war political system.

On the other side was Foreign Minister Bouwayz, who was staunchly opposed to the establishment of the ME, in no small measure because it removed a realm of authority from his ministry. His response to the law during these discussions may be best characterized as "correct." This was the government's law, he stated, and hence as a cabinet minister he was supportive, although he did register his surprise that the law had not first been submitted to the Foreign Affairs committee. He also noted the

---

[96] See Al-Jumhuriyyah al-Lubnaniyyah, Majlis al-Nuwwab, *al-Dawr al-Tashri'i al-Thani 'ashr, al-'Aqd al-'Adi al-Awwal, 16 March 1993*.
[97] Ibid., pp. 343, 347.

problem with the word *ishraf* in this controversial article, which he said raised problems of sovereignty, as well as jurisdiction. What exactly did the word *ishraf* mean, and why was it to be accorded to the ME when, for all other ministries, the prerogative of legal oversight resided with the Ministry of the Interior?[98]

As the debate continued, Berri made clear that he wanted to find language that would work and move ahead. At one point, and in a dramatic move, he turned his speaker's chair over to his deputy and stepped down to speak from the floor as a parliamentary deputy. His displeasure with the WLCU (and the MFA) was clear as he argued that there were Lebanese expatriates who used their second citizenship as a cover for "certain political positions." What the deputies needed to do was to give the ME some oversight authority regarding the WLCU:

In the past at times, we have been impotent vis-à-vis the WLCU because when there was a problem, it would say that it was a private institution. However, when the WLCU members wanted benefits from the Lebanese state, they went back to relying on their Lebanese passports. There have been some insolent statements from the WLCU regarding the legitimacy of the parliament, as well as statements that accuse the Lebanese government of positions it has not taken. Yet we have heard no response from the MFA. It says it is a private institution. But the WLCU has an office in the MFA and is under the oversight of an ambassador responsible for the associations. This is what needs to be better controlled.[99]

In the end, it was agreed to change the controversial word *ishraf* to *ri'ayah* (which has a similar meaning, but one that connotes taking care of, rather than controlling), and the law passed; but the battle lines were clear.

Thus, more than four decades after the first Phalange expatriate conference had issued its call, a separate ministry had finally been established, problems and opposition notwithstanding. Its charge was broad and challenging: to energize the role of Lebanese emigration, to oversee the affairs of Lebanon's expatriates, to work to strengthen the ties between expatriates and Lebanon, to develop cooperation and exchange with them and with the authorities/bodies produced by the emigrants, and to participate in international activities related to emigration.[100]

The new ministry had five bureaus or divisions (*masalih*). The division of expatriates and emigration was concerned with expatriate interests both inside and outside Lebanon. That of property and registration/documentation was to follow up the registration of Lebanese at the consulates and to be responsible for procedures related to personal status

---

[98] Ibid., p. 344.   [99] Ibid., p. 347.   [100] Al-'Aql, p. 272.

as well as property. The bureau for public relations and emigration affairs was to strengthen ties and develop cooperation with émigré institutions, associations and clubs and to oversee the work of bodies that developed out of the émigré communities and were registered in Lebanon. It was also responsible for recognizing the bodies that had a right to represent Lebanese emigrants and speak in their name (a responsibility which, as we have already seen, created problems with the WLCU). The division of culture and information was to develop ties with the émigré media, play a role in publishing émigré work in Lebanon and encourage the study of Arabic.[101]

Finally there was the bureau for émigré attachés, which was not officially established until 15 February 1996. These attachés, who became a serious bone of contention in ME activity, were supposed to gather information on the size of the communities and their activities, establish close ties with the communities, help solve problems when possible – these community members were not all Lebanese citizens, so the degree to which Lebanese diplomats were empowered/allowed to be involved varied – and provide information to encourage investment. They were also to coordinate with the MFA cultural attachés on relevant programs, including strengthening the teaching of Arabic language, and reinforcing the ties of the community to the homeland.[102]

Conflict with the Ministry of Foreign Affairs

The establishment of the ME meant that there were now three institutions with special tasks vis-à-vis the Lebanese diaspora: the MFA, the new ME and the WLCU. The conflicts among them took their toll on all three, but expatriate affairs were also a casualty, since none of the institutions was really in a position to address existing problems and concerns. The competition and conflict among the three also prevented Lebanon from benefitting as it might have from these communities' resources.

From the beginning, the MFA dealt with the ME as something that had been imposed, refusing to acknowledge it as a legal, organizational reality. Indeed, it obstructed its role by continuing to monopolize the responsibilities that were to have devolved to the ME. Among some of the most serious results was that the new ministry was unable to activate its property and documentation bureau because the MFA's parallel bureau continued to control all registers and documents through the consulates. In addition, because of problems in hiring employees, the ME's bureaus

---

[101] Ibid., pp. 272–74.   [102] Ibid., p. 281.

of property and documentation and personal status remained empty.[103] Finally, there was a controversy over the attachés which spanned the life of the ME.

The problem of overlap of functions between parts of the new ministry and the ministry of Foreign Affairs' Directorate of Expatriate Affairs (which continued to exist) surfaced almost immediately. Wahid's vision of the division of labor was that the MFA's role concerned relations between states and the problems expatriates had with their host government, whereas the ME was concerned with the LEs as human beings and as human groupings.[104] To attempt to address the overlap, the Ministry of State for Administrative Reform undertook a study of a slightly different administrative structure for the ME, and some minor adjustments to the original proposal for the ministry were introduced, but most were of a techno-administrative, not a political, nature.

The ministry continued to encounter obstacles and opposition along the way, even after the problem of duality had ostensibly been solved. Most crippling was the continuing opposition of Bouwayz. As noted earlier, his concerns were in part turf-based, related to the fact that the establishment of the ministry overlapped with and therefore potentially undermined the functioning of his ministry. He was also clearly concerned that the ME represented a challenge to the WLCU. On this subject it seems likely that the political/confessional consideration mentioned above was the major bone of contention. Ambassador Fu'ad al-Turk underlined this point in the blunt, confessional terms in which it was understood by many: the Christians had been the first to call for a ministry of emigration years earlier, yet when the ministry was established, the minister and director-general were Shi'a, so the Christians were outraged. In such circumstances they felt that it was better to dispense with a separate ME and return responsibility for the diaspora to the MFA.[105]

That said, some prominent religious leaders were supportive of the establishment of the ME. The Maronite Patriarch Sfeir had decried the national divisions that had plagued the WLCU and had long called for a separate ministry to look after expatriate issues. After the experience with conflicts and duality of the ministries, however, he demanded a clarification of the relations between the two to prevent further problems. The Greek Catholic Patriarch Maximus Hakim felt that concern with expatriates was a national duty. The Sunni mufti, Qabbani, denied that there was any problem in establishing the ministry alongside the MFA as long

---

[103] Ibid., pp. 299–300.   [104] *Al-Safir*, 7 March 1993.   [105] Al-'Aql, p. 292.

as the law made clear the demarcation of responsibilities to avoid the conflicts or duality in responsibilities which would ultimately have negative repercussions for the Lebanese abroad.[106]

The controversies surrounding the establishment of the ministry explain in large part the fact that decrees and decisions relating to making the ministry truly operational were frozen for a long time. Even efforts to find a building for the ministry were hampered. It was first given merely *a room* in the Ministry of Information. From there it moved to an apartment offered to it in the al-Ramla al-Bayda area, then to a building offered temporarily by 'Ali Sabbah, a former WLCU president, finally to settle into a seven-story building in the al-Junah area, at the entrance to the heavily Shi'i southern suburbs of Beirut.[107] There were also problems with appointing employees that were related to confessional considerations: the Civil Service board was unwilling to make certain appointments because of the need to maintain a confessional balance among employees in the ministry.[108]

By early 1995, one source argued that the state was interacting with the ministry as if it had been stillborn, as if there were no need for it to carry out its functions, using a variety of pretexts. There were many examples of President Hrawi's ignoring the ministry, such as not inviting the minister on the occasion of visits to Lebanon by ranking members from the expatriate communities. Moreover, the MFA continued to deal with the WLCU, despite the fact that Wahid had dissolved it and had charged a number of its leaders with falsely claiming to speak in its name. Wahid ultimately stopped attending cabinet meetings because of threats, violations of protocol, and the obstruction of his ministry's work.

One of the most contentious issues was Wahid's hiring of twenty-four émigré attachés in November 1994 after they had taken a six-month training course and exam overseen by university professors. The MFA cried foul, as the exam was not overseen by the Civil Service council, and it alleged high-level corruption. Moreover, the MFA provided evidence of the poor preparation of these candidates, six of whom had failed more than once the formal foreign service exam supervised by the Civil Service council in conjunction with the MFA. The MFA also objected to the introduction into the diplomatic corps of émigré attachés (at high ranks) who had not passed this exam. In addition, there were many unanswered questions about the attachés: did they enjoy diplomatic immunity?; did their work overlap with that of the consuls?; and who had the ultimate authority abroad, the ambassador or the ME?[109] While the MFA's

---

[106] Ibid., pp. 294–95.   [107] *Al-Liwa'*, 24 February 1995; Al-'Aql, p. 291.
[108] *Al-Liwa'*, 24 February 1995.   [109] Al-'Aql, pp. 301–3.

objections may have had confessional, political or even personal bases, they were justified on legal grounds, and it is clear that there were numerous irregularities in the attaché appointment process.[110] One ambassador reported that on one occasion an attempt was made to force him to take a woman as an attaché in his embassy simply because her husband had taken a job in a nearby city.[111]

'Ali Khalil took over the ministry in late May 1995 and inherited all of the unfinished business with the MFA – most importantly, the status of the WLCU and the attachés. After the confidence vote, he and Bouwayz held a series of meetings to work out the interrelated problems of the two ministries. As a result, the ME recognized the WLCU, and, in exchange, the MFA recognized the legitimacy of the attachés, on the condition that they be subject to an oral exam before an official committee composed by the MFA to examine the extent of their understanding of emigration, and their knowledge of foreign languages, especially French and English, among other qualifications.[112]

As for effective action by the ME during Khalil's tenure, there were several notable achievements. The ME was able to provide security guarantees to protect the community in Sierra Leone after strikes threatened it. It was also able to convince the Zairian authorities to allow a large number of the Lebanese who had been expelled to return. It examined the situation of the community in Liberia through a visit undertaken shortly after the war there ended, and during a visit to the USA in cooperation with the communities there it worked, through meeting with various senators and representatives, to convince the USA to lift the travel ban to Lebanon.[113]

The "cease-fire" between Bouwayz and Khalil continued into the period of the next government, when Talal Arslan, a former Minister of Health (1990–92) took over the ME (1996–98). This was a period of considerable activity. In a 1997 address, Arslan laid out his goals for the ministry as: continuing to strengthen the staff (including the role that the expatriate attachés were to play); addressing the problems of personal status in order to stop the loss of Lebanese identity; and insisting that Lebanese nationality be given to every *mughtarib* who had the right to recover it.[114] He initiated summer camps in Lebanon for Lebanese expatriate youth, conferences of emigrant clubs and associations, and

---

[110] *Al-Diyar*, 27 May 1997.

[111] From the interviews for this study. I chose to leave this anonymous.

[112] Al-'Aql, p. 304. The additional requirements – an absence of physical defects and maladies, proper attire, and an intelligence test – certainly raise questions about just exactly who had been recruited.

[113] *Al-Anwar*, 14 April 1996.   [114] Wizarat al-mughtaribin, p. 128.

emigration seminars. He played an active role in opening such meetings and in follow-up so that these activities became a continuing feature of the ministry's work.[115]

It was also under Arslan that the attaché issue was finally settled, by a unanimous decision of the cabinet. According to the formula, the attachés were to be attached to full diplomatic missions (not consulates), but were not given diplomatic passports. This met the demand of Nabih Berri (whose daughter had been in charge of the attachés), who insisted that they receive their appointments, while it also placated Hrawi and Bouwayz, who had insisted that they be attached to full missions but not be given diplomatic passports.[116]

The ministership of Salim al-Huss and the reintegration of the ME into the MFA

As the government in which Arslan participated was nearing an end with the approach of new presidential elections, rumors began to circulate about the possible reintegration of the ME into the MFA. Arslan himself stated: "It is not a question of needing a separate ministry, the two ministries can be recombined. The issue is to have a single expatriate policy."[117]

In the new government, veteran politician Salim al-Huss took over the ME and MFA portfolios in December 1998 *in addition to* his prime ministerial position.[118] He then formed an expatriate committee, both to put in place an emigration policy and to look into the continuing paralysis in the WLCU. Discussions about integrating the two ministries continued as part of a larger administrative reform program aimed at reintegrating other ministries between which there was an overlap of functions.[119]

---

[115] Al-'Aql, p. 305.

[116] The account of this accord in *al-Nahar* suggests that Syrian pressure played a role, as it was reached after the return of Buwayz from consultations in Damascus. See *al-Nahar*, 28 May 1997.

[117] Arslan's statement was no doubt in reaction to a then-recent trip by Hrawi to Brazil in which he had promised the community there Lebanese citizenship, but had then backed down: "we promise them citizenship and then delay. We ask them to learn Arabic. And there are officials who want investment from the expatriates. But if this is not put in the context of state policy, it remains the policy of individuals, and this is where conflicts enter in": *Al-Nahar*, 15 December 1997.

[118] *Al-Diyar*, 14 February 1999. Al-Huss also admitted that as PM as well as MFA and ME he did not have much time to devote to expatriate affairs.

[119] On several occasions, Al-Huss noted the difficulties encountered in trying to implement the administrative reform program. See *al-Wasat*, 22 May 2000; *al-Nahar*, 24 November 1999. It is also worth noting that several of the other new ministries – municipalities, technical training, and transport – were also folded back into other ministries.

This situation continued until 7 August 2000, when the ME, with all its employees and property, was formally reintegrated into the MFA (to become again the MFAE) under al-Huss. The reasons given were the continuing problems with dualities of functions and the unwillingness of the MFA to cede responsibilities.[120] The issue of the attachés was addressed through their integration into the MFAE, although not without complaints from members of the diplomatic corps, who were concerned about their positions and seniority.[121] According to al-Huss's counselor for expatriate affairs, Ahmed Tabbara, the hope was that this step of reintegration would reactivate the ties between expatriates and their country and put an end to the ghosts of past differences through the implementation of a comprehensive emigration policy through the MFAE. A number of steps had already been taken in the field: a call for a meeting of expatriate businessmen, and a request that the diplomatic missions collect statistics on expatriate competencies (some of which had begun to be completed) and reinvigorate the WLCU through reorganization of branches and new elections in preparation for a new world congress/conference.[122]

During its final years, the ME had initiated or continued a number of activities. It held four camps (1997–2000) for emigrant and resident Lebanese youth.[123] The ministry also organized two conferences for émigré clubs and associations, the first in March 1998, in which 150 people participated, and the second in May 1999 in which 250 people representing 130 different associations took part. The second conference established the Lebanese Emigrant Council for Investment, which was intended to attract and facilitate foreign and expatriate investment, and was to have its headquarters in the ME. In turn, along with other Lebanese economic bodies and the ME, this Council succeeded in preparing the first conference of Lebanese and *mutahaddir* businessmen, the Lebanese International Business Council (LIBC). Held at the beginning of June 2000, it attracted 600 businessmen from 60 countries in addition to 200 resident Lebanese. Among its recommendations were: implementing administrative reform, activating the role of diplomatic missions; issuing treasury bonds especially for LEs with symbolic interest rates; establishing mixed public and private sector companies with expatriate participation; taking emigrant interests into account when the Lebanese government entered into agreements with the host countries; and making LEs aware of tenders issued by the Lebanese government.[124] Most

---

[120] Al-'Aql, pp. 336–37.   [121] Ibid., p. 310.
[122] *Al-Diyar*, 9 April 2000.   [123] Al-'Aql, pp. 318–21.
[124] Ibid., pp. 325–7. The LIBC's meetings are now called "Planet Lebanon."

recently, this Council has begun to call for parliamentary representation of the diaspora.[125]

The ME also took over responsibility for providing material support and participating in festivals honoring émigrés, which local associations and municipalities organize each summer in different parts of the country and which are intended to encourage émigrés to visit Lebanon and to see the various rebuilding and development projects underway in the country. Finally there was also a magazine, *Al-Mughtarib*, which was supposed to be published regularly in several languages. In fact, it appeared only four times, and only in Arabic. The problems were, not surprisingly, financial and administrative.[126]

Conclusions

Unlike what we saw in the two Maghrebi cases, the macro-historical explanations, or stages of emigrant community development, do not seem to account for the emergence of state institutions in the Lebanese case, nor do developments in regional or bilateral relations with host states. Domestic upheaval, on the other hand – the new cabinet following the 1958 civil war and the reshaped government resulting from the Ta'if accords following the 1975–90 conflict – does appear to have opened the way to the establishment of both the WLU and the ME. Nevertheless, the significance of the role of civil unrest in the country for the evolution of these institutions can only be understood against a broader background.

Throughout the years concerns had been expressed regarding Lebanon's small size and limited domestic resources. For a country with a large and wealthy diaspora population, one way to overcome the capital gap was to enlist expatriates in the service of national development. During the course of the research on Lebanon, I was repeatedly told that the state's view of the expatriates was the now familiar milk-cow image, that of a source of funds and little more. It is certainly the case that, in preparation for the founding of the WLU, greatest care was given to studies of an economic nature, aimed at providing expatriates with information to facilitate investment. There is also no doubt that, as rebuilding began following the civil war, those both inside and outside government circles stressed the key economic role that expatriates could play in assisting with Lebanon's post-war recovery.

Given the historical evolution that we have seen in the Moroccan and Tunisian cases, one would expect that communities settled even longer,

---

[125] *Daily Star*, 26 July 2004. The proposal is for two seats for each of the six continents.
[126] Ibid., pp. 332–35.

but who still identify themselves as Lebanese, would be in an even stronger position economically to support the home state than would be groups of relatively recent arrivals. Yet, when one examines the Lebanese state's record, the degree of milk-cow exploitation is shockingly small. Even with the importance of potential émigré contributions following the Ta'if accords, there has been neither a successful marshaling of resources by the state, nor serious, sustained policies to attract expatriate investment. Expatriate contributions continue and are substantial, but they are directed to more parochial, or personal, rather than national, goals. This is no doubt in part due to a continuing lack of confidence in the political situation in Lebanon, but the problem runs deeper than this.

Two interrelated factors must be kept in mind in understanding Lebanon's approach to its expatriates, both of which are closely linked to the question of state sovereignty. The first is the long-standing minimalist role of the Lebanese state.[127] In the economic realm, as we have seen, this has meant a laissez-faire approach intended to minimize the state's ability to constrain the activities of capital. Indeed, one could make the argument that Lebanon had no need to engage in special programs or policies to encourage expatriate investment because, unlike the situation in many developing countries, there were few bureaucratic hurdles to overcome. In addition, calls for economic support did not directly threaten to privilege or displace any particular confessional group; so to this extent, focusing on the economic as opposed to the political was far "safer." For better or for worse, the Lebanese state's sovereign control over or involvement in domestic economic development was far more limited than that of any other state in the region.

But the effect of a weak state went far beyond the economic realm in the Lebanese case. In the political realm, it meant that the state bureaucracy and its functions also remained relatively limited. This was no accident, but instead owed to the thinking that underpinned the National Pact. In a multi-confessional society in which the elite had an interest in seeing political affiliation crystallize along religio-confessional lines, and in which the confessions held very different views of the country's history, identity and future, a weak state was, ironically, one way to hold the system together. What in other countries were *state* responsibilities – education for example – in Lebanon devolved in large part to communally based institutions, or were not undertaken at all. The state provided a

---

[127] As in other cases, the private or NGO sector has spawned numerous organizations, perhaps the oldest of which in the Lebanese case is the Maronite League, established in 1952 with the aim of strengthening cooperation between Maronites inside and outside of Lebanon.

superficially unifying framework for what were in fact groups who had very different ideas of what Lebanon or Lebanese were or should be. There was no single Lebanese national narrative or myth; indeed, the focus of nationalism itself divided the population as some looked to a larger Arab entity, while others clung to a more parochial affiliation, but one that nonetheless identified with the West. The divisions that arose over the Syrian role in the country during, and that have continued since the end of, the civil war, are clear manifestations of this basic fracture line.[128]

In a situation in which loyalty is primarily to territory and family or confession, but not to the political entity, the establishment or development of state sovereignty will be at best problematic. The fact that in the Middle East the sense of primary affiliation was long to family, tribe, or village bears repeating, for a critical part of the state-building process in the region has involved creating a sense of the "national" that can compete with sub-national or communal identity markers. The degree to which states have succeeded in instilling such national attachments varies, but there is little question that Lebanon has been the least successful in doing so, in part because the very premise underlying the state–society contract runs counter to such a project. All the greater the problem then, if one is talking about dual nationals or those of Lebanese origin who no longer hold Lebanese citizenship. What can the bases of their sense of attachment and identification be? In such circumstances it should not be surprising that what pass for "national symbols" have nothing to do with politics or history and everything to do with a non-confessionalized folklore: 'araq (the anis-flavored alcoholic drink), tabbouleh (the parsley, bulghar and tomato salad); and the dabkeh (a well-known dance).

The problems of bureaucratic turf wars, weak institutional capacity and patrimonialism manifested in the Lebanese case were also present in the previous two cases to varying degrees. That they seem to tell so much more of the institutional evolutionary story in the Lebanese case must be at least hypothesized to derive from this same problem of a weak, highly penetrated and minimally sovereign state. However, and to return to the role of internal unrest, the specificity of the Lebanese case resides in the role that the structure and composition of the domestic political system have played in the evolution of these institutions. Although there were certainly exceptions, in general it appears that key actors in the

---

[128] It must be noted, however, that as the Ta'if-proposed deadlines for Syrian redeployment were violated, and the Syrian role in Lebanese domestic politics grew broader and deeper, even many who initially supported the Syrian presence became weary and critical of this continuing, clear "infringement" of Lebanese sovereignty.

development of the expatriate institutions were far less concerned with
the situation of LE communities and what their participation could mean
for the country's needs at large than with what LE numbers and resources
meant for the confessional/political power balance back in Lebanon. This
was certainly the basic explanatory element in the story of why the
WLCU rather than a ministry was founded in the early 1960s; it also
explains a good deal of the opposition that the ME encountered from
certain actors in Lebanon as well as some key elements in the LE communities. State actors as well as political party and confessional ones have
tended to view the expatriate communities through this domestic political
lens, and, what is arguably worse, to transfer domestic struggles to the
émigré field.

In such circumstances, the associations themselves become political
prizes; and undertaking any serious émigré-related work becomes at best
a secondary consideration. The result has been that, on the one hand,
despite the tremendous resources (human and financial) found in the
diaspora communities, the government's ability to draw directly on them
is limited (although expatriate remittances that go through official channels do help alleviate balance of payments problems), and the state still
has few accurate statistics on them. Everyone insists upon the importance
of having reliable information on the expatriates in order to develop
proper policies, yet everyone also knows (or at least believes) that con-
ducting such studies is too politically sensitive for the system to bear.

Lebanon is still involved in a process of national definition and reconfiguration of the state–citizen relationship at the most basic level. One
manifestation of the problem has been the series of regional actors who
have, in violation of Lebanon's Westphalian sovereignty, if often at the
invitation or through the acquiescence of internal actors, openly interfered
in or even physically occupied parts of the country. A second, less obvious,
but critical aspect is the implication for domestic sovereignty of the state's
continuing failure to define clearly who is and who is not part of the polity,
whether they are the disenfranchised within the territorial boundaries[129]
or members of the widespread and wealthy émigré communities.

---

[129] See Maktabi in Butenschon et al., pp. 162–64 on the numbers of Muslims – Kurds,
Bedouin and others – who resided in Lebanon's border regions with Syria, but who, for
political reasons, were counted as foreigners, not citizens, in the 1932 census. A more
recent example is that of some 400,000 naturalizations that took place in 1994, and
which were overwhelmingly of Syrians, although some Palestinians also received citizenship as a result. Under pressure from anti-Syrian groups in Lebanon, efforts are currently underway to review these naturalizations with an eye to overturning many of
them. Finally, there is the issue of the several hundred thousand Palestinians living in
Lebanon – 1948 refugees and their descendants – who remain stateless.

In sum, while the establishment of these institutions and their focus on mobilizing expatriate resources, both human and material, may be understood as one means of attempting to reinforce or rebuild state sovereignty, in the Lebanese case the history of the ME and WLCU is best understood as an integral part of the story of the highly circumscribed sovereignty, and the battles over it, that have long characterized (and plagued) the country's politics. For years, a state that was weak militarily, politically and in terms of national identity served both the economic and political interests of an elite whose vision of Lebanon intersected in little other than the perceived need for minimal state sovereignty. However, even in its weakness or limited scope, the state could not comfortably accommodate serious efforts to claim the political allegiance of Lebanese abroad. All communities sought to extend the political community to include their expatriate members, but the danger was so great that none could allow any other to succeed in the effort. Indeed, only when civil war has shaken the country and opened the way for formal reconfiguring of power relations has the way also been opened for more serious state involvement with its nationals (and their descendants) abroad.

6   Jordan: unwilling citizens, problematic expatriates

Limited resources, successive waves of Palestinian refugees, and proximity to the Gulf oil-producing region all played key roles in Jordan's development into a labor-exporting state. While British financial support during the Mandate and into the independence period established the bases for structural characteristics that contributed to the emergence of outmigration, it was the 1947–49 Palestine War that introduced the problems and possibilities of unanticipated human resources. First, as a result of the war that dismembered Palestine, some 70,000 Palestinians took refuge directly on the East Bank of the Jordan. More important, however, were the territorial changes that followed the war. At the time of the cease-fire, the Arab Legion (Jordan's British-commanded Army) was in occupation of the rump of Eastern Palestine, subsequently known as the West Bank. Through a series of legal and administrative measures, by 1950 this area was annexed by the Hashemite Kingdom. Jordan's King 'Abdallah had long sought a realm larger than that given him by the British, and his incorporation of the territory and subsequent enfranchisement of the population of the West Bank (some 800,000 at the time) was in keeping with those aspirations.

Whatever dynastic ambitions may have been thereby fulfilled, the postwar period was one of economic crisis for both banks of the expanded kingdom. Nearly half of 'Abdallah's new subjects were refugees, many of them destitute. An additional 160,000 had been separated from their productive land by the armistice lines, but did not qualify for UNRWA (United Nations Relief and Works Agency for Palestine Refugees in the Near East) assistance because they were not refugees. Just as devastating, the establishment of the state of Israel disrupted transport and commercial lines between Jordan and its outside markets. The fact that the conflict ended in the absence of a peace treaty also meant that Jordan found itself with a 650-kilometer border with Israel that required a diversion of resources for defense. With limited domestic economic resources, the kingdom, still heavily reliant on aid from Britain, was hardly in an economic position to absorb the refugees swiftly.

176

These developments coincided with the early stages of development of the oil industry in the states of the Persian Gulf region. With small and generally low-skill populations, these states needed assistance to expand their governmental and commercial infrastructures and could pay for expatriate workers with their new-found oil wealth. The desperate need of the poor and/or unemployed of the Arab East, especially the then-recently displaced Palestinians, thus dovetailed with a growing demand for labor in the Gulf.

In addition, the Hashemite role in the Palestine War had been at best murky, and at worst traitorous, in the eyes of many Palestinians. Stories abounded of the British-commanded Jordanian Arab Legion's fighting Palestinian irregulars rather than the new Israel Defense Forces. Rumors of deals struck between King 'Abdallah and the Zionist leadership over the partition of Palestine – rumors which later proved to be largely true[1] – further alienated many of the kingdom's new Palestinian subjects from "their" king. Nor had there been consensus regarding the West Bank's annexation by Jordan. Some Palestinian notables had been supportive, either having been pro-Hashemite from the beginning or believing, after the disaster of 1948, that the only hope for the future lay in throwing their lot in with 'Abdallah. For those less privileged, there was little love lost for the new sovereign in Amman.

Hence, although Jordan enfranchised these Palestinians by the mid-1950s, few identified with Jordan as an entity. Moreover, as part of the annexation process, the word "Palestine" disappeared from official Jordanian documents referring to the new territory of the kingdom. Indeed, if 'Abdallah's project was to be successful, these people had to be *Jordanians*. Thus, from the beginning, there was a question of difference of identity between the two banks, based not only in historical experience, but also in differential relations with the regime in Amman.[2] This lack of sense of belonging reinforced by a regime focus on East Bank development, while not triggering migration, nonetheless played a key role in its evolution and in the claims the regime could make on those who left.

In the Moroccan and Tunisian cases, we saw regimes which counted on their nationals' sense of attachment to their homeland, if not necessarily to its political system. The Jordanian case is quite different in this respect, for the Palestinian sector of the population was in effect appropriated by the Jordanian state without its consent (and in the aftermath of a war in which its homeland had been lost); moreover, the refugee part of this population

---

[1] See Avi Shlaim, *Collusion Across the Jordan: King Abdullah, the Zionist Movement and the Partition of Palestine* (New York: Columbia University Press, 1987).

[2] For a discussion of the identity issue see Laurie A. Brand, "Palestinians and Jordanians: A Crisis of Identity," *Journal of Palestine Studies* 24/4 (96) 1995: pp. 46–61.

(those who came from the area that became the state of Israel) could not identify *territorially* with Jordan, even after the annexation of the part of Mandate Palestine that came to be known as the West Bank. Enfranchised without their consent rather than, in the case of some Tunisians and Moroccans, born under a political system which they might not support, the Palestinians, until 1988 (when the king disengaged from the West Bank), constituted 70–75 percent of the kingdom's population. The real and potential challenges to sovereignty from this situation alone were daunting. Yet, in addition, the Hashemite Kingdom failed to engender moral or political legitimacy among some of its own, indigenous population through the first several decades of its existence, and in 1970–71, in several episodes of bloody civil war, not only Palestinians, but also some Transjordanians, fought the regime. If these were not sufficient challenges, until 1994 Jordan was officially at war with Israel and, indeed, in 1967 lost to Israeli occupation the West Bank it had annexed in 1950. The king's 1988 decision finally to disengage legally and administratively from the occupied West Bank, which constituted a renunciation of its claim to sovereignty over the territory, has few modern precedents and should be seen as indicative of the larger complex of challenges to state authority and control.

Hence, like Lebanon, but for very different reasons, from its beginnings Jordan struggled with a degree of sovereignty that was highly circumscribed even by developing world standards: a lack of allegiance (or in some cases a split allegiance after the 1964 establishment of the Palestine Liberation Organization) from a majority of its population; civil strife within; regional military conflict and loss of territory; and an extremely limited economic base from which to build state wealth. As in the other countries, emigration emerged as one means of securing additional resources, but in the Jordanian case the emergence of large communities abroad that were overwhelmingly of Palestinian origin was addressed with these challenges to sovereignty – especially those that proceeded from the communal divide at home – clearly in decision-makers' minds.

The beginnings of emigration

High rates of unemployment – estimated at 25% in the early 1950s[3] and probably conservatively at 17% in 1955 by the International Bank for

---

[3] Salih Khasawneh, "Labor Migration in Jordan: Policies, Flows, Organization," a paper presented at the ILO/UNDP Seminar on Migration Policies in the Arab Labor-Sending Countries, Cairo, 2–4 May 1992, cited in Seteney Shami, *Emigration Dynamics in Jordan, Palestine and Lebanon*. Paper no. 4, IOM/UNFPA Policy Workshop on Emigration Dynamics in the Arab Region (Geneva: IOM, 1996), p. 17.

Reconstruction and Development – and underemployment, coupled with low levels of capital investment, encouraged a gradual labor outflow from the kingdom. Much of the emigration was from West Bank sub-districts, for the reasons mentioned above. According to the results of the November 1961 census, 80% of all Jordanian migrants were from the West Bank, which had a migration level of 6%, as opposed to 1.4% for the East Bank. Kuwait and Saudi Arabia hosted more than 72% of the almost 63,000 Jordanians who were counted as resident abroad,[4] and, in the Arab states, those of West Bank origin represented 82% of all Jordanian migrants.[5]

Although political crises triggered fluctuations, the Jordanian economy did make moderate progress in the 1950s and 1960s. Some of the growth owed precisely to the exodus for work in the Gulf. As elsewhere, such migrants not only reduced unemployment at home, but also added to the country's foreign exchange coffers with their remittances.[6] Migration continued, with annual net departures averaging 26,000 in the three years prior to 1967; over the period 1960–66 these workers' remittances reached JD 52.8 million, while exports totaled only JD 41.8 million.[7] Nonetheless, the country continued to be heavily dependent upon its original source of external support, foreign aid. (See Table 6.1.)

The moderate progress of the economy was completely upset by the 1967 war. The consequent Israeli occupation of the West Bank deprived Jordan of a region that had contributed about 45% to GNP in 1966, and in which the major tourist sites – Jerusalem, Bethlehem, Hebron – were located. Coupled with these losses was the influx of an additional 250,000 to 300,000 Palestinian refugees who had been driven out of the West Bank to the East Bank by the war. The political instability that followed – the rise of the Palestinian *fida'iyyin*, continuing Israeli military strikes against the East Bank, and ultimately the showdown between the regime and the Palestinian resistance in September 1970 – all further under-mined prospects for economic growth. When the regime moved against the *fida'iyyin* in 1970, Kuwait and Libya suspended their financial sub-sidies, while Iraq and Syria closed their borders and airspace, thus

---

[4] See Ian J. Seccombe, "Labour Emigration Policies and Economic Development in Jordan: From Unemployment to Labour Shortage," in Bichara Khader and Adnan Badran (eds.), *The Economic Development of Jordan* (London: Croom Helm, 1987), p. 119.

[5] Françoise de Bel-Air, "Expression, émigration, état rentier. Migration et politique en Jordanie depuis 1973," paper presented at the Third Mediterranean Social and Political Research Meeting, Florence, 20–24 March 2002, Mediterranean Programme, Robert Schuman Centre for Advanced Studies, European University Institute, p. 7.

[6] Laurie A. Brand, *Palestinians in the Arab World: Institution Building and the Search for State* (New York: Columbia, 1988), p. 157.

[7] Seccombe in Khader and Badran, p. 119.

Table 6.1. *Jordanian expatriate remittances (in millions of JDs and as percentage of GNP)*

	JD	% of GNP
1961	5.3	4.2
1962	6.2	4.7
1963	6.2	4.5
1964	9.3	5.8
1965	9.1	5.0
1966	10.6	5.7
1967	6.6	4.6
1968	4.1	2.7
1969	6.9	3.5
1970	5.5	3.0
1971	5.0	2.5
1972	7.4	3.4
1973	14.7	6.1
1974	24.1	8.6
1975	53.3	14.2
1976	136.4	24.3
1977	154.8	23.4
1978	159.4	20.4
1979	180.4	19.6
1980	236.7	19.9
1981	340.9	23.0
1982	381.9	22.8
1983	402.9	22.8
1984	475.0	25.6
1985	402.9	21.8
1986	414.5	21.6
1987	317.7	17.0
1988	–	–
1989	306.0	13.0
1990	285.0	10.9
1991	265.0	9.3
1992	515.0	14.7
1993	667.0	17.5
1994	699.0	16.6
1995	797.0	17.1
1996	1024.0	23.2
1997	1031.7	23.7
1998	947.0	20.9

Source: from De Bel-Air, Table 3.

severely limiting Jordan's sphere for exports. This conflict was an extension of the problem noted above: the large numbers of Jordanians of Palestinian origin and their uneasy relationship with the Jordanian state, in the context, of course, of the Israeli occupation of their homeland. The stage had been set for a future clash by the 1964 establishment of the Palestine Liberation Organization (PLO), a development that King Husayn had accepted only grudgingly: there was a clear contradiction between the Hashemite insistence upon its sovereign claim over these Jordanians of Palestinian origin and the growing Palestinian desire for political self-assertion on a Palestinian nationalist basis.

Following the 1970–71 civil war, it was not until the 1974 Arab League Summit Conference in Rabat, Morocco, during which King Husayn acquiesced (formally, although not effectively) in the designation of the PLO as the sole, legitimate representative of the Palestinian people, that Jordan was economically and politically rehabilitated by its Arab neighbors. By this time, the oil boom was well underway and Jordan had begun to witness an even larger outflow of labor. In 1972 unemployment stood at over 14 percent nationally, while the number of Jordanians working abroad had increased to over 80,000 with 41,000 in Kuwait alone.[8] Increased liquidity in the Gulf drew expatriate workers but also, in a kind of quid pro quo, led governments there to make available substantial amounts of financial assistance to the labor-sending Arab states. As a result, Jordan experienced a dramatic rise in remittances in addition to becoming a primary candidate for Arab development assistance.[9]

At the same time, however, as a domestic response to the 1970 civil war, changes had begun to be instituted in the Jordanian administration. An "East Banker first" period was initiated during which subsidies to the West Bank (which Jordan had continued to pay even after the occupation) were cut, the ratio of Jordanians of Palestinian origin in the cabinet dropped, and some Palestinian government personnel were replaced by Transjordanians. The army was also largely Transjordanized, even though its Palestinian members had not defected during the confrontations with the guerrillas. These changes further reinforced the feeling among many of Jordan's citizens of Palestinian origin that the state was neither of nor for them.

Thus, for many expatriates, the relationship to Jordan was one of an imposed nationality, while political loyalty belonged to one of the factions

---

[8] Ibid., p. 119. Seccombe looks at the number of trade proficiency certificates for labor abroad issued by the Ministry of Labor and argues that in the late 1970s, annual net labor outflow was in excess of 10,000 per year: p. 120.

[9] Brand, *Palestinians in the Arab World*, p. 160.

of the PLO. One might well own an apartment or a home in Jordan, but this was because to do so in Palestine was much more difficult or impossible. Jordanian embassies were places where passports had to be renewed, but which were otherwise to be avoided. The state was increasingly associated with a Transjordanian-staffed internal intelligence service that impounded passports, harassed, and at times tortured suspected political activists. The East Bank was where one went to visit family for the summer (or through which one had to pass in order to enter the West Bank), but it was not a place which for many Jordanians of Palestinian origin engendered a sense of affection or attachment beyond whatever family members might live there. Hence, Jordan had a growing expatriate population abroad, overwhelmingly in the Gulf states, which was at best only formally attached to the kingdom.

Kuwait was a special case among the host states for Palestinian expatriates. In the first place, it came to host the largest Palestinian community in the Gulf, with estimates of its numbers in some cases as high as 400,000. Not all the Palestinians in the Gulf or Kuwait more specifically were Jordanian citizens, but it was estimated that about 85% of all Jordanians in Kuwait were of Palestinian origin. While the community in Saudi Arabia was also large, it did not approach the proportions of that in Kuwait, nor were Palestinians there allowed to organize themselves as Palestinians. The greater resultant politicization in Kuwait was viewed as potentially dangerous by the Jordanian regime, as was its wealth, which enabled it and the other Palestinian Gulf communities to become important financial stays of the PLO. The remittances sent back to the kingdom certainly played a key role in Jordan's economic stability, but the same economic success enabled Jordanians of Palestinian origin to contribute to an organization that was the king's greatest competitor for political loyalty.[10]

It is important to note here that the situation of a Jordanian or any other non-Gulf national in the Gulf states is quite different from that of a Maghrebi migrant in Europe. While the categories of legal and illegal do exist and are relevant, it is the laws ordering legal immigration that have set the Gulf experience apart. In the case of Kuwait, for example, in the years immediately following the 1948 war, visas were required for entry. Abu Odeh argues that the British, who were responsible for security and foreign affairs in a number of Gulf states in the 1950s, including Kuwait, used their influence to assure priority in employment for Palestinians – especially members of the intelligentsia and, above all,

---

[10] For a fuller discussion of the community in the Gulf during this period, see ibid., chs. 6–8.

those who became Jordanians – over other Arabs.[11] For those who
obtained work contracts, the securing of such a visa was not a problem;
however, the dire economic circumstances on the West Bank drove many
without work contracts to try to enter Kuwait illegally. Many succeeded,
and were ultimately able to obtain legal residency. Others attempted to
enter and were left by unscrupulous guides – not unlike some of the
"coyotes" working the US–Mexican border today – to die in the desert.
Finally, in 1958–59, an agreement was concluded between Jordan and
the amirate, according to which any Jordanian could go to Kuwait as long
as s/he had a valid Jordanian passport.

As is typical of immigration stories, those Palestinians/Jordanians who
arrived in the Gulf first then paved the way for relatives and friends to
follow. Migration up until the 1967 war was largely a single male affair, as
one family member would be charged to go to the Gulf to establish
himself and ultimately serve as the financial mainstay of what were
often entire extended families. In the wake of the 1967 war, family
unification – the departure of families from the occupied territories for
the Gulf – became more common.

This process of gradual family reunification ultimately led Gulf states
to impose increasingly tighter control over the entry of foreigners. First, a
laborer/worker had to secure a work contract before s/he could obtain a
visa. Second, upon arrival the worker's passport had to be surrendered to
the employer or guarantor (*kafil*). The worker's continued residence in
the country then depended upon the satisfaction of the *kafil*, a host-state
national, who alone made decisions regarding extending or terminating
contracts and even about travel, since it was s/he who held the passport.
In a group of countries in which, with only a few exceptions, labor
organizing was banned or heavily circumscribed and where, in any case,
non-national workers were not eligible to join unions, the worker was and
is extremely vulnerable, as any excuse may be used as a pretext for
expulsion. Furthermore, since the Gulf states have extremely strict nation-
alization requirements, there has been little if any chance of an expatriate's ever securing citizenship. Once employment was terminated, unless
a new *kafil* could be found (and generally a worker could not easily switch
jobs), the worker and his family had only a few days to pack and leave.
The Gulf states did provide a needed economic safety valve through the
employment opportunities they afforded; however, unlike some of the
European states to which Maghrebi workers emigrated, they did not offer
the possibility of obtaining citizenship. Nor did the Gulf states offer the

---

[11] Adnan Abu-Odeh, *Jordanians, Palestinians, and the Hashemite Kingdom in the Middle East Peace Process* (Washington, DC: United States Institute for Peace, 1999), p. 63.

same atmosphere for non-national investment, since owning immovable property was forbidden them, and businesses needed to be registered with 51 percent ownership in the hands of a national.

Therefore, for those Palestinian Jordanians who went to the Gulf, political "exit" in the form of acquisition of host-country citizenship was not an option.[12] Since full citizenship was also unobtainable from the kingdom's authoritarian regime, the "exit" of these people in the form of extended exile and political silence was an acceptable alternative both for the regime and for some of the expatriates. However, another option, "voice," was pursued by some expatriates through contributing to the PLO, or by involvement in one of its constituent factions. The goal was not so much to overthrow the Hashemites (although some more radical groups called for this) as an end in itself, but rather to fight their political program as a step toward establishing a Palestinian state. Throughout this period, the throne in Amman both politically (through its cooperation with the USA and Israeli Labor party leadership) and geographically (through the incorporation of the West Bank into the kingdom) effectively blocked such a goal. For all of these reasons, the dynamics and stakes of the Jordanian state – Jordanian expatriate relationship directly concerned not only regime/state security but also the kingdom's territorial integrity.

Perhaps because the primary dynamic was understood to be regime and territorial security, the main channel for "relating" to the communities overseas was the embassies and informers who worked for internal security and reported on community members' political activities. Since Arab states have not looked kindly upon the establishment within their borders of political organizations affiliated with other states, there was no attempt by the Jordanian state to establish anything like the *amicale* structures we saw in the Moroccan and Tunisian cases in Europe. Also playing a role, no doubt, was the realization that these heavily Palestinian communities would have had little interest in cooperating with institutions founded around the notion of a Jordanian identity.

Close security cooperation between Jordan and these Gulf states characterized their relationship, and, unlike in Europe, there were no democratic norms at work to constrain what that might involve. As a result of the monitoring efforts, whether carried out by the embassies or by the Gulf state security services, those involved in political activities abroad were often subjected to lengthy questioning upon return to the kingdom for summer vacation or business. These sessions were intended to

---

[12] Albert O. Hirschman, "Exit Voice and the State," in *Essays in Trespassing: Economics to Politics and Beyond* (Cambridge: Cambridge University Press, 1981), pp. 246–65.

intimidate the expatriate into either giving up his/her activities or informing on others. Resident citizens who engaged in political behavior deemed seditious often had their passports confiscated. In the case of expatriates, however, at least after 1962 (see below), it seems the state preferred that they maintain their jobs abroad and make money, rather than be forcibly detained at home. In this way, then, there is a political safety valve argument to be made in parallel to the socio-economic safety valve discussed above. Emigration to the Gulf not only reduced economic hardship at home, it also opened up the possibility that political discontents would "exit," doing less harm from abroad – especially in the authoritarian contexts of the Gulf states – than at home, all the while contributing to the kingdom's stability through remittances.

Labor and migration policy

The creation of employment sufficient to absorb all or most new entrants into the market requires medium- to long-term changes in government spending priorities and/or changes in legislation to encourage investment in job-creating activities and sectors. Because such a restructuring strategy requires time to work and can be subversive of the existing political order, it is often avoided, implemented half-heartedly, or given only lip-service. With the exception of short periods in the 1960s, for reasons related both to the limited resource base, and to the increasingly entrenched rentier nature[13] of the state, Jordan pursued a strategy of encouraging or allowing employment abroad rather than promoting serious economic restructuring at home.[14]

In examining Jordanian development policies of the 1960s, one is struck by the explicit emphasis, which subsequently disappears, on the problem of excessive dependence on foreign aid, on the desire to expand the indigenous productive base, and, therefore, on the need to increase domestic job creation. Such a focus was the hallmark of the development approach of Wasfi al-Tall, who served as prime minister in 1962–63 and

---

[13] A rentier state is one in which a substantial part (40 percent or more) of state revenues accrues as the result of non-productive activity. Rents include foreign aid, payments for the use of military bases, transit fees, as well as income that results from purely extractive industries such as oil. For a fuller discussion of Jordan as a rentier economy, see Laurie A. Brand, "Economic and Political Development in a Rentier State: The Case of the Hashemite Kingdon of Jordan," in Denis Sullivan and Iliya Harik (eds.), *Privatization and Liberalization in the Middle East* (Bloomington: Indiana University Press, 1992).

[14] For a fuller discussion of the economic and political implications of internal restructuring versus an externally directed strategy, see Laurie A. Brand, *Jordan's Inter-Arab Relations: The Political Economy of Alliance Making* (New York: Columbia University Press, 1994), p. 37. For an application to labor exporting, see de Bel-Air, pp. 3 and 13.

again in 1965–67. Indeed, Jordan's first initiative in economic development, the 1962–67 "Five year program for economic development" coincided with al-Tall's assumption of the prime ministership. In the realm of employment, it acknowledged that one-third of the labor force was unemployed[15] and stressed the importance of vocational education, but with *domestic* needs, existing and expected, in mind. The only mention of those working abroad was in relation to the role of their remittances in providing income back home.[16] The lack of emphasis on those working abroad probably owed both to the focus on domestic job creation and to the small numbers of expatriates, since, as noted earlier, the 1961 census placed the total number of those *living, not just working*, abroad at only 63,000.

The political context of the time also must be borne in mind. In the mid-1950s, Jordan began to experience a period of domestic turmoil, which culminated in a coup attempt in 1957 and the subsequent imposition of martial law. Given the crackdown at home, a Jordanian opposition to the regime developed abroad, just as Jordan's regional rivals sought to cultivate support against the Hashemites within the kingdom: "In a country where the government [was] the major employer and the political activists [came] mainly from the intelligentsia, it was easy under martial law for the government to control the opposition by firing suspects from their government posts."[17] Not surprisingly, control of expatriates was also a key concern, and, during this period, the government's main instrument of control was the exit permit, without which one could not travel abroad.

Any suspicion about an applicant's political affiliation or activity was sufficient to deny him or her the travel permit, and (for an expatriate home for a visit) this essentially would mean the loss of a much needed job. Many people lost their jobs or contracts under this security system. Understandably, such a measure was also resented not only by the punished expatriates and their families, but also by all the other expatriates who identified with them. From their point of view, the government, which had failed to provide them with jobs, was now depriving them of the jobs they had been able to get or were about to get. The same system was applied to students who attended universities outside the country. Many either had to drop their studies because they were denied a travel permit, or refrained from returning home during the summer holidays.[18]

---

[15] Al-Mamlakah al-Urdunniyyah al-Hashimiyyah, Majlis al-ʾIʿmar al-Urdunni, *Barnamij al-Sanawat al-Khamis l-il-Tanmiyah al-Iqtisadiyyah, 1962–67* (n.p., n.d.), p. 15.
[16] Ibid., p. 37.   [17] Abu-Odeh, p. 83.   [18] Ibid., pp. 83–84.

Here again, al-Tall's role was significant for, in addition to trying to curb elements of rentierism, he introduced several measures increasing personal freedoms. Among these, the most important for our purposes was the 1962 abolition of this exit permit requirement, which thereby opened the way for easier movement of Jordanians between the kingdom and their host states.[19]

In the context of Jordan's dependence upon US budgetary support during this period, a Kennedy administration plan to reduce US aid to Jordan forced the scrapping of the 1962–67 program. Its replacement, intended to cover the 1964–70 period, continued to acknowledge the problem of unemployment, but noted the existence of a training division in the Labor Bureau in the Ministry of Social Affairs which was responsible for improving workers' skills for employment either at home or abroad. In addition, a new Employment Division was to be established in the Ministry, although the document noted only domestic employment as a goal.[20] A strong emphasis was also placed on expanding the school system and on training additional teachers.

The 1967 war marked a critical turning point. It caused work to stop on a number of key development projects outlined in the 1964–70 document and, according to the 1973–75 plan, led to a drop in remittances from Jordanian workers abroad from JD 13 million in 1966 to JD 5 million in 1971.[21] In addition to this loss of remittance income, the Jordanian economy lost West Bank industries, while the East Bank received a new wave of refugees, estimated by this document at 400,000, but which is generally given as 250,000–300,000.[22] The plan discusses the need to link secondary education to the needs of Jordanian society for technical trained labor power, and the imperative to channel more students into vocational rather than academic education, but at no point does it state that such training is to be for export.[23]

The war also undermined whatever commitment remained to institutionalizing a form of economic development that was driven more by domestic factors than by external aid. After 1967, the Arab oil states intervened to provide aid to Jordan to address the immediate military

[19] Paul Kingston, "Rationalizing Patrimonialism: Wasfi al-Tall and Economic Reform in Jordan, 1962–67," in Tariq Tell (ed.), *The Resilience of the Hashemite Rule: Politics and the State in Jordan, 1946–67*. Les Cahiers du Cermoc 25 (Amman: Centre d'Etudes et de recherche sur le Moyen-Orient Contemporain, 2001), pp. 120–21.

[20] Al-Mamlakah al-Urdunniyyah al-Hashimiyyah, Majlis al-ʾIʿmar al-Urdunni, *Barnamij al-Sanawat al-Sabiʿl-il-Tanmiyyah al-Iqtisadiyyah 1964–1970* (n.p., 1965), p. 390.

[21] Wizarat al-Thiqafah w-al-ʾIʿlam, Al-Mamlakah al-Urdunniyyah al-Hashimiyyah, *Mujiz Khittat al-Tanmiyah al-Urdunniyyah, 1973–75* (n.p., n.d.), p. 3.

[22] Ibid., p. 4.   [23] Ibid., p. 41.

and refugee impact of the war. For the next two decades, the focus on military spending, combined with the impact only a few years later of skyrocketing oil prices, meant that the basic rentier nature of the state would be reinforced rather than supplanted by the development of domestic productive forces.

Prior to the 1970s, to the extent that emigration for employment was discussed in formal documents, it was regarded as an expedient means of reducing the labor surpluses triggered by regional or domestic political crises. However, by the early 1970s, what had initially been an individual response to such developments had become a part, if not always explicitly stated, of state economic policy. The increasing number of Jordanians abroad on secondment from government jobs clearly attests to this. For example, those from the Ministry of Education sent to the oil-rich Arab states grew from 271 in 1970 to 810 in 1974, and by 1983 the number exceeded 2,330.[24]

The 1973–75 plan was the first to mention in any detail the importance of workers abroad, calling them a "not small part" (*juz' ghayr qalil*) of the Jordanian labor force and classifying their financial remittances to Jordan as an important source of hard currency. This was also the first planning document to note that the government needed to attend to the interests of expatriate workers and to protect their rights. Indeed, to ensure that the workers would benefit as much as possible from the advantages of host-country labor laws, it proposed that the Jordanian government conclude bilateral labor accords with the receiving countries and charge the Jordanian diplomatic missions in them with following up on workers' concerns.[25]

This plan also continued to stress the need to reduce unemployment and underemployment. While there was no explicit link drawn between the government's continued emphasis on vocational education and labor for export, the section on education did state that developing human resources was considered one of the most important factors in producing and increasing hard currency income.[26] While the relationship between human resources and foreign currency may also be understood as deriving from foreign investment attracted by the presence of a well-trained labor force, the first explanation was probably what was intended.

The fact that private recruitment agencies were illegal and that the state was only sectorally-specifically engaged in recruitment for work abroad meant that labor emigration from the kingdom was largely the product of

---

[24] Seccombe in Khader and Badran, p. 122.
[25] Al-Mamlakah al-Urdunniyyah al-Hashimiyyah, Al-Majlis al-Qawmi l-il-Takhtit, *Khittat al-Tanmiyah al-Thulathiyyah, 1973–75* (n.p., n.d.), p. 271.
[26] Ibid., p. 223.

individual initiative, undertaken through personal contacts in or visits to the importing countries.[27] Even so, skill scarcity in the kingdom, as well as wage inflation and inflows of non-Jordanian replacement and other labor, began to characterize the domestic market.[28] As a result, the authors of the 1976–80 plan confronted a very different set of circumstances than those prevailing at the time the 1973–75 plan had been drafted. Indeed, in 1976 the National Planning Council forecast labor *shortages* and concluded that such shortages would have a negative impact on the implementation of the plan. In response, some brakes were placed on the otherwise laissez-partir policy. For example, in 1976 a prohibition against publishing ads. for employment abroad in Jordanian newspapers was issued,[29] and professionals in certain specializations were required to secure the permission of the Ministry of Labor to take jobs abroad, permission which was in some cases refused if the domestic sector was suffering from a particularly acute labor shortage.[30] Nonetheless, these appear to be limited exceptions to a policy otherwise based in freedom of movement.

The government maintained its overall commitment to a largely open-door emigration policy for a number of reasons. First was the level of remittances and their significance to the Jordanian economy: in a number of years these levels were higher than external budgetary aid. Second, placing restrictions on labor outflows might have had negative repercussions on the level of external support from the oil states, as a close relationship between foreign aid receipts and the supply of labor was noted in several official reports. Third, domestic labor market expansion alone could not absorb the growing labor force, given the paucity of resources and the high birth rate. Moreover, the post-1970 emphasis on recruiting Transjordanians rather than Jordanians of Palestinian origin into the civil and military bureaucracies meant that an increasing percentage of the unemployed would be from the latter community, with all that meant for stability at home. As a result, a restrictive emigration policy would have been politically difficult to police and enforce as well.[31]

In recognition of the importance of the labor force's role in the process of economic and social development, a separate Ministry of Labor was established in February 1976. Concern with expatriate labor was clearly part of the ministry's mission, as in 1978 it signed bilateral labor agreements with both Pakistan and Libya. Just as significant, in order to keep

---

[27] Frank Czichowski, "Migrations internationales et répartition du revenue en Jordanie," in Gilbert Beaugé and Friedmann Buttner, *Les migrations dans le monde arabe* (Paris: CNRS, 1991), p. 311.

[28] Seccombe in Khader and Badran, p. 122.

[29] Czichowski in Beaugé and Buttner, p. 311.   [30] De Bel-Air, p. 12.

[31] Seccombe in Khader and Badran, pp. 123–24.

abreast of the conditions of Jordanians working abroad, the ministry began to appoint labor attachés to key embassies, first in Kuwait and the UAE.[32] The attachés were to help solve problems of individual Jordanians in their jobs, such as dismissal or failure to receive compensation, to gather information on the labor markets in these countries, and to report on conditions and trends.[33]

Despite these efforts, in its diagnosis of Jordan's labor problems, a subsequent plan noted the "lack of a common Arab framework or of integrated Arab programs aimed at training and remunerating the labor force in such a manner as to meet the development needs of the Arab countries." It lamented the lack of bilateral agreements regulating labor-power mobility and emphasized the need to intensify the Ministry of Labor's efforts to look after the interests of Jordanian workers at home and abroad, with the organization of recruitment and education a central goal. The document further mentioned the need to pay attention to labor-power planning studies and stressed that such studies should take into consideration the expected demand of Arab countries.[34]

The 1976–80 plan ultimately proved correct in its expectations of domestic labor shortages. During the period the outflow of Jordanian workers increased at an average of 8,000–10,000 annually, while growing demand for labor at home continued to require the importation of workers from other Arab and non-Arab countries. In 1980, the number of foreign workers was estimated at 70,000 or about 15 percent of the total labor force on the East Bank.[35]

In response, the 1981–85 plan placed special emphasis on the domestic development of vocational and technical skills to achieve a balance between high- and medium-level cadres and to increase women's participation. Compulsory education was to be expanded, enrollment capacities of institutions of higher education increased, and measures taken to upgrade and expand post-graduate programs.[36] The document estimated that additional labor power needed over the planning period would reach 254,000 workers, broken down as follows:[37]

[32] Hashemite Kingdom of Jordan, National Planning Council, *Five Year Plan for Economic and Social Development 1981–1985* (Amman: Royal Scientific Society Press, n.d.), p. 295.
[33] Interview with Taysir 'Abd al-Jabir, Former Minister of Labor, Commissioner of the Jordan Securities Commission, Amman, 12 July 1999.
[34] Hashemite Kingdom of Jordan, *Five Year Plan for Economic and Social Development 1981–1985*, pp. 297–99.
[35] Ibid., p. 293.
[36] Ibid., p. 38.
[37] Ibid., p. 294.

Professional, technical and their equivalent	45,695
Managerial and administrative	5,275
Clerical	20,835
Sales	27,165
Agricultural	15,235
Production, transport, communications, services, etc.	139,795
Total	254,000

Based on the numbers of graduates expected and the numbers of additional women entering the labor force, a shortage of about 70,000 was anticipated. It was projected that this would be met by the further inflow of workers from abroad as well as by the return of Jordanian expatriates and perhaps by an even greater increase in female participation. Among the measures proposed to address the shortages were "providing incentives to draw trained workers into the domestic labor market and to attract Jordanians working abroad to return," and "permitting Arab and foreign workers to work in Jordan in accordance with the requirements of the labor market to prevent bottlenecks, especially in the agriculture and construction sectors."[38] Had regional conditions not changed, the 1981–85 plan would likely have proven accurate in its projections. However, the continuing Iran–Iraq war, the regional economic downturn and the resultant dwindling of aid to Jordan from the oil-producing states intervened to transform the domestic employment situation from one of shortages to again one of surplus.[39]

The economic crisis of 1988–89, which led to Jordan's conclusion of a debt rescheduling agreement through the IMF, forced new economic development priorities on the kingdom's policymakers. Hence a perusal of the 1993–97 and 1999–2003 plans reveals the imperatives of structural adjustment. The 1993–97 plan talks about the need to create profitable jobs, to tie education to policies of production, and to diversify the kingdom's productive base.[40] There is a discussion of organizing the labor market, and this includes finding work opportunities abroad to absorb a part of the excess labor force, but the need to train Jordanians to take the place of the large numbers of non-Jordanians working in the kingdom is

[38] Ibid., pp. 294–95, 297.
[39] Hashemite Kingdom of Jordan, Ministry of Planning, *Five Year Plan for Economic and Social Development, 1986–1990* (Amman: National Press, n.d.), p. 165.
[40] Al-Mamlakah al-Urdunniyyah al-Hashimiyyah, Wizarat al-Takhtit. *Al-Khittah al-Iqtisadiyyah w-al-Ijtima'iyyah 1993–1997* (n.p., n.d.), pp. 86–89.

also stressed.[41] The 1999–2003 plan treats the same themes, but also emphasizes the role of privatization in economic development. The only significant reference to workers abroad (whose presence is not mentioned in a section detailing the characteristics of the workforce) is a call to appoint labor consultants in Jordanian embassies in countries having large numbers of Jordanian workers.[42]

In conclusion, while there was no migration policy in the strict sense of the term, certain practices were clearly intended to influence the flow of labor, depending upon period. From the early requirement that all citizens obtain exit visas, to a more open-door policy regarding departure, the state's efforts at control for political reasons shifted from a desire to, in effect, "imprison at home" those who were viewed as threatening, to a willingness to undercut the possibilities for the development of domestic discontent by removing obstacles to departure. In the economic realm, the conclusion of bilateral labor accords, the attempts to restrict flows from some sectors while promoting vocational training seemingly for export in others, and modifications in public sector salaries and retirement provisions all targeted some aspect of the labor market.[43] Nonetheless, what medium- or long-range planning in the field of labor-power development was implemented was on several occasions overtaken by regional economic or political events: the 1967 war, the 1970 civil war, the jump in oil prices, and the recession accompanying the Iran–Iraq war.

In the meantime, the composition of the communities abroad changed. Parallel to what we saw in the Moroccan and Tunisian cases, following the Israeli occupation of the West Bank in 1967, the Jordanian/Palestinian expatriate communities began to be more family-, rather than single-male-, based. Moreover, despite Gulf state restrictions on residence and the franchise, they also began to assume a multi-generational and, after 1973, an increasingly economically successful, character. At the same time, the establishment of the PLO, the rise of the Palestinian resistance after the 1967 war, and the civil war in 1970 made clear that there was a political alternative to the Hashemite monarchy and that its appeal among Palestinian Jordanians was growing. Nevertheless, more than a decade passed before economic and political circumstances led the

---

[41] Ibid., pp. 94 and 98.

[42] Al-Mamlakah al-Urdunniyyah al-Hashimiyyah, Wizarat al-Takhtit, *Mulakhkhas Khittat al-Tanmiyah al-Iqtisadiyyah w-al-Ijtima'iyyah l-il-A'wam, 1999–2003* (n.p., n.d.), pp. 208 and 210. The labor attachés in the Gulf states prior to 1990 would presumably have been expelled or brought home, given the anger of the oil producers over Jordan's position on the Iraqi invasion of Kuwait and the expulsion of large numbers of Jordanian workers as a result.

[43] Shami, p. 56.

Jordanian state to take greater institutional interest in the overwhelmingly Palestinian-in-origin expatriate communities.

Backdrop to the émigré conferences

By 1983, the Iran–Iraq war and the drop in oil prices had begun to take their toll on the Arab regional economy. Oil states were pumping huge sums into Iraq to support it in its battle with Iran to impede the exportation of the Islamic revolution. That they were doing so at a time of declining oil revenues meant that they were forced to engage in belt-tightening elsewhere, and several of these areas directly affected the Jordanian economy. In the first place, the oil producers who had made annual aid commitments to Jordan, the PLO and Syria in 1979 at an Arab summit in Baghdad began to fall into arrears, and Amman, accustomed to aid infusions to balance its accounts, began to feel the pinch. Second, the oil states, which had drawn large numbers of Jordanians and other Arabs into the labor force, began to reduce recruitment. Remittances, therefore, dropped *and* some expatriates began to return home, thus constituting a new source of demand for jobs in the kingdom. Finally, capital actually *invested* by expatriates in Jordan had not been of great magnitude in the past – with the exception of land purchases and construction – and there had been increased hesitancy on the part of expatriates to invest, in the wake of several then-recent scandals and failures of government companies.

The content of the successive economic development plans reviewed above attests to a long-standing lack of serious state involvement with this sector: during the early years the expatriate numbers had not been large, and when their numbers and contributions skyrocketed, the Jordanian government seemed content to observe while the good times rolled. The economic rationale behind the first real manifestation of special state interest in the expatriate communities – a series of conferences for nationals abroad – was that, in conditions of increasing economic difficulties, inviting these people, (re)acquainting them with Jordan, listening to them, making them feel welcome and having the king himself attend, would generate goodwill sufficient to interest them in more serious investment.[44]

On the political front, however, "it [wa]s also clear that the conferences [were] intended to assist Jordan in asserting sovereignty over the large Palestinian-Jordanian community in the Gulf states, particularly Kuwait,

---

[44] Interview with Adnan Abu-Odeh, Former Minister of Information, Court Chamberlain and Advisor to King Husayn and King 'Abdallah II, Amman, 15 May 2003.

where many [had] lived all or most of their lives and [had] little or no sense of identification with Jordan."[45] While the expatriates' problems of where to educate children and how to reintegrate into the overburdened Jordanian job market upon their return were relatively new owing to the growing economic crisis in the Gulf, other expatriate problems had existed for a long time, and the Jordanian government had never before shown such an interest in serving its sons and daughters abroad.[46]

To understand the political context, one must first consider that it was a substantially weakened PLO whose National Council met in Amman in November 1984. Dispersed from what had been its base of power in Beirut by the 1982 Israeli invasion and then riven by internal fighting that had turned bloody in the Biqaʿ Valley and in Tripoli in 1983, Yasir ʿArafat's PLO was in need of mending fences with Arab states to strengthen its position. Capitalizing on this weakness, King Husayn entered into discussions with ʿArafat that produced in mid-February 1985 an accord to guide Palestinian–Jordanian coordination aimed at leading to Arab–Israeli peace negotiations. It was, therefore, also an ideal time to try to mend political fences with the Jordanian/Palestinian communities in the Gulf states.[47]

The expatriate conferences

To lay the groundwork for the first conference, the government formed a preparatory committee headed by the Minister of Labor and Social Development, Khalid al-Hajj Hasan, and with the participation of the previous Minister of Labor, Taysir ʿAbd al-Jabir, during whose term the idea for the conference had first been discussed. The committee was responsible for determining the topics of and preparing the five working papers, registering participants and following up on all activities and programs in order to make sure the conference met its goals.[48] It was to work both to familiarize the expatriates with Jordan and to make the relevant Jordanian officials and other leaders aware of the problems or difficulties faced by the expatriates. The official press indicated that more

---

[45] Brand, *Palestinians in the Arab World*, pp. 175–76.   [46] Ibid., p. 176.

[47] In my interview with Abu-Odeh, he mentioned the policy of giving passports to selected Gazans. Unlike West Bankers, Gazans, having lived under Egyptian military administration from 1949 to 1967, carried only Egyptian travel documents, not passports. The awarding by the king, upon advice from the pro-Hashemite Gazan notable Rashad al-Shawwa, of passports to financially successful Gazans (most of whom resided in Saudi Arabia) was part of the regime's strategy to cultivate Palestinian loyalty.

[48] See *Awraq ʿAmal wa Munaqashat al-Muʾtamar al-Awwal l-il-Mughtaribin al-Urdunniyyin* ("Working Papers and Discussions of the First Conference for Jordanian Expatriates") (Amman, 1985).

Table 6.2. *Jordanian expatriate numbers*

	Expatriates in Arab countries	Expatriates in non-Arab countries
1980	261,500	43,900
1983	271,500	–
1985	276,000	52,000

Source: Annual Statistical Bulletin, Hashemite Kingdom of Jordan, selected years.

than 800 people were expected to attend the three-day meeting held at the Palace of Culture at the Al-Husayn Youth City, although in the end only 506 attended this First National Conference on Jordanian Expatriates.[49]

Welcoming banners in the Palace of Culture were signed by the Housing Bank, the Ministry of Labor and Social Development, the Social Security Corporation, the Islamic Bank and the Al-Husayn Youth City. The conference was officially opened by Royal Court Chief Marwan al-Qasim, who read an address from King Husayn which praised the expatriates for their patriotism, achievements and reputation abroad and said they had reflected positively on Jordan's national standing and commitments: "Our country lacks natural resources, but its richness stems from its people, who are highly educated and have proved themselves to be the best technicians, professionals, businessmen, and intellectuals, whether inside or outside Jordan." The speech also mentioned the February 11 Accord between the PLO and the kingdom.[50]

The first working paper, presented by Foreign Minister Tahir al-Masri (a Jordanian of Palestinian origin), was intended to give the attendees a clear idea of Jordan's political positions on a variety of issues, but especially the Palestinian question. A question and answer session followed, during which the issue of permission to hold dual nationality was raised.[51] The second day was devoted to papers on the economy. The first was on general economic conditions and investment opportunities and the second reviewed the kingdom's development plans, while also presenting the various investment incentives offered by the government.[52] A third paper examined the social, economic and legal reality of the labor force in Jordan, including that of foreign workers, and discussed plans for job-creating activities.

[49] Ibid., p. 9.   [50] *Jordan Times*, 21 July 1985.   [51] Ibid.   [52] *Jordan Times*, 22 July 1985.

A fourth paper looked at the problems that expatriates faced abroad, as well as those they encountered upon visits to the kingdom. The paper argued that these problems abroad "were mainly caused by labor conditions, world-wide inflation and recession, living conditions abroad, and bureaucracy in Jordanian embassies," which the paper charged with "delays and complicating the issuance of new passports, legal papers, military service booklets, and birth certificates." A then-recently passed law requiring that the General Intelligence Directorate (the *mukhabarat*) in Amman approve the issuing of any Jordanian passport abroad was criticized for increasing delays. Concerns were also expressed regarding the difficulties in obtaining family documents abroad.[53] In response, a government official announced an extension of the deadline for renewals. He also said that the children of expatriates who wished to enroll in Jordanian universities and community colleges would be exempt from having to show their family document (which was supposed to remain with the head of household).[54]

Underlining the importance the government accorded this meeting, the king, who generally showed little interest in economic affairs not related to the military, addressed the last day of conference in person and received a four-minute standing ovation. This was a key part of the overall public relations aspect to this conference. Indeed, one official noted that some people attended just to see the king and have the opportunity to have their picture taken with him.[55]

In their recommendations at the end, the participants emphasized the importance of holding such a conference regularly – annually, if possible. They also called for numerous changes. First, they asked that the efficiency and staff of Jordanian embassies abroad be improved. Numerous complaints expressed during the conference had focused on embassy employees, whose numbers were noted as being high, but whose quality was criticized as low. Some expatriates had expressed a willingness to pay to have their papers processed without having to "be subjected to humiliation and delay."[56] A second recommendation stressed the importance of establishing a higher-profile government department dedicated to expatriates' needs and concerns. (The Ministry of Foreign Affairs had established a special expatriate section in 1981.) They asked that efficient people be placed at border and airport entries to facilitate expatriate affairs, and they requested that the government find solutions to the

---

[53] A family document is issued only to a male head of household – all dependents are included on it – and it is required in order to complete virtually any government procedure.
[54] *Jordan Times*, 23 July 1985.   [55] Abu-Odeh interview.   [56] Ibid.

difficulty of issuing Jordanian passports and civil registration documents for expatriates.[57]

Among other recommendations were calls for expatriates to increase their investment in local projects and establish a public shareholding company to fund investment projects and carry out feasibility studies regarding investing in Jordan. The importance of establishing housing complexes to be financed by the expatriates was noted, but more important was a call for the establishment of a private university to be financed by Jordanian expatriates (JEs) so that their children would have easier access to higher education. A call was also issued to establish Jordanian secondary schools abroad through coordination between the Ministry of Education in Jordan and its counterparts in the host countries.[58] In addition to the conference itself, several cultural and informational programs were arranged for the participants during their stay: a visit to Jordan University, where they were to view films about the kingdom's premier research institute, the Royal Scientific Society; tours of Yarmuk University in the northern city of Irbid and the agriculturally rich Jordan Valley; and attendance at the national cultural festival at the archeological site of Jerash.

For a first attempt at mobilizing members of the Gulf communities, the conference appeared to be a success. In terms of attendance, the numbers were not huge, but respectable. Key concerns of both the expatriates and the government were discussed and solutions or further consideration were promised. Finally, the political atmosphere was positive and high-level participation seemed likely to ensure a momentum that could carry over to the next year, generating the interest and goodwill the state hoped would translate into increased investment. But politics would intervene to thwart the government's designs.

Political challenges

While the economic climate did not change between the 1985 and 1986 meetings – the regional recession and its various effects continued to be felt – Jordan's relations with the PLO deteriorated markedly. Even before the formal suspension of Jordanian–PLO cooperation, which came in February 1986, renewed competition between the PLO and Amman began to surface in the expatriate communities. For example, the Jordanian embassy set up a branch of the *Jordanian* Writers' Union in Kuwait and then attempted to establish other unions, as alternatives to

---

[57] *Jordan Times*, 24 July 1985.   [58] Ibid.

existing Palestinian ones. In addition, certain prominent "Jordanians," who had previously referred to themselves as Palestinians, began to speak of the large *Jordanian* community in Kuwait. It should be noted that those who stressed their Jordanian identity at this time demanded concessions from the government in exchange: special arrangements for their children to enroll in Jordanian universities and privileges in the fields of importing and property holding.[59]

The most dramatic event of the period was the king's 19 February 1986 suspension of the political coordination with the PLO outlined in the 11 February Accord, as Jordan moved to repair relations with Syria, then 'Arafat's arch-enemy. Husayn laid the blame for the termination of the accord at 'Arafat's feet. Whatever the real story, what followed was the closure of the offices of Fateh, the largest constituent group of the PLO, in Jordan; the declaration of some PLO officials *personae non gratae*; and the adoption by the regime of a Fateh rebel, 'Atallah 'Atallah (Abu Za'im), to try to split Fateh ranks in the kingdom. In the meantime, a new electoral law was promulgated which made East Bank refugee camps separate electoral districts, but counted them among the quota of seats allotted for *West* Bank representation in the Jordanian parliament. Moreover, East Bank resident Palestinians were explicitly prohibited from running for East Bank parliamentary seats. In addition, in spring 1986, Jordan approved of Israel's appointment of pro-Jordanian Palestinians to municipal posts on the occupied West Bank.

On the Palestinian side, the March 1986 funeral of a prominent West Bank politician turned into a demonstration of militant Palestinian nationalism, a rejection of both the Israeli occupation and Jordanian designs. The following September, a major public opinion poll dramatically showed the minimal support Amman enjoyed in the West Bank.[60] Such developments were a major embarrassment to the Jordanian regime, as they clearly gave the lie to Hashemite pretensions to speak for the Palestinians instead of the PLO. The formal manifestation of Jordanian sovereignty over the Palestinians abroad – citizenship – remained, but its corollary, political loyalty, was clearly absent.

These developments had serious implications for relations between the regime and the largely Palestinian Jordanian expatriate business community in the Gulf. While such businessmen were unlikely to be sympathetic to the more radical factions of the PLO such as George Habash's Popular

---

[59] Brand, *Palestinians in the Arab World*, p. 176.

[60] According to the survey, support for King Husayn was just over 3 percent. See "The Al-Fajr Public Opinion Survey," Document B-1, *Journal of Palestine Studies* 16 (2) Winter 1987: pp. 196–207.

Front for the Liberation of Palestine or Nayef Hawatmeh's Democratic Front for the Liberation of Palestine, Fateh was a broad and generally conservative movement, which attracted the loyalty and the support of many members of the Gulf communities. Forcing them to choose between Husayn and 'Arafat under such conditions was likely to alienate all but the most opportunistic or most compliant with the regime.

During this same period, the Jordanian government announced a JD 461 million West Bank development plan, which regime officials hastened to note had first been conceived in April 1985 with the *approval* of the PLO as a response to the reduction of 1979 Arab summit financial commitments to the kingdom and 'Arafat. The plan called for liberalizing Jordan's policy toward West Bank industries and channeling low-interest loans and grants to education, industry, agriculture, housing and services in the West Bank. As for financing, the USA had pledged only a small amount to support the plan, but the reception in Europe had been much warmer. Contributions from the Jordanian treasury were projected at a very modest level,[61] while Gulf-based expatriates were seen as a logical potential source of funding.

However, following the break with 'Arafat, the plan could no longer be seen (nor was it intended) as a cooperative effort between the Jordanian regime and the PLO to support the population under occupation. Instead, it was viewed by 'Arafat supporters as a Hashemite attempt to coopt West Bankers. Given the consequently high stakes the Jordanian regime saw in successfully making its case before the Palestinians of the West Bank and the diaspora bourgeoisie, it is not surprising that the king addressed the opening of the 1986 expatriate conference in person. However, tensions were high. While the PLO had not actively encouraged attendance at the first conference, it accused those present at the second of selling out; 'Arafat called the meeting nothing more than an attempt to steal Palestinian representation from the PLO.[62]

The king's address contained numerous indirect references to the existing tensions between Jordan and the PLO. He repeatedly talked about Jordanians as a "united family" – always an indication of problems between Transjordanians and Jordanians of Palestinian origin. He mentioned the negative impact of the continuing deterioration in the regional economy, as well as the development plan, and he stressed Jordan's commitment to the Palestinian people, "irrespective of the political differences in positions and objectives between us and the various leaderships [note the plural] of the PLO"; "Support for our brethren's

---

[61] *Jordan Times*, 10–11 July 1986.   [62] Ibid., p. 176.

steadfastness will remain divorced from these differences. We will continue to live up to our duties toward our brethren, with persistence and awareness."[63]

In terms of less high-profile issues, two days before the second conference began, Prime Minister Zayd al-Rifaʿi reported that the government had implemented most of the recommendations adopted by the first conference. According to him, the government's position was that there should be no difference between Jordanians living in the country and those living abroad: they both had the same rights and responsibilities. Like the first conference, this one would be a chance for the expatriate delegates to discuss their living and working conditions and to seek assistance. For the government, it was to be another chance to familiarize the expatriates with areas and incentives for investment.[64]

Officially, 521 expatriates attended the conference, although a *Jordan Times* article reported that no more than 220 were in attendance any given day.[65] The participants were generally wealthy businessmen and traders, company owners, intellectuals, and economists. The Ministry of Tourism and Antiquities had instructed hotels to offer special rates to conference attendees, while Alia (Royal Jordanian Airlines) announced that it had made special arrangements to facilitate expatriate visits and stays in the kingdom. The expatriates were also taken on tours of several development projects, the free zone in Zarqa, and the Sahab Industrial City; and the state media, in the form of Jordan Television, produced a special broadcast the first day of the conference to acquaint viewers, especially those visiting Jordan, with development experiments and investment incentives offered to expatriates.[66]

As for activities by the expatriates themselves, the first meeting had called for establishing a range of committees to coordinate with Jordan in the areas of culture, the economy, industry, housing, social security, manpower planning, and expatriate councils and clubs. At this second meeting, representatives of the Jordanian communities in the UAE, Kuwait, Saudi Arabia, Denmark and West Germany reported that they had accomplished this. Other initiatives were also noted. JEs living in the UAE had agreed to establish a housing company in which they would invest to set up housing units for occupation upon their return to the kingdom, and on the third day of the conference the expatriates announced the establishment of two holding companies, capital for which was to be raised by selling shares to expatriates living in the Gulf states. Both companies' resources were to be channeled into socio-economic development projects in the kingdom.

---

[63] *Jordan Times*, 16 July 1986.   [64] *Jordan Times*, 12 July 1986.
[65] *Jordan Times*, 17–18 July 1986.   [66] *Jordan Times*, 14 July 1986.

These initiatives promised to be the first concrete results of the three-day meeting; however, no subsequent progress was made.[67]

There were requests by a majority of delegates that the government provide more information on investment facilities and customs and income tax exemptions offered on investment projects. There was also a call for streamlining a variety of bureaucratic procedures. Several delegates asked that the Central Bank tighten its control on moneychangers in view of the then-recent collapse of two local establishments in which, reportedly, a large number of expatriates had lost money. A number of JEs also expressed fears regarding the future of Jordan's leading public shareholding companies and requested that the government provide guarantees for such companies.[68] On the positive side of the ledger, the expatriates acknowledged that the government had responded to some of their major demands of the previous year, especially regarding permitting dual nationality[69] and expanding the number of seats in higher education institutions to accommodate their offspring. Other issues on which the government had worked included the provision of social security coverage, customs exemptions, expanded investment facilities, and problems with security checks at the borders.[70]

At the end of the meeting, the recommendations issued called on expatriates: to channel their investment priorities into Jordan in view of increased government incentives; to support efforts to set up housing societies for Jordanian expatriates in coordination with the government; to help promote economic integration between the host countries and Jordan; to buy Central Bank of Jordan development bonds; and to participate in efforts to set up a joint committee for consultations on investment affairs. (At the conclusion of the conference the government announced that an office would be set up at the Ministry of Industry and Trade to encourage investments and to facilitate the issuing of licenses for industrial businesses.) The recommendations also called on the concerned authorities to take legal measures against all those who refused to honor their commitments in areas related to financial

---

[67] *Jordan Times*, 17–18 July 1986.   [68] *Jordan Times*, 17–18 July, 19 July 1986.

[69] This was not finally ratified by the senate until 16 July 1987. Newspaper reports indicated that the law was originally devised as an incentive for Jordanian expatriates. The new law granted Jordanian nationality to women married to Jordanians after three years for Arabs and five years for non-Arab women. According to the same law, a Jordanian woman who married a non-Jordanian and obtained her husband's nationality would be able to keep both nationalities unless she chose to give up one of the two. She would retain the right to her Jordanian nationality in the case of divorce or death of the non-Jordanian husband. Children under eighteen who obtained a foreign nationality would keep their Jordanian nationality (*Jordan Times*, 18 July 1987).

[70] *Jordan Times*, 19 July 1986.

remittances and buying land and real estate. They asked Royal Jordanian Airlines to review its pricing policy on routes that linked expatriates with the homeland, and to operate flights to destinations where there were large Jordanian communities. They also requested more information from the government – through Jordanian embassies abroad – on socio-economic developments in the country.[71]

In the political realm, the expatriates called upon the government to extend to them the right to vote in parliamentary as well as professional association and municipal elections. They expressed their gratitude for the then-recent government order allowing people from Gaza and Beersheba residing in Jordan the right to own land and property, and called on the government to issue a similar order to be applied to all Palestinians who used Palestinian travel documents.[72] Regardless of the problems that had arisen between Husayn and 'Arafat, these JEs (most of whom were, according to a *Jordan Times* article, of Palestinian origin) reaffirmed their total support for the king and his efforts to strengthen the steadfastness of the people living under occupation. They also voiced their gratitude for the open-bridges policy which facilitated movement of goods and people between the West and East Banks.[73] That said, what the official press failed to mention was that most of these delegates were handpicked by the Jordanian embassies and consulates in the host countries. In this way, the likelihood of contentious exchanges or expressions of opposition to the regime was kept to a minimum.[74]

The third expatriate conference, 1987

Although the political and economic contexts are particular to the kingdom, it is clear from the record of the first two conferences that neither specific expatriate concerns (customs exemptions, provisions for children's education, etc.) nor stated government interests (attracting investment monies) differ substantially from what we have seen in the other case-country experiences. Moreover, as one examines the records of successive conferences, the repetition of topics of concern (from both the JE and the government sides) is as striking as it is, by the end,

---

[71] Ibid.
[72] Gaza came under Egyptian military administration after the 1948 war, and its residents, whether refugee or indigenous, were given Egyptian travel documents. As a result of the 1967 war, several thousand Gaza refugees ended up in Jordan but, without citizenship, had very limited rights. It is to this situation that the conferees' comments refer.
[73] *Jordan Times*, 19 July 1986.
[74] Mazen Salamah, "Al-Fashl Yulahiq Mu'tamarat al-Mughtaribin," *Al-Urdunn al-Jadid*, no. 10 Spring 1988, p. 70.

tiresome. The third conference did not differ markedly from its predecessors, except that no political or economic developments had intervened dramatically to affect the context. The opening speech at the 1987
conference was given by Crown Prince Hasan, the traditional patron of
economic development meetings in the kingdom. He reviewed the process of encouraging the private sector to participate in development
efforts in agriculture, industrial production, telecommunications and
other fields. On the political front, he reaffirmed Jordan's unwavering
role in support of the people of the occupied territories and underlined
the kingdom's measures to help Palestinians maintain their steadfastness
in the face of the Israeli occupation.[75]

In subsequent sessions, the government presented several working
papers on economic and regional political questions. Here the content
was clearly intended to reach out to a Palestinian population, in effect
reassuring them of the kingdom's commitment despite the continuing
strain in relations with the PLO. Foreign Minister Tahir al-Masri reaffirmed Jordan's rejection of separate talks to settle the Middle East conflict. He also reiterated Jordan's refusal to represent the Palestinian
people in peace negotiations, saying that since the Palestinians were a
large part of the conflict they should take part in talks to settle the
problem.[76] Minister of Occupied Territories Affairs Marwan Dudin
(also a Jordanian of West Bank origin)[77] presented a paper on the
Occupied Territories and Jordan's role in supporting Palestinian steadfastness. He rehearsed the kingdom's record of support for the West Bank
over the previous twenty years of occupation, although the expatriate
contribution had far surpassed that of the government: during this period,
a total of JD 470 million had been channeled into the West Bank by
expatriates, while during the same period the government had pumped
JD 125 million into the West Bank in the form of salaries and pensions,
and funds for development projects. The presence of Masri and Dudin,
top ministers of Palestinian origin, detailing Jordan's record of diplomatic
and economic support for the Palestinians under occupation, was not
accidental. It was clearly a part of the kingdom's on-going competition
with the PLO for the hearts and minds of the West Bankers.[78]

On the third day of the conference, Prime Minister Zayd al-Rifaʻi
retrained the focus on the domestic economy. Given that the Jordanian

---

[75] *Jordan Times*, 14 July 1987.   [76] *Jordan Times*, 15 July 1987.

[77] The Dudin family was associated with the infamous and ultimately failed Village
Leagues, a crude attempt by the Israelis in the early 1980s to give the appearance of
instituting a form of autonomy in the West Bank.

[78] *Jordan Times*, 15 July 1987.

dinar lost half of its value only a year later, and only a few months thereafter the kingdom was forced to conclude a structural adjustment agreement with the IMF in order to avoid insolvency, the error (if not the cynicism) in his praise for the Jordanian economy is striking. Al-Rifaʿi urged expatriates to convert their foreign currency funds into dinars and increase their contribution toward the prosperity of the country through investments in development projects. In another particularly egregious miscalculation, he argued that unemployment did not constitute a serious problem in the long run because the kingdom had embarked on a series of domestic and foreign policy measures to address this situation.[79]

In other sessions, in detailing the achievements of the past year and in fulfillment of JE demands, the government reported that it had taken measures to provide housing and higher education for expatriates and their children, in addition to implementing recommendations concerning dual nationality and social security services for JEs. It had increased the time that children of expatriates could postpone military service from one to two years, exempted expatriates from paying duty on their belongings if they returned to settle in Jordan, and extended facilities to issue passports to expatriates and to help them move their capital and belongings into and out of the country. The government had agreed to the opening of a private university to absorb more expatriate children (although the first such university did not actually open until 1991), and the Council of Higher Education had decided to increase the numbers of expatriate students admitted into Jordanian universities and community colleges.[80]

The final resolutions of the 600 or so attendees gave unqualified support to the kingdom's political stands on the Palestine question and peace efforts as well as to the development plans for Jordan and the West Bank. The conferees also backed the controversial open-bridges policy as well as organic links with the West Bank aimed at supporting Palestinian steadfastness under Israeli occupation. Other resolutions included praise for government steps granting expatriates tax exemptions on personal belongings, furniture and household appliances repatriated to Jordan. The conference recommended the establishment of an expatriate fund in the host countries to promote social ties among members of Jordanian communities in coordination with the Jordanian government and its diplomatic missions there. Finally, the expatriates called upon the government to increase its support of the JE communities and protect their interests through cooperation with host governments and through

---

[79] *Jordan Times*, 16–17 July 1987.   [80] *Jordan Times*, 13 July 1987.

increasing and improving services provided by Jordanian embassies and consulates.[81]

The fourth conference, 1988

Following the 1987 meeting, and in response to the discussions that had taken place during it, the cabinet decided to establish an Expatriates Directorate (mudiriyyat al-mughtaribin) in the Ministry of Labor and Social Development to prepare subsequent conferences, to follow up with the concerned parties, and to devote special concern to expatriate affairs.[82] Far more significant, however, five months after the end of the third conference, what came to be known as the Palestinian intifada began. This revolt against the Israeli occupation was viewed with concern, not only by the Israelis, but on the East Bank as well. First there was the potential for spill-over of discontent, given the Palestinian origins of a sizeable sector of the East Bank population. More important for the long term, however, the intifada sounded the death knell of the development plan (already on life support owing to lack of international and diaspora support), for it made clear – as if further evidence were needed – once and for all that the Palestinians of the West Bank were not interested in Hashemite political or economic "sponsorship." The intifada's leadership and message were purely Palestinian nationalist in character, leaving no place for the traditional notables who had served Amman.

Both Dudin and Al-Masri addressed the fourth expatriate conference, but their position and Jordan's had substantially changed. In addition to the ongoing intifada, the previous May, an Arab League summit had decided to channel directly to the PLO, rather than the PLO–Jordanian joint committee, whatever funds were still being contributed by Arab states as part of their 1979 summit commitments. Moreover, the kingdom's long-standing role in support of the West Bank was completely ignored in the Arab leaders' summit statements. Against the backdrop of the intifada, this political and economic slap in the face helped trigger the decision announced by King Husayn only two weeks after this conference (31 July 1988) to sever administrative and legal ties with the West Bank.

According to a paper prepared by the new Expatriates Directorate of the Ministry of Labor, the number of Jordanian expatriates had by this time reached 1 million. Owing to the recession in the Gulf, the number of expatriates returning home each year stood at about 3,000, and

---

[81] *Jordan Times*, 18 July 1987.
[82] Wizarat al-'Amal (w-al-Tanmiyah al-Ijtima'iyyah), *Al-Taqrir al-Sanawi 1987* (Amman: Da'irat al-Abhath), p. 61.

remittances had declined 23.4 percent from the previous year, although new Central Bank regulations were expected to boost remittances from expatriates and to liberalize financial procedures for them.[83] In the event, however, such measures ended up having little significance. Whatever steps the government had taken over the previous year in response to expatriate demands, and whatever decisions this fourth conference made regarding assistance, coordination and economic investment – and they were similar to those of conferences past – were suddenly irrelevant for a large number of expatriates after 31 July 1988. For, as a result of King Husayn's disengagement decision, all of those expatriates whose normal place of residence was the West Bank were, overnight, deprived of their citizenship – the largest mass disenfranchisement since the Second World War – and a dramatic "innovation" in what one could call population policy broadly defined, insofar as it redefined the kingdom's citizenship base.[84] It was also a dramatic move in terms of territorial sovereignty, as it meant a relinquishment of Amman's political claim to the West Bank. In such a context, the relevance of tax exemptions, university seats, and the possibility of dual nationality quickly dissipated.

Indeed, massive Palestinian capital flight followed, contributing to the economic crisis and ultimately to the dinar's precipitous drop in value. A new crisis with the PLO was triggered, and, by February 1989, the kingdom was forced to seek IMF assistance to reschedule its debt. Expatriates were neither the cause of nor the solution to the kingdom's economic woes; however, a different policy toward the PLO in the wake of the Arab summit might have forestalled economic collapse. In the event, however, the pressures were simply too great, and the relatively high standard of living (in comparison with the kingdom's resource base) that Jordanians had enjoyed for several decades came to an end.

The fifth conference, 1989

By the time the fifth conference was held, major changes were underway in Jordan as a result of the developments noted above. The downward economic spiral had ultimately produced riots in mid-April 1989 that shook the kingdom. The response was a gradual opening of what had become a stifling political system and the announcement that parliamentary elections, the first since the 1967 war, would be held in the fall. Clearly shocked by the domestic unrest, which had erupted in Transjordanian areas whose support the regime had long taken for granted, the government's attentions

[83] *Jordan Times*, 12 July 1988.   [84] See De Bel-Air, p. 19.

were absorbed by issues other than expatriates, which had in any case become less and less central since the 1987 conference.

This fifth (and final) conference in the series was reportedly attended by more than 800 expatriates from 29 countries. Crown Prince Hasan opened the meeting with wide-ranging remarks covering both economic and political topics. In an example of unusual frankness, the Crown Prince reviewed Jordan's economic difficulties and admitted, "In all honesty ... some of us may have exaggerated in our spending and consumption [patterns] ... and some may have initiated productive projects which did not operate at their maximum capacity."[85]

He noted that the kingdom had decided to return to parliamentary life, although he did not mention the reasons for it. He also paid tribute to the Palestinians in the Occupied Territories, saying that Jordan supported them fully, but he then had to place this Jordanian commitment in the context of the disengagement. According to the Crown Prince, Jordan's decision had come as a step toward the establishment of a Palestinian state. (This was the official, ex-post rationalization, which few Jordanians, whether of Palestinian or Transjordanian origin, accepted.) He went on to say that the close relations and true unity between Jordan and Palestine were strong and could not be divided easily: "That is why some of the measures which we opted to apply were the subject of controversy by those whom they affected, especially those working abroad ... Undoubtedly we are open-hearted and open-minded enough to do whatever we can without tampering with the spirit, aim and content of the disengagement ... Jordan is more than willing to reconsider some of these decisions in order to facilitate matters."[86] In fact, the issue of passports and nationality took several years to sort out, in part because the Jordanian state as well as its embassies and consulates abroad were deliberately vague in their interpretation of who would be allowed to maintain his/her citizenship. The lack of clarity allowed for deliberate manipulation of the issue by the bureaucracy, especially the security forces, as a form of intimidation or harassment.

Perhaps as an expression of the "Amman spring" the country was experiencing, Tahir al-Masri's address to this meeting stressed the government's interest in enhancing the dialogue and exchange of views with Jordanians working abroad: the government was keen to have expatriate opinions and advice on possible legislation to give them privileges and incentives to return. The deputy governor of the Central Bank (CBJ), Mohammed Saleh Hourani, urged the expatriates to contribute to

[85] *Jordan Times*, 8 July 1989.   [86] *Jordan Times*, 9 July 1989.

helping their country through its then difficult circumstances. He indicated that the CBJ had begun to prepare a draft plan to issue bonds in foreign currency to attract expatriate interest. His was followed by several other presentations on various aspects of the economy: taxes, science and technology, agriculture and industry.[87] At the end, participants made numerous recommendations regarding use of remittances, stabilizing the national economy, and more systematic follow-up.[88] On the political level, the conference reaffirmed Jordan's position regarding the Palestinian problem and the kingdom's efforts to help convene an international peace conference on the Middle East. Attendees also expressed pride in the king's letter of appointment to the government, especially on the issues of resuming parliamentary life, the reorganization of the country's administration, and on the elimination of favoritism.[89]

Proclamations of successes and expectations aside, this 1989 conference was the last in the series. It had been clear by 1987 that the state's desired goal of attracting large-scale investment from the expatriates through the instrument of this conference had not worked. Domestic and regional developments had played a role in undermining the attractiveness of launching projects in Jordan, but the regime's decision-makers themselves had also erred in their failure to understand that public relations efforts alone would not ensure investment.[90] Certainly, the domestic economic context – laws, institutions, procedures as well as the general bureaucratic climate – needed to become more investor friendly in order to attract interest. However, the domestic political environment was also in need of serious attention, just as were the nature and bases of Jordanian–PLO relations. The annual conferences had generated a great deal of seasonal sound and fury, but in the end had signified nothing in terms of a serious change in economic or political approach that might secure greater investment. In the meantime, the king had disengaged from the West Bank, thereby removing the state's claim on the loyalty and resources of its residents, while raising the suspicion and sometimes the ire of many other Jordanians of Palestinian origin regarding the regime.

The 1990s

The economic and political climate changed considerably in the kingdom over the next decade during which no expatriate meetings were held. Jordan had still been in the early stages of both its political liberalization and the painful process of structural adjustment when Iraq invaded

---

[87] *Jordan Times*, 10 and 11 July 1989.   [88] *Jordan Times*, 8 July 1989.
[89] *Jordan Times*, 12 July 1989.   [90] Abu-Odeh interview.

Kuwait in August 1990, and the complexion of the Jordanian presence in the Gulf was brutally disfigured. Some Jordanian expatriates fled Kuwait, while others were expelled owing to the positions taken by the kingdom and by the PLO on the invasion. While statistics varied markedly, especially in the early days, some 200,000 Jordanians returned to the kingdom as a result of the Iraqi invasion. For most, it was the end of an era. Relations with the previous Gulf state hosts, particularly Saudi Arabia and Kuwait, remained strained for a number of years, and hence expatriate return to them was generally impossible, despite King Husayn's efforts at repairing the damage. The Directorate of Jordanians Working Abroad, a re-creation of the previous Directorate of Expatriates, coordinated administrative efforts to assist Jordanian workers/businessmen in submitting claims, and in many cases ultimately receiving compensation, for losses owing to their expulsion from the Gulf states.[91] However, not until 'Abdallah succeeded his father in 1999 were relations with the Gulf states fully repaired and new campaigns undertaken to reopen Gulf labor markets to Jordanian workers.

Another important difference ushered in by the 1990s concerned the progress toward settling the identity and sovereignty question between the Hashemite regime and the Palestinians. Husayn's disengagement had effectively terminated his claim to the West Bank and to the loyalty of its Palestinian residents. This had led the PLO to declare a state in late 1988; however, it also ultimately opened the way for the PLO to negotiate over territory, leading to the secret discussions which produced the Oslo accords of 1993. By 1998, when the Palestinians began to run their own series of expatriate conferences, a nascent quasi-government, the Palestinian National Authority, exercised some control over limited segments of the West Bank and Gaza. While economic relations between the Palestinian Authority and the Jordanian state continued to be of critical concern to both, Jordan was no longer competing for political influence on the West Bank, at least not to the same extent or with the same goals as before. Added to this clarification of relations was the somewhat freer political atmosphere in the kingdom, including the holding of relatively clean parliamentary elections in 1989. Add to that the impact that King Husayn's refusal to support the international coalition against Iraq had had in 1990–91 in boosting his popularity with his entire population, Transjordanian and Palestinian alike, and the basis was laid for a gradual change in perception of the regime by important sectors of the population, resident and expatriate.

[91] See Wizarat al-'Amal (w-al-Tanmiyah al-Ijtima'iyyah), *Al-Taqrir al-Sanawi*, 1990 onward.

Expatriate businessmen's conferences

Over the years, a legal structure intended to encourage expatriates to invest, rather than simply consume, had been elaborated. The first element had been the Encouragement of Investment Law no. 53/1972, designed to attract capital flows for investment, which exempted fixed assets from customs duties on imports, and profits from income tax for a period of six years. Next was the Post Office Fund introduced in 1973 and development bonds issued in 1974. These served to encourage the in-flow of remittances and to channel such cash balances into productive investment via the state. Finally, in general, the Central Bank of Jordan adopted liberal policies, such as those allowing workers abroad to hold accounts in foreign currencies with commercial banks.[92] Nevertheless, even following the Iraqi invasion of Kuwait, the investment initiatives of many of the newly returned expatriates – outside the realm of construction – failed.

Important changes were introduced into the kingdom's investment law in the 1990s, following the beginnings of structural adjustment. The 1995 Investment Promotion Law is the centerpiece of the new approach, which actively seeks to attract foreign investment. In this regard, the Jordanian approach has differed from that of Tunisia and Morocco, in that no special incentives are offered to expatriate Jordanians to invest back home. Instead, all investors are treated alike, regardless of nationality. The intent is not to discriminate against Jordanians who seek to invest; rather, the emphasis is on attracting what have been labeled strategic partners, perhaps individuals, but more likely companies, that are willing to make major, rather than small or modest, financial commitments, particularly to the on-going process of privatization.[93]

In this context, in 1998 a new series of conferences was launched, this time targeting only expatriate businessmen, not the communities abroad in general. Indeed, the initiative originated with the Jordanian Businessmen's Association (JBA), and sought to reestablish or strengthen ties that had been broken when the series of conferences in the 1980s ended. The sponsorship also changed, as the new meetings were organized jointly by the JBA, a private sector organization, and the government, through the Investment Promotion Corporation (IPC). A basic problem they faced in trying to organize this first conference was the lack of a database on expatriate businessmen. The organizers had to be creative, going to embassies, Jordanian institutions abroad, prominent individuals with good

---

[92] M. A. J. Share, "The Use of Jordanian Workers' Remittances," in Khader and Badran, p. 41.
[93] Abu-Odeh interview.

networks overseas, as well as the large and powerful Arab Bank. As a result of their efforts they assembled a list of more than 1,000 names.[94]

The first meeting, held in summer 1998, entitled "Building Jordan's Future Together," had as its primary goal that of attracting foreign investment. President of the JBA Hamdi Tabba' chaired the conference's preparatory meeting and expressed hope that the meeting would mark a turning point in Jordan's drive to bolster the economy at a time when the kingdom was pursuing efforts to open up further to the outside world and implement a partnership agreement with Europe while seeking an Arab free-trade zone.[95] In the event, the meeting produced a number of recommendations to encourage investment. The first was the establishment of an efficient information system to keep businesses updated on the latest investment opportunities. Second was a call for amending the tax and customs laws to attract investors and reduce red tape. Businessmen wanted to be able to count on prompt business arbitration as well as more and better banking facilities, and they stressed that progress depended in large part upon how serious the government was. Complaints about time-consuming procedures as well as lack of cooperation from government-owned companies were common.[96]

The second in this new series of conferences was held three (rather than the initially planned two) years later, in August 2001. The name was changed slightly to the "Conference for Jordanian Businessmen and Investors" and was held under the slogan "Together to Build Jordan of the Future." Expatriate businessmen were a primary target, but the meeting, still a joint project of the JBA and the IPC, was directed at investors in general. Both the government and private sectors had investment proposals on offer at this three-day meeting. However, newspaper coverage of the meeting made clear that many of the same impediments to investment of which businessmen had complained in the 1980s persisted: a complicated and inefficient bureaucracy, inadequate legal protections, lack of reliable investment information, excessively high interest rates, small market size, and the like.[97]

By the time of this meeting, the Ministry of Planning had inaugurated a project aimed at liaising better with the expatriates. The ministry realized that in order to work in the expatriate and investment sector, basic information was needed, and the latest data available at this point dated to 1993. The basis of the project was a questionnaire, to be available through the

[94] Interview with 'Ali Yusuf, General-Director, Jordanian Businessmen's Association, Amman, 28 June 1999.
[95] *Jordan Times*, 5 September 1998.   [96] *Jordan Times*, 10–11 September 1998.
[97] *Al-Ra'y*, 15 August 2001. The next conference in the series was held 11–13 August 2003.

embassies/consulates, the businessmen's meetings, as well as the Internet, to collect information on expatriates. The hope was that through this project the ministry would be able to develop a better idea of where the major concentrations of Jordanians abroad were, as well as of their background, employment type, and the like. The ministry was less interested in securing figures about the size of investments and/or remittances than in putting in place relationships that would ensure the continued flow of funds.[98] The series of conferences continued in 2003, with similar content and goals.

Conclusions

Of the case countries covered in this study, the extent of institutionalized government involvement with the expatriates is the most minimal in the Jordanian case, while the percentage of Jordan's active working population abroad (in its heyday in the 1980s, some one-third of the total active labor force) was clearly the largest. How may we explain this?

While it is certainly the case that the numbers were small in the early years, so was the overall Jordanian population; hence the absolute numbers say nothing about their relative importance. (As we have seen, Tunisia launched its *amicales* among a very small expatriate population.) Moreover, it is clear from the planning documents that, like their Maghrebi counterparts, Jordanian bureaucrats were well aware of both the role of external labor markets in attracting what might otherwise have been redundant labor and that of expatriate remittances in the kingdom's economy. Unlike what we saw in the Moroccan and Tunisian cases, however, the emergence of more family-based communities abroad did not play a direct role in attracting state interest: this family composition of the communities was clear by the early 1970s, yet it was not until the mid-1980s that the state began paying greater attention to them, and even then it was not with the primary goal of addressing social concerns. Certainly, the presence of the overwhelming proportion of Jordanian expatriates in Arab countries meant that questions of language, religion and cultural identity were not posed for Jordanians as they were for Maghrebis in Europe. Nor, given that enfranchisement was not an option, was permanent resettlement or adoption of a second nationality. Nevertheless, the explanation for the lack of more elaborate state involvement and for the ultimate timing of state intervention seems to lie elsewhere.

While calls from within the expatriate communities themselves may have preceded the convening of the conferences of the 1980s, this series

---

[98] Interview with Naseem Rahahla, National Competitiveness Team, Ministry of Planning, Amman, 23 June 1999.

of meetings was clearly a government initiative. The catalyst was the regional recession, not a sudden recognition that there was a large Jordanian expatriate community or that as a community of families it had special problems. While the role of remittances was acknowledged, until the 1980s external financial support from the Arab oil states had meant that the state had not felt the need to demand or ask more from its private sector nationals/workers abroad. Given the distrust that characterized Transjordanian–Palestinian or state vs. citizens of Palestinian origin relations, especially after the 1970 civil war, the regime was likely relieved at their exit and content with their residence abroad, if at times suspicious of the use of some expatriate resources. However, with the drop in funds from Arab states, the beginning of the gradual closing of Gulf labor markets to expatriate workers, and the return home of others after work contracts were not renewed, the Jordanian economy began to suffer. One obvious, but untried, strategy was to attempt actively to mobilize resources from within the expatriate community. As we saw above, this also meant finessing or attempting to reshape Jordan's relations with the PLO, and with large numbers of expatriates who had been second-class citizens simply because they were of Palestinian origin.[99] In other words, the regime felt it necessary to imbue with some content what had to that point been largely empty proclamations – often contested – of sovereignty over this population. In order to make claims on the resources of these expatriates, it had also to begin to make them more fully citizens by giving them reason to identify with the Jordanian state and its needs.

That said, the identity question was framed differently in the Jordanian case than it was in the Moroccan or Tunisian examples. While the calls for investment were real, they did not employ the rhetoric of a Jordanian national responsibility to contribute to Jordan. Most of these expatriates were Palestinians, and it was that identity that commanded their deepest loyalty. Moreover, many of these JE's identified territorially only with the West Bank and not with the kingdom as a whole. A Jordanian regime that over the years had fought most expressions of separate Palestinian identity because of the threat it posed to regime legitimacy and sovereignty had to treat the identity issue with care, if its calls for investment by these Palestinians were to succeed. The fact that the initial investment push attempted to focus JE interest on the West Bank development program,

---

[99] Given that Palestinians represent somewhere around half the population, their numbers in the parliament, the cabinet and the senate are well below what one would expect, and there is clearly discrimination in public sector recruitment as well as in numerous daily bureaucratic procedures. Nevertheless, some sectors of the Palestinian bourgeoisie have traditionally been close to the Hashemite throne and others have secured various forms of influence as a result of financial success.

and not so much on East Bank opportunities, suggests that the state understood this quite well. How better to mobilize Palestinian money for Jordan's development than by proposing that it be channeled to a part of former Mandate Palestine?

The record clearly demonstrates that the expatriates and the government came to these conferences with different goals and expectations. The regime in effect wanted money and political support, while the expatriates sought a series of bureaucratic and administrative concessions. The results were repeated statements of intent, but few concrete results. The kingdom's ostensibly free-market orientation was not able to overcome a strong protectionist tendency prevailing in the government circles responsible for economic policy implementation. Moreover, bureaucratic suspicion of the private sector was further exacerbated by the fact that the state was staffed largely by Transjordanians, while the private sector was largely Palestinian. One anecdote was certainly emblematic of the tensions in this relationship. In an argument between an expatriate and a government official the expatriate reportedly said: "If you want our money for investment in the country, then in return we want university seats for our children." The official replied, "We don't want your money or your children."[100]

Given the divergence between state and expatriate interests, as well as the problematic relationship between the Jordanian state and its nationals in the Gulf, it is not surprising that the series of expatriate conferences boasted only minimal achievements. Indivisible from these failures, however, were the regional developments noted above: the failure of the development plan to attract significant international support; a surging Palestinian nationalism that, most clearly through the intifada, rejected Hashemite attempts at influence; the subsequent (and to a certain extent, consequent) disengagement from the West Bank; the devaluation of the dinar; and the economic riots that led to a political opening in 1989. The tension between Transjordanians and Palestinians after the disengagement also led to charges against some Jordanians of Palestinian origin of dual loyalty – to both Jordan and the PLO.[101] Given the large Palestinian contingent among the expatriates, such an atmosphere hardly encouraged their participation in regime-sponsored gatherings. From the state's perspective, the failures of these conferences were clear at a time when the most immediate challenges required devoting all energy to the domestic front. It was nearly a decade before domestic and regional conditions led the regime to refocus attention on its expatriates.

---

[100] Salamah, p. 71.   [101] ʿAbd al-Jabir interview.

When the expatriate conference series was revived, it was under different sponsorship, and with more focused goals that related, not to expatriates in general or to the communities, but to only a particular sector and to investment in the kingdom. In this respect as well, Jordan's experience with expatriate-directed institutions differs markedly from the other three cases where, over time, state fields of interest have broadened. In the case of the kingdom, its institutional target audience has narrowed to solely that of potential investors.

Sensitivities between the two communal groups in the kingdom persist, and the wealth of former and current (largely Palestinian[102]) expatriates is viewed by some Transjordanians as a threat, but the issue of competition with the PLO is no longer pressing, nor is the identity of West Bankers. The current investment attraction efforts are certainly part of regime maintenance and hence cannot be seen as apolitical, but they are much more clearly economically oriented than were some of the policies of the 1980s. Questions may remain about the loyalty of Jordanians of Palestinian origin, but, at this point, there are no developments that force them to declare or choose. The most important issue from the mid-1990s onward in this regard has been the political role that the long-time, largely politically marginalized, Palestinian bourgeoisie – particularly those who returned from the Gulf states in 1990–91 – might play in effecting political change in the kingdom, either through pushing for a more open system, or through replacing the Transjordanian bureaucracy as the mainstay of the soft authoritarian Hashemite regime. To date, to the surprise of many, at least in terms of formal politics, abdication of responsibility or lack of interest has been the most common response. Only time will tell if changes in regional conditions – developments in the Israeli–Palestinian theatre or a revival of the internal political liberalization process – may open the way for more active expatriate involvement in the kingdom's domestic politics. For now, however, the challenge of Palestinian identity to Jordanian state sovereignty is largely settled or muted; the continuing focus of efforts to reinforce regime authority has, therefore, returned to the more economic/technocratic considerations of pure investment attraction both to assist with socio-economic development and to bolster the balance of payments bottom line.

---

[102] The majority of expatriates continues to be of Palestinian origin, but in recent years there have been growing numbers of Transjordanians among the emigrant population as well.

Conclusions: transnationalism, security and sovereignty

A focus on the sending states, and not just the societies, of the global South has a great deal to contribute to our understanding of the multi-faceted phenomenon of international migration. The traditional European/US bias of political science studies of border controls and immigration policy, combined with the civil-society and network emphasis of much of the transnationalism literature, leaves significant parts of the migration story untold. First, because the majority of migration is South–South, not South–North; and second because the *state* plays a preeminent role in shaping employment and investment, as well as identity and security policy, all of which have been shown to contribute to the nature and magnitude of emigration as well as the subsequent management of communities of nationals abroad.

In attempting to discern the forces behind the establishment of state institutions involved in expatriate affairs, this work first derived a general proposition from the transnationalism literature that such structures could be understood as the product of a particular stage of capitalist development, that of the late twentieth – early twenty-first centuries. While there has certainly been a recent proliferation of these institutions, a close examination of the historical record of our four case countries demonstrated that such structures are not new. Indeed, the initial initiatives by the Tunisian, Lebanese and Moroccan states appear to have been driven by decolonization, not more recent economic globalization.

Another juncture of profound importance in the history of some of these institutions was the 1973 oil crisis. The consequent closing of Europe's borders to further, legal immigration, combined with relatively liberal family reunification policies, laid the bases for the development of more family-based Maghrebi communities. As the emigration horizons of these Tunisians and Moroccans then shifted, so did their governments' involvement with them. No longer were they simply agglomerations of a natural resource (human capital) that could be passively counted on as a stable source of remittances. Indeed, as European states successively changed laws governing immigrant integration, the Maghrebi states faced the prospect of declining loyalty among their nationals. In response, new institutions and policies were put in place or existing ones were redefined.

None of this is to deny transnationalism's contention that economic factors have played an important role in state institutional development, although they seem to have been less of a driving force than one might initially imagine. Depending upon period, all four states acknowledged the importance of expatriate contributions and manifested an interest in maximizing emigrant contributions to the national economy; however, Jordan offers the only clear example of economic imperatives' actually triggering institutional development (beyond the Bank al-'Amal in Morocco). The kingdom had long ignored the needs of its expatriate communities, but when regional recession in the early 1980s reduced aid infusions from the oil-producers, the state finally began to court its largely Gulf-state-resident nationals. The goal was to convince them to increase investment to prop up Amman's sagging financial fortunes and contribute to a controversial development plan.

As for the argument from the literature on political transnationalism that sending states establish such institutions as a means of creating lobbies abroad, the cases offered several relevant examples: Morocco apparently hoped that its nationals would lobby for its claim to the Western Sahara; Tunisia called upon its émigrés to serve as ambassadors for Tunisian values and economic development abroad; and US-based Lebanese communities played a role in having a US government travel ban lifted. However, with the exception of Tunisia, which has truly pushed the ambassadorial role of its expatriates, these are rather limited examples, and were felicitous, but unplanned, outcomes of the presence of institutions established for other reasons. This is not to say that such a function could not be further energized in the future, but it does not seem to have been central to the states' *initial* decisions to establish or revamp institutions involved with expatriates.

Domestic politics, the fourth factor discussed in chapter 1, was far more important, but largely as an intervening variable, not as a driving reason for the founding of new institutions. In Lebanon, it was the aftermath of the 1958 civil war that gave rise to the establishment of the WLU, just as it was factors particular to the post-Ta'if arrangements that led to the proliferation of new ministries that included the Ministry of Expatriates. There is no question that the diaspora communities had long interested certain members of the Lebanese elite, but it took dramatic changes on the domestic political scene to open the way for the establishment of institutions that, because of confessional sensitivities, had been viewed as too provocative before.

Similarly, in Tunisia, under Bourguiba there had been a gradual evolution of bureaucratic involvement in emigration and in the communities abroad, but it was the coup of 1987 which served to shake many government bureaus out of their malaise, and which set in motion new policies aimed at expanding the state's role in the lives of its nationals abroad. It may also be that, in Morocco, the gradual political opening begun in the late 1980s paved the way for a transformation of the *makhzen*'s view of the émigré from that of subject to one of citizen to whom the state had to be more responsive, through both a ministry dedicated to Moroccans resident abroad and the Fondation Hassan II.

The cases suggested two additional generalizations, both regarding the *host* states and institutional development. The first involves the possibilities of social and political integration. In the case of Jordan, the timing and quality of whose institutional attention to its nationals lagged well behind that of Tunisia and Morocco, the vast majority of its expatriates were living in culturally similar, although authoritarian and exclusivist (i.e., not offering the possibility of enfranchisement) countries. The host states, therefore, offered little economic or political competition to Jordan's ties to its expatriates. Maghrebis, on the other hand, migrated overwhelmingly to the social democracies of Western Europe in which they were offered more rights and possibilities for economic, social and even political integration. Seemingly in response, Tunisia and Morocco took a more active and service-oriented interest in their emigrants. While further research is needed, the lesson appears to be that a sending state is more likely to establish separate expatriate-related institutions if its nationals are concentrated in countries that offer the possibility of meaningful integration, for only in such circumstances do the host states constitute serious competitors for the emigrants' loyalty and resources.

In this regard, regime type in the receiving state is also critical. For both Morocco and Tunisia the vast majority of expatriates lived in democracies. While there is no doubt that the French security services cooperated with these states on issues ranging from labor union activism to Islamist organizations, the fact that the Maghrebis resided in democracies meant that the fields for organizing and activism were by definition more open than they would have been for Jordanians in the Gulf or Lebanese in the Gulf, Africa and Latin America. Not only did local law not forbid organizing by foreigners, it increasingly offered them more opportunities and protections. In such a climate, the sending states had to resort to their own devices to monitor their nationals. Thus, it seems that separate institutions, particularly those with a security function, are more likely to be established among communities from authoritarian states but resident in more politically open systems.

It was the initial discovery of the primacy of the security function manifested by the North African *amicales* that led this study gradually to move toward an exploration of the connection between these state institutions and the larger issue of state sovereignty. The relationship between sovereignty and immigration has been explored, but, as noted above, it has been in the context of questions of frontier control. While not discounting the importance of borders, this work has focused instead on "the people," another traditional basis of sovereignty, and demonstrated how the sending states' concern with maintaining some sovereignty claim to them has in effect redefined the political community.

Traditionally, sovereignty as applied to a population has referred to the loyalty or allegiance of those resident within a territorially bounded area. Who was included in or excluded from the polity was based on place of residence and exclusive citizenship. Certainly there have long been exceptions to this rule, but the current extent of human movement beyond the frontiers of states of origin constitutes a challenge to the long-accepted notion of sovereignty as exercised over a population located within a single, recognized territorial unit. Not only are the numbers greater, but developments in transport and communication have rendered far easier a continued flow of people, goods, messages and images across and between states. As a result, the line between home and abroad blurs, in both cultural and political terms, thereby also calling into question the shape and nature of the boundaries of the national community.

This work has suggested that the emergence of expatriate-related institutions with their differing histories and functions may be best understood as indications of the degree of state sovereignty or as manifestations of resilience in the face of economic and political challenges to state authority: through these institutions, states demonstrate their robustness by attempting to renegotiate their role, thereby reshaping and redefining their claims over groups of nationals (and even their descendants) who live beyond their territorial boundaries. The four case countries' emigration experiences make clear that while the expatriate may be the largely forgotten "other" in general accounts of national political development, emigrants have in fact been key actors in these histories. Although the authority of these four states has been most *obviously* forged or contested over the years by forces within or attempting to infringe upon their borders, the communities abroad have also substantially affected and been affected by the state, and their relationship to it has been an increasingly important part of the historical evolution of the content and practice of sovereignty.

In Morocco, the preservation of domestic stability (through exporting excess labor), a component of domestic sovereignty, explains the earliest institutional involvement by the state in the form of labor coordinating offices. It also explains the emergence of the *amicales*, which were first established as it became clear that security at home required a heavier hand in dealing with anti-regime activity among the communities abroad. The monarchy manifested little other interest in its expatriates until economic and political developments in Europe challenged Hassan II's sovereign claim to these "subjects." Although with a certain lag, probably owing to lack of institutional capacity, Rabat ultimately did move through institutional channels to assert the tie of allegiance (*bay'ah*) binding Moroccans to their king. Around the same time, given the economic crisis, remittances began to assume greater importance, thus giving the state an additional reason to insist on the Moroccanness of its emigrants, and a domestic political opening was initiated, a discursive part of which changed the terms used to refer to expatriates from those of subjects to those of citizens. Thus, in the face of opportunities for political integration into the European host states, where they could also, increasingly, maintain the cultural ties most important to them through association with Islamic, rather than specifically Moroccan, institutions, Rabat sought to reassert its ties and, by extension, its sovereign rights, to its nationals abroad.

The Tunisian state's early efforts to organize emigration and prepare its nationals for work outside the country may also be understood in the context of a newly independent state's attempts to marshal its resources for the challenging state-building and sovereignty-consolidating process. Tunisia sought both to do well by its citizens (in the context of an inability to generate sufficient domestic employment) and to maintain order at home, both key elements of sovereignty. Indeed, the security aspect of sovereignty-maintenance in these institutions is preeminent in the Tunisian case as, within five years of independence, it established *amicale* structures that were extensions of the PSD in the areas of greatest Tunisian expatriate concentration. While the efficiency and effectiveness of these institutions clearly waned as the Bourguiba regime sank into malaise, they were restructured and revived following the 1987 coup. Still in the early stages of structural adjustment and in need of the cultural ties, business skills and political weight of its nationals abroad, the new regime initially embraced a more inclusionary discourse to try to win back those who had been alienated by the coercive methods of the *ancien régime*. Nevertheless, the security rationale continued to predominate. Tunis used its institutions to propagate the politically correct version of its mission at home and abroad of promoting "tolerance" (while brutally suppressing al-Nahdah) and "pluralism" (in which state-sponsored NGOs often strong-armed legitimate civil-society actors). At the same time, the state insisted upon

Tunisians' continuing cultural, economic and political responsibilities to the homeland: one could become successful abroad and integrate into the host state, but assimilation was unacceptable.

In the case of Lebanon, one sees again the importance of post-independence sovereignty-reinforcing exigencies in the early attempts to reach out to what were at the time already established diaspora communities. The difference in this case is that, given the confessional composition of the diaspora and the role that confession came to play in domestic politics, attempts by the Lebanese state to extend its writ to include its emigrants and their descendants more fully in the political community were far more politically charged than in the Maghrebi cases. Indeed, the formula initially conceived to ensure Lebanon's independence, the National Pact, in fact lay the bases for the most highly penetrated, least sovereign state among the four cases examined here. Lebanese efforts may be seen, in part, as initiatives to mobilize émigré resources, but they were driven by a particular segment of the economic and political elite that was eager to integrate the émigrés more fully into the domestic power balance to their own advantage, not to the advantage of the country as a whole.

The relationship between the émigré communities and state sovereignty is also problematic in the case of Jordan, since the provenance of a majority of its expatriates was the West Bank, a part of Mandate Palestine that had been annexed to the Hashemite Kingdom. As the case study noted, of the four countries considered here, Jordan's institutional involvement with its expatriates was minimal, consisting for decades simply of its consular network, which also monitored the community for anti-regime activities. This low level of institutional involvement seems to have derived directly from the insecure bases of sovereignty in the kingdom. The most obvious challenges to Amman have come from periodic Israeli military incursions, the most disastrous of which resulted in the occupation of the West Bank during the 1967 war. However, had the regime not suffered from a deficit of domestic legitimacy – manifested most strikingly by the 1970 civil war – its involvement with its expatriates over the years would likely have been quite different. Indeed, it was precisely the question of the allegiance of nationals of Palestinian origin, and the consequent imperative to suppress expressions of separate Palestinian identity in the context of Husayn's competition with the PLO for the emigrants' loyalty, that precluded the regime from assuming that Jordan was an entity for which a majority of its citizens had any particular affection. Despite formal proclamations to the contrary, its sovereignty over the Palestinian part of its population rested on tenuous foundations at best.

After flirtations in the 1960s with attempts to restructure the economy, the regime seems to have acquiesced in the desire of increasing numbers of its citizens, the vast majority of whom were of Palestinian origin, to seek work abroad. While with Gulf state assistance it certainly monitored their political activities, to have attempted to organize them under Jordanian auspices and a Jordanian identity could well have provoked dissent, and in any case would likely have been an embarrassing failure. The kingdom was fortunate that, given the immigration situation in the Gulf, few of its citizens had the option to invest, much less settle permanently, in the oil-producing states. In addition, its primary competitor was a non-state actor, the PLO, which could offer neither a stable, sovereign territory into which to integrate, nor remunerative investment opportunities. Hence, unlike the Maghrebi states, Jordan had no real competitors for expatriate remittances or for an alternative citizenship. Its complacency was not shaken until the regional recession of the 1980s began to hit home. In these conditions Amman launched its sole expatriate-targeted institutional initiative aimed at reaching out to wealthy communities abroad. In the event, however, the efforts were mostly of a public relations nature. There was little effective change in the approach of the bureaucracy and, still suspicious of most of its expatriates of Palestinian origin, it carefully monitored participation to make sure the conferences counted large numbers of loyalist elements.

States with large populations of nationals abroad face myriad challenges in formulating their policies to deal with these communities. This work has shown that while there are some striking similarities, state responses are quite varied, deriving from a combination of their own histories, the history of their emigration, their domestic political structures, the host-state regime, and the extent and nature of their sovereignty. The experiences of the four cases examined here suggest that it may be precisely those states that are relatively more secure in their sovereignty vis-à-vis "the people" (Morocco and Tunisia) that are likely to launch such institutions. Is it mere coincidence that it was Jordan and Lebanon, both of which have suffered wars related to the lack of clear boundaries of the "national" political community – a clear indication of highly impaired sovereignty – which have the more checkered record in their relations with large and wealthy communities of expatriates? This question requires further study, but it does appear to be a lesson of this comparative work.

Whatever form state response may take, it appears that the nature of sovereignty in the international system is being reconfigured, not only by economic, military, religious and environmental developments, but by the presence of substantial expatriate communities actively leading transnational lives. More in-depth work is needed on expatriate-related institutions established by other states to determine if the lessons drawn here hold. In the meantime, for the foreseeable future, communities or networks of nationals abroad and their descendants seem destined to grow in number and significance. These members of "the people," those in whom ultimate sovereignty is supposed to rest, but who officially rest outside the sovereign, are, inadvertently, mounting significant challenges to sovereignty's meaning and practice as the twenty-first century unfolds.

Bibliography

SOURCES IN ENGLISH, FRENCH AND SPANISH

Abou Fadel, Henri, Jean Malha and Ibrahim Kaidy (eds.). *Lebanon: Its Treaties and Agreements* (Beirut: Maktab Khayyat, 1966).

La République Libanaise et ses relations extérieures: traités et conventions internationaux conclus par la République Libanaise 1966–1972, 2 vols. (Beirut: Librairie du Liban, 1972).

Abu-Odeh, Adnan. *Jordanians, Palestinians, and the Hashemite Kingdom in the Middle East Peace Process* (Washington, DC: United States Institute for Peace, 1999).

Alouane, Youssef. *Droits de l'homme et émigrés tunisiens en Europe* (Tunis: SAGEP, 1992).

L'Annuaire de l'émigration marocaine, ed. Kacem Basfao and Hinde Taarji (Rabat: Fondation Hassan II pour les Marocains Résidant à l'Etranger, 1994).

Appadurai, Arjun. *Modernity at Large: Cultural Dimensions of Globalization* (Minneapolis: University of Minnesota Press, 1996).

Arango, Joanquin, and Martin Baldwin-Edwards. *Immigrants and the Informal Economy in Southern Europe* (New York: Frank Cass, 1999).

L'Association Marocaine d'Etudes et de Recherches sur les Migrations. *La migration clandestine: enjeux et perspectives* (Rabat: Papeterie Al Karamah, 2000).

Baccar, Tawfic, and Ali Sanaa. "La genèse des politiques d'emploi et d'émigration en Tunisie," in *Emploi, émigration, éducation et population* (Tunis: Ministère du Plan et du Développement, 1990).

Barkin, J. Samuel, and Bruce Cronin. "The State and the Nation: Changing Norms and the Rules of Sovereignty in International Relations," *International Organization* 48 (1) Winter 1994: 107–30.

Basch, Linda, Nina Glick Schiller and Cristina Szanton Blanc. *Nations Unbound: Transnational Projects, Postcolonial Predicaments, and Deterritorialized Nation-States* (Langhorne, PA: Gordon and Breach, 1994).

Bauböck, Rainer. *Transnational Citizenship: Membership and Rights in International Migration* (Brookfield, VT: Edward Elgar, 1994).

"Towards a Political Theory of Migrant Transnationalism," *International Migration Review* 37 (2) Fall 2003: 700–23.

Beau, Nicolas, and Jean-Pierre Tuquoi. *Notre ami Ben Ali* (Paris: Editions de la Découverte, 1999).

Beaugé, Gilbert, and Friedmann Buttner. *Les migrations dans le monde arabe* (Paris: CNRS, 1991).

Belguendouz, Abdelkrim. *La communauté marocaine à l'étranger et la nouvelle marche marocaine* (Kenitra: Boukili Impressions, 1999).

Les marocains à l'étranger: citoyens et partenaires (Kenitra: Boukili Impressions, 1999).

L'ahrig du Maroc: l'Espagne et l'UE, plus de Europe ... securitaire (Kenitra: Boukili Impressions, 2002).

Bendourou, Omar. *Le régime politique marocain* (Rabat: Dar al-Qalam, 2000).

Bennouna, Mehdi. *Héros sans gloire: échec d'une révolution, 1963–73* (Casablanca: Tarik Editions, 2002).

Bensimon, Agnes. *Hassan et les juifs: histoire d'une émigration secrète* (Paris: Editions du Seuil, 1991).

Biersteker, Thomas J., and Cynthia Weber (eds.). *State Sovereignty as Social Construct* (Cambridge: Cambridge University Press, 1996).

Boehning, Roger. "The ILO and the New UN Convention on Migrant Workers: the Past and Future," *International Migration Review* 25 (4): 698–709.

Boubakri, Hassan. "Le Maghreb et les nouvelles configurations migratoires internationales: mobilités et réseaux," *Correspondances* 68 (October–December 2001): 8–15.

Boukhari, Ahmed. *Le Secret: Ben Barka et le Maroc, un ancien agent des services spéciaux parle* (Neuilly-sur-Seine: Editions Michel Lafou, 2002).

Bourchachen, Jamal. *Statistiques sur la migration internationale dans les pays mediterranéens: rapport de mission Algérie, Maroc, Tunisie*, Eurostate Working Papers, Population et conditions sociales 3/1999/E/n*11 (n.p.: European Commission, 1999).

Brand, Laurie A. *Palestinians in the Arab World: Institution Building and the Search for State* (New York: Columbia, 1988).

Jordan's Inter-Arab Relations: The Political Economy of Alliance Making (New York: Columbia University Press, 1994).

"Palestinians and Jordanians: A Crisis of Identity," *Journal of Palestine Studies* 24/4 (96) 1995: 46–61.

Braziel, Jana Evans, and Anita Mannur. *Theorizing Diaspora* (Oxford: Blackwell, 2003).

Brettell, Caroline, and James F. Hollifield (eds.). *Migration Theory: Talking Across Disciplines* (New York: Routledge, 2000).

Brubaker, William Rogers. *Citizenship and Nationhood in France and Germany* (Cambridge, MA: Harvard University Press, 1992).

"Comments on 'Modes of Immigration Politics in Liberal Democratic States,'" *International Migration Review* 24 (4) winter 1995: 903–8.

Brubaker, William Rogers (ed.). *Immigration and the Politics of Citizenship in Europe and North America* (New York: University Press of America, 1989).

Butenschon, Nils A., Uri Davis and Manuel Hassassian (eds.). *Citizenship and the State in the Middle East: Approaches and Applications* (Syracuse: Syracuse University Press, 2000).

Buzan, Barry, Ole Waever and Jaap de Wilde. *Security: a New Framework for Analysis* (Boulder: Lynne Reinner, 1998).

Carlsnaes, Walter, *et al.* (eds.). *Handbook of International Relations* (Thousand Oaks: Sage, 2002).

Cassarino, Jean-Pierre. *Tunisian New Entrepreneurs and their Past Experiences of Migration in Europe: Resource Mobilization, Networks, and Hidden Disaffection* (Burlington, VT: Ashgate, 2000).

Castles, Stephen. *Here for Good: Western Europe's New Ethnic Minorities* (London: Pluto Press, 1984).

Castles, Stephen, and Mark Miller. *The Age of Migration: International Population Movement in the Modern World* (London: Macmillan, 1998).

Centre de Documentation Tunisie-Maghreb. *La communauté maghrebine immi-grée en France et ses perspectives d'insertion dans l'Europe de 1993* (Tunis: CDTM, 1990).

Centre d'Etudes et de Recherches Economiques et Sociales (CERES). *Migration internationale, contenu – effets – enjeux: cas de la Tunisie*, Série Géographie 16 (Tunis: Cahiers du CERES, 1996).

CERES and Communauté Economique Européenne (CEE). *Analyse des mouve-ments migratoires dans le sud et le sud-est du basin mediterranéen en direction de la CEE: le cas de la Tunisie* (Tunis: CERES, 1992).

Chattou, Zoubir. *Migrations marocaines en Europe: le paradoxe des itinéraires* (Paris: L'Harmattan, 1998).

Cohen, Robin. *Global Diasporas: An Introduction* (Seattle: University of Washington Press, 1997).

Cornelius, Wayne A., Philip L. Martin and James F. Hollifield (eds.). *Controlling Immigration: A Global Perspective* (Stanford: Stanford University Press, 1994).

Davis, Uri. *Citizenship and the State: A Comparative Study of Citizenship Legislation in Israel, Jordan, Palestine, Syria and Lebanon* (Reading: Ithaca Press, 1997).

Discours et interviews de S. M. le Roi Hassan II (Rabat: Ministère de la Communication, 1998).

Dowty, Alan. *Closed Borders: The Contemporary Assault on Freedom of Movement* (New Haven: Yale University Press, 1987).

El-Khazen, Farid. *The Communal Pact of National Identities: The Making and Politics of the 1943 National Pact* (Oxford: Centre for Lebanese Studies, 1991).

Fellat, Fadlallah Mohammed. "Le Maroc et son émigration," in *L'annuaire de l'Afrique du Nord*, Volume XXXIV (Paris: CNRS, 1995), 981–92.

Feldblum, Miriam. *Reconstructing Citizenship: The Politics of Nationality Reform and Immigration in Contemporary France* (Albany: State University Press, 1999).

Finnemore, Martha. "Norms, Culture and World Politics: Insights from Sociology's Institutionalism," *International Organization* 50 (2) spring 1996: 325–47.

Fitzgerald, David. *Negotiating Extra-Territorial Citizenship: Mexican Migration and the Transnational Politics of Community*, CCIS Monograph 2 (La Jolla: University of California, San Diego, Center for Comparative Immigration Studies, 2000).

Freeman, Gary. "Migration Policy and Politics in the Receiving States," *International Migration Review* 26 (4) winter 1992: 1144–67.

"Modes of Immigration Politics in Liberal Democratic States," *International Migration Review* 29 (4) winter 1995: 881–902.

"Rejoinder," *International Migration Review* 29 (4) winter 1995: 909–13.

Garcia Griego, Manuel. "The Importation of Mexican Contract Laborers to the United States, 1942–1964," in David G. Gutierrez (ed.), *Between Two Worlds: Mexican Immigrants in the United States* (Wilmington, DE: Scholarly Resources, Inc., 1996): 45–85.

Gemayel, Pierre. "Libanais de l'étranger: le Congrès des Emigrés," *Cahiers de l'Est* 2 1945: 171–73.

Gildas, Simon. *L'éspace des travailleurs tunisiens en France: structures et fonctionnement d'un champ migratoire international* (Poitiers: l'Université de Poitiers, 1979).

Goytisolo, Juan, and Sami Nair. *El peaje de la vida: integración o rechazo de la emigración en España* (Ediciones El País: Aguilar, 2001).

Groupe d'Etudes et de Recherches appliquées de la Faculté des Lettres et des Sciences Humaines, "Etude des mouvements migratoires du Maroc vers la Communauté Européenne. Résumé du rapport final." Etude pour le compte de la Commission des Communautés Européennes, 5 January 1992.

Guarnizo, Luis Eduardo. "The Rise of Transnational Social Formations: Mexican and Dominican State Responses to Transnational Migration," *Political Power and Social Theory* 12 1998: 45–94.

"The Economics of Transnational Living," *International Migration Review* 37 (3) Fall 2003: 666–99.

Guarnizo, Luis Eduardo, Arturo Ignacio Sanchez and Elizabeth M. Roach. "Mistrust, Fragmented Solidarity, and Transnational Migration: Columbians in New York City and Los Angeles," *Ethnic and Racial Studies* 22 (2) March 1999: 367–96.

Hall, Rodney Bruce. *National Collective Identity: Social Constructs and International Systems* (New York: Columbia University Press, 1999).

Hanagan, Michael, and Charles Tilly (eds.). *Extending Citizenship, Reconfiguring States* (New York: Roman and Littlefield, 1999).

Hashemite Kingdom of Jordan, Ministry of Planning. *Five Year Plan for Economic and Social Development, 1986–1990* (Amman: National Press, n.d.).

Hashemite Kingdom of Jordan, National Planning Council. *Five Year Plan for Economic and Social Development 1981–1985* (Amman: Royal Scientific Society Press, n.d.).

Hollifield, James F. *Immigrants, Markets and States: The Political Economy of Postwar Europe* (Cambridge, MA: Harvard University Press, 1992).

Hourani, Albert, and Nadim Shehadi (eds.). *The Lebanese in the World: A Century of Emigration* (London: I. B. Tauris, 1992).

Humphrey, Michael. *Islam, Multiculturalism and Transnationalism: From the Lebanese Diaspora* (London: Center for Lebanese Studies and I. B. Tauris, 1998).

Hurewitz, J. C. *The Middle East and North Africa in World Politics: A Documentary Reader* (New Haven: Yale University Press, 1979, 2nd edn.).

Institut de Recherche sur le Maghreb Contemporain. *L'étranger: Actes des Journées d'études organisées dans le cadre du séminaire annuel de l'IRMC "Identités et territoires: les catégorisations du social,"* Tunis, 16–17 fevrier 2002 (Tunis: IRMC, 2002).

International Migration Organization (OIM). *Rapport final de l'atelier sur La migration tunisienne en Europe: enjeux actuels et futurs* (Tunis: OIM, 2002).

Interviews de M. le Ministre Rafiq Haddoui, 1991–1993. Ministère des Affaires de la Communauté Marocaine à l'Etranger. Work produced by Mme. Alaoui Noufissa (photocopy, n.p., n.d.).

Ireland, Patrick R. *The Policy of Ethnic Diversity: Immigrant Politics in France and Switzerland* (Cambridge, MA: Harvard University Press, 1994).

Itzigsohn, José. "Immigration and the Boundaries of Citizenship: The Institutions of Immigrants' Political Transnationalism," *International Migration Review* 34 (4) Winter 2000: 1126–54.

Itzigsohn, José, Carlos Doré Cabral, Esther Hernández Medina and Obed Vázquez. "Mapping Dominican Transnationalism: Narrow and Broad Transnational Practices," *Ethnic and Racial Studies* 22 (2) March 1999: 316–39.

Jacobson, David. *Rights Across Borders: Immigration and the Decline of Citizenship* (Baltimore: Johns Hopkins University Press, 1996).

Jones-Correa, Michael. "Under Two Flags: Dual Nationality in Latin America and Its Consequences for Naturalization in the United States," *International Migration Review* 35 (4) Winter 2001: 997–1029.

Joppke, Christian. *Immigration and the Nation-State: The United States, Germany and Great Britain* (New York: Oxford University Press, 1999).

Kennedy-Brenner, Carliene. *Les travailleurs étrangers et les politiques d'immigration: le cas de la France* (Paris: Centre de Développement de l'Organisation de Coopération et de Développement Economiques, 1989).

Kepel, Gilles. *Allah in the West: Islamic Movements in America and Europe.* Trans. by Susan Milner (Stanford: Stanford University Press, 1997).

Khader, Bichara, and Adnan Badran (eds.). *The Economic Development of Jordan* (London: Croom Helm, 1987).

Khagram, Sanjeev, James V. Riker and Kathryn Sikkink (eds.). *Restructuring World Politics: Transnational Social Movements, Networks and Norms* (Minneapolis: University of Minnesota Press, 2002).

Kharoufi, Moustafa. "Les effets de l'émigration sur les sociétés de départ au Maghreb: nouvelles données, nouvelles approches," an article from *Correspondances, bulletin scientifique de l'IRMC,* from the website of l'Institut de Recherche sur le Maghreb Contemporain: www.irmcmaghreb.org/corres/textes/karoufi.htm.

Khater, Akram Fouad. *Inventing Home: Emigration, Gender, and the Middle Class in Lebanon, 1870–1920* (Berkeley: University of California Press, 2001).

Kingdom of Morocco, Prime Minister, Ministry Attached to the Prime Minister's Office in Charge of Planning, Directorate of Planning. *Orientation Plan for Economic and Social Development, 1988–92* (Mohammedia: Imprimerie de Fedala, 1988).

Kingdom of Morocco, Royal Cabinet, Economic Coordination and Planning Division. *Three-Year Plan, 1965–67* (Imprimerie Nationale, 1965).

Koslowski, Rey. *Migrants and Citizens: Demographic Change in the European State System* (Ithaca: Cornell University Press, 2000).

Krasner, Stephen D. "Sovereignty: An Institutional Perspective," *Comparative Political Studies* 21 (1) April 1988: 66–93.

Sovereignty: Organized Hypocrisy (Princeton: Princeton University Press, 1999).

Labaki, Boutros. "L'émigration depuis la fin des guerres à l'intérieure du Liban (1990–1998)," *Travaux et Jours* 61 spring 1998: 81–142.

Labaki, Boutros, and Khalil Abou Rjeily. *Bilan des guerres du Liban, 1975–1990* (Paris: l'Harmattan, 1993).

Laguerre, M. S. "State, Diaspora and Transnational Politics: Haiti Reconceptualized," *Millennium Journal of International Studies* 28 (3) 1999: 633–51.

Levitt, Peggy. "Transnational Migration: taking stock and future directions," *Global Networks* 1 (3) 2001: 195–216.

López-García, Bernabé. *Atlas de la inmigración magrebi en España*. Taller de Estudios Internacionales Mediterraneos (Madrid: Ministerio de Asuntos Sociales, Dirección General de Migraciones. Observatorio Permanente de la Inmigración, 1996).

Mahler, Sara J. "Constructing International Relations: The Role of Transnational Migrants and Other Non-state Actors," *Identities* 7 (2) 2000: 197–232.

Marshall, T. H. *Class, Citizenship and Social Development* (New York: Doubleday, 1964).

McMurray, David A. *In and Out of Morocco: Smuggling and Migration in a Frontier Boomtown* (Minneapolis: University of Minnesota Press, 2001).

Menassa, Gabriel. *Pour une rénovation économique libanaise avec la collaboration du Liban d'outre mer* (Beirut: Editions de la Société Libanaise d'Economie Politique, 1950).

Migration internationale et changements sociaux dans le Maghreb, International Colloquium, Hammamet–Tunisia, 21–25 June 1993 (Tunis: Université de Tunis I, 1997).

Moannack, Georges. "Libanais de l'étranger: point de vue d'un émigré," *Cahiers de l'Est* 4 1946: 176–86.

Nielsen, Jørgen S. *Muslims in Western Europe* (Edinburgh: Edinburgh University Press, 1992).

Toward a European Islam (New York: St. Martins, 1999).

Norton, Augustus Richard. *Amal and the Shi'a: Struggle for the Soul of Lebanon* (Austin: University of Texas Press, 1987).

L'Office de la Formation Professionnelle et de l'Emploi. *L'Office de la Formation Professionnelle et de l'Emploi*, brochure (n.d., n.p.).

L'Office des Tunisiens à l'Etranger. Compilation of press articles on the "Séminaire Nationale des Travailleurs Tunisiens à l'Etranger," 1988 and 1989.

Ögelman, Nedim. "Documenting and Explaining the Persistence of Homeland Politics among Germany's Turks," *International Migration Review* 37 (1) Spring 2003: 163–93.

Organisation for Economic Cooperation and Development. *Trends in International Migration* (Paris: OECD Publications, 1999).

Østergaard-Nielsen, Eva. "The Politics of Migrants' Transnational Political Practices," *International Migration Review* 37 (3) Fall 2003: 760–86.

Petran, Tabitha. *The Struggle Over Lebanon* (New York: Monthly Review Press, 1987).

Philpott, Daniel. *Revolutions in Sovereignty: How Ideas Shaped Modern International Relations* (Princeton: Princeton University Press, 2001).

Portes, Alejandro. "Conclusion: Towards a New World – the Origins and Effects of Transnational Activities," *Ethnic and Racial Studies* 22 (2) March 1999: 463–77.

Portes, Alejandro, Luis E. Guarnizo and Patricia Landolt. "The Study of Transnationalism: Pitfalls and Promise of an Emergent Research Field," *Ethnic and Racial Studies* 22 (2) March 1999: 217–37.

Pries, Ludger (ed.). *New Transnational Social Spaces: International Migration and Transnational Companies in the Early Twenty-first Century* (New York: Routledge, 2001).

Public Culture 8 1996 (special issue on "Cities and Citizenship").

Rabbath, Edmond. *La formation politique du Liban politique et constitutionnel* (Beirut: Librairie Orientale, 1986).

Ramadan, Tariq. *To Be a Muslim in Europe* (Leicester: Islamic Foundation, 1999).

Republic of Tunisia. *Plan for Economic and Social Development, 1982–1986*, Volume I (Tunis, n.d.).

République Libanaise, Ministère du Plan. *Plan sexennal de développement 1972–1977* (n.p., n.d.).

République Tunisienne, *Plan de développement économique et social, 1967–1972, rapport de synthèse*, Volume I (Tunis, n.d.).

Plan de développement économique et social, 1973–1976 (Tunis, n.d.).

Plan de développement économique et social, 1977–1981 (Tunis, n.d.).

Septième plan de développement économique et social, 1987–91 (Tunis, n.d.).

Huitième plan de développement, 1992–1996 (Tunis, 1992).

Neuvième plan de développement, 1997–2001, Volume II, *Continue sectoriel* (Tunis, 1997).

République Tunisienne, Ministère des Affaires Sociales. *Office des tunisiens à l'étranger* (a brochure) (Tunis, 1995).

Rex, John, Daniele Joly and Czarina Wilpert (eds.). *Immigrant Associations in Europe* (Brookfield, VT: Gower, 1987).

Risse, Thomas, Stephen C. Ropp and Kathryn Sikkink (eds.). *The Power of Human Rights: International Norms and Domestic Change* (Cambridge: Cambridge University Press, 1999).

Risse-Kappen, Thomas (ed.). *Bringing Transnational Relations Back In: Non-State Actors, Domestic Structures and International Institutions* (Cambridge: Cambridge University Press, 1995).

Royaume du Maroc, Ministère de l'Economie Nationale, Division de la Coordination Economique et du Plan, *Plan quinquennal, 1960–64* (Rabat, 1960).

Royaume du Maroc, Ministère de la Prévision Economique et du Plan, Direction de la Programmation. *Le plan de développement économique et social, 2000–2004*, Volume I, *Les orientations et les perspectives globales de développement économique et social*; Volume II, *Le développement sectoriel* (Sale: Print-Diffusion, 2001).

Royaume du Maroc, Premier Ministre, Ministère de la Prévision Economique et du Plan et L'Institut National de Statistique et d'Economie Appliquée (INSEA), *Les marocains résidant à l'étranger: une enquête socio-économique* (Rabat: El-Maarif al-Jadidah, 2000).

Royaume du Maroc, Premier Ministre, Ministère des Affaires Economiques du Plan et de la Formation des Cadres. Division de la Coordination Economique et du Plan. *Plan quinquennal, 1968-72,* Volume I (Mohammedia: Fedala, n.d.).

Royaume du Maroc, Premier Ministre, Ministère du Plan et du Développement Régional, Direction de la Planification. *Plan de développement économique et social, 1981-85* (n.p., n.d.).

Royaume du Maroc, Premier Ministre, Secrétariat d'Etat au Plan, au Développement Régional et à la Formation des Cadres. *Plan de développement économique et social, 1973-77,* Volume I (Casablanca: Dar El-Kitab, n.d.).

Royaume du Maroc, Premier Ministre, Secrétariat d'Etat au Plan et au Développement Régional. *Plan de développement économique et social, 1978-80,* Volume I (n.p., n.d.).

Ruggie, John Gerard. "Continuity and Transformation in the World Polity: Toward a Neo-Realist Synthesis," in Robert O. Keohane (ed.), *Neo-Realism and its Critics* (New York: Columbia University Press, 1986).

Saade, Edmond Khalil. *Le Liban dans le monde: guide des émigrés libanaises et syriens en Afrique Occidentale et Equatoriale* (Beirut: Universelle, 1952).

Safa, Elie. *L'émigration libanaise* (Beirut: Université Saint-Joseph, 1960).

Saidi, Abdelatif. "Les stratégies des associations marocaines bruxelloises: une comparaison avec les Noirs Americains et les Franco-Maghrebins," extracts from unpublished thesis, Namur, June 1997; www.users.skynet.be/suffrage-universel/bmar02.htm.

Salibi, Kamal. "Lebanon Under Fuad Chehab, 1958-1964," *Middle Eastern Studies* 2 (3) April 1966: 211-26.

A House of Many Mansions: The History of Lebanon Reconsidered (London: I. B. Taurus, 1988).

Saouda, Joseph. "Importance de notre émigration, services rendus à la mère-patrie," *Cahiers de l'Est* 1 1945: 162-63.

Sassen, Saskia. *Globalization and its Discontents* (New York: The New Press, 1998).

Schulz, Helena Lindholm. *The Palestinian Diaspora* (New York: Routledge, 2003).

Shadid, W. A. R., and P. S. van Koningsveld. *Religious Freedom and The Position of Islam in Western Europe* (Netherlands: Kok Pharos, 1995).

Shafir, Gershon (ed.). *The Citizenship Debates* (Minneapolis: University of Minnesota Press, 1998).

Shain, Yossi. *Marketing the American Creed Abroad: Diasporas in the US and their Homelands* (New York: Cambridge University Press, 1999).

Shami, Seteney. *Emigration Dynamics in Jordan, Palestine and Lebanon,* Paper no. 4, IOM/UNFPA Policy Workshop on Emigration Dynamics in the Arab Region (Geneva: IOM, 1996).

Smith, Michael Peter, and Luis Eduardo Guarnizo (eds.). *Transnationalism from Below,* Comparative Urban and Community Research 6 (New Brunswick, NJ: Transaction Publishers, 1998).

Smith, Robert C. "Migrant Membership as an Instituted Process: Transnationalization, the State and the Extra-Territorial Conduct of Mexican Politics," *International Migration Review* 37 (2) Summer 2003: 297-343.

Soysal, Yasemin Nuhoğlu. *Limits of Citizenship: Migrants and Postnational Membership in Europe* (Chicago: University of Chicago, 1994).

Spruyt, Hendrik. *The Sovereign State and Its Competitors: An Analysis of Systems Change* (Princeton: Princeton University Press, 1994).

Stoakes, Frank. "The Supervigilantes: The Lebanese Kataeb Party as a Builder, Surrogate and Defender of the State," *Middle Eastern Studies* 11 (3) October 1975: 215–36.

Taamallah, Khemais. *Les travailleurs tunisiens en France: aspects socio-démographiques économiques et problèmes de retour* (Tunis: Imprimerie Officielle de la République Tunisienne, 1980).

Tell, Tariq (ed.). *The Resilience of the Hashemite Rule: Politics and the State in Jordan, 1946–67*, Les Cahiers du Cermoc 25 (Amman: Centre d'Etudes et de recherche sur le Moyen-Orient Contemporain, 2001).

Van de Laan, H. L. *The Lebanese Traders in Sierra Leone* (The Hague: Mouton & Co., 1975).

Van Hear, Nicholas. *New Diasporas* (Seattle: University of Washington Press, 1998).

Waever, Ole. "Identity, Integration and Security: Solving the Sovereignty Puzzle in EU Studies," *Journal of International Affairs* 48 (2): 389–431.

Walker, R. J. B. *Inside/outside: International Relations as Political Theory* (Cambridge: Cambridge University Press, 1993).

Walker, R. J. B., and Saul H. Mendlovitz (ed.). *Contending Sovereignties: Redefining Political Community* (Boulder: Lynne Reinner, 1990).

Weil, Patrick. *La France et ses étrangers: L'aventure d'une politique de l'immigration 1938–1991* (Paris: Calmann-Levy, 1991).

Weiner, Myron. "Security, Stability and International Migration," *International Security* 17 (3) winter 1992/93: 91–126.

The Global Migration Crisis: Challenge to States and to Human Rights (New York: Harper Collins, 1995).

"Ethics, National Sovereignty and the Control of Immigration," *International Migration Review* 30 (1) Spring 1996: 171–97.

Weiner, Myron, and Sharon Stanton Russell (eds.). *Demography and National Security* (New York: Berghahn Books, 2001).

Weiner, Myron, and Michael S. Teitelbaum. *Political Demography, Demographic Engineering* (New York: Berghahn Books, 2001).

White, Gregory. "Risking the Strait: Moroccan Labor Migration to Spain," *Middle East Report* 218 Spring 2001: 26–29, 48.

Wihtol de Wenden, Catherine. *Les immigrés et la politique* (Paris: Presses de Sciences Po, 1988).

La citoyenneté européenne (Paris: Presses de Sciences Po, 1997).

Faut-il ouvrir les frontières? (Paris: Presses de Sciences Po, 1999).

Wihtol de Wenden, Catherine, and Remy Leveau. *La beurgeoisie: les trois âges de la vie associative issue de l'immigration* (Paris: Editions CNRS, 2001).

Zamir, Meir. *The Formation of Modern Lebanon* (Dover, NH: Croom Helm, 1985).

Zevelev, Igor. *Russia and Its New Diasporas* (Washington, DC: US Institute of Peace Press, 2001).

Zolberg, Aristide. "New Waves of Migration: Migration Theory for a Changing World," *International Migration Review* 23 (3) fall 1989: 403–30.

MATERIALS IN ARABIC

Abu Jabir, Kamil, Salih Khasawnah and Mateus Bubeh. *Suq al-'Amal al-Urdunni: Tatawwuruhu, Khasa'isuhu, Siyasatuhu, wa-Afaquhu al-Mustabaliyyah* (Amman: Dar al-Bashir, 1991).

Al-'Aql, Jihad Nasri. *Al-Hijrah al-Hadithah min Lubnan wa-Ta'ati al-Mu'assasat al-Rasmiyyah w-al-Ahliyyah ma'aha 1860–2000* (Beirut: Dar wa-Maktabat al-Turath al Adabi, 2002).

Awraq 'Amal wa Munaqashat al-Mu'tamar al-Awwal l-il-Mughtaribin al-Urdunniyyin (Working Papers and Discussions of the First Conference for Jordanian Expatriates) (Amman, 1985).

Awraq 'Amal wa Munaqashat al-Mu'tamar al-Thani l-il-Mughtaribin al-Urdunniyyin, (Working Papers and Discussions of the Second Conference for Jordanian Expatriates) (Amman, 1987).

Harfush, Nabil. *Al-Hudur al-Lubnani f-il-'Alam,* Volume I (Juniyyah: Dar Kurayyam, 1974); Volumes II and III (Beirut: Dar al-Funun, n.d.).

Al-Jumhuriyyah al-Lubnaniyyah, Majlis al-Nuwwab. *al-Dawr al-Tashri'i al-Thani 'ashr, al-'Aqd al-'Adi al-Thani, 1992, Mahdar al-Jalsah al-Thalithah,* 9–10 November 1992.

al-Dawr al-Tashri'i al-Thani'ashr, al-'Aqd al-'Adi al-Awwal, 16 March 1993.

Al-Kitab al-Abyad: Wizarat al-Mughtaribin – matlab wa-'athirat wa-baramij 'amal (Beirut: Ministry of Expatriates, 1994).

Al-Lajnah al-Qita'iyyah l-il-Tanmiyyah al-Ijtima'iyyah w-al-Tadamun al-Watani, Wizarat al-Shu'un al-Ijtima'iyyah. *Mutabi'at Tanfiz al-Mukhattat al-Tasi' (1997–98)* (Tunis, 1998).

Majlis al-Inma' w-al-'I'mar. *Mashru' al-'I'mar* (Beirut: n.p., 1978).

Al-Mamlakah al-Urdunniyyah al-Hashimiyyah, Majlis al-'I'mar al-Urdunni. *Barnamij al-Sanawat al-Khamis l-il-Tanmiyah al-Iqtisadiyyah, 1962–67* (n.p., n.d.).

Barnamij al-Sanawat al-Sabi'l-il-Tanmiyyah al-Iqtisadiyyah, 1964–1970 (n.p., 1965).

Al-Mamlakah al-Urdunniyyah al-Hashimiyyah, Al-Majlis al-Qawmi l-il-Takhtit. *Khittat al-Tanmiyah al-Thulathiyyah, 1973–75* (n.p., n.d.).

Al-Mamlakah al-Urdunniyyah al-Hashimiyyah, Wizarat al-Takhtit. *Al-Khittah al-Iqtisadiyyah w-al-Ijtima'iyyah 1993–1997* (n.p., n.d.).

Mulakhkhas Khittat al-Tanmiyah al-Iqtisadiyyah w-al-Ijtima'iyyah l-il-A'wam, 1999–2003 (n.p., n.d.).

Al-Mukhattat al-Ruba'i, 1965–1968 (Tunis: Kitabat al-Dawlah l-il-Takhtit w-al-Iqtisad al-Watani, n.d.).

Al-Mukhattat al-Thulathi, 1962–1964 (Tunis: Kitabat al-Dawlah l-il-Tasmim w-al-Maliyyah, n.d.).

Al-Mu'tamar al-Khamis i-il-Urdunniyyin al-'Amilin f-il-Kharij (Amman: Ministry of Labor, n.d.).

Al-Mu'tamar al-Rabi' l-il-Mughtaribin al-Urdunniyyin (Amman: Ministry of Labor, Expatriate Affairs Bureau, n.d.).

Sa'adeh, Antun. *Zad al-Muhajir* (Beirut: Dar Fikr l-il-Abhath w-al-Nashr, 2002).

Salamah, Mazen. "Al-Fashl Yulahiq Mu'tamarat al-Mughtaribin," *Al-Urdunn al-Jadid* 10 Spring 1988: 70–73.

Wizarat al-'Amal (w-al-Tanmiyah al-Ijtima'iyyah). *Al-Taqrir al-Sanawi*. (Amman: Da'irat al-Abhath), 1980–97.

Wizarat al-Mughtaribin. *Watha'iq min Mahfuzat al-Wizarah* (Beirut: Manshurat Wizarat al-Mughtaribin, 1998).

Wizarat al-Thiqafah w-al-'I'lam, Al-Mamlakah al-Urdunniyyah al-Hashimiyyah. *Mujiz Khittat al-Tanmiyah al-Urdunniyyah, 1973–75* (n.p., n.d.).

NEWSPAPERS AND PERIODICALS

A dossier of brochures from La Fondation Hassan II describing its activities.

L'Action (Tunisia)
Al-'Alam (Morocco)
Al-Anba' (Morocco)
L'Annuaire de l'Afrique du Nord
Al-'Amal (Tunisia)
Al-Anwar (Lebanon)
Al-Bayan (Morocco)
Al-Bayane (Morocco-French)
Billedi (Tunisia)
Les Cahiers de L'Est (Lebanon)
Daily Star (Lebanon)
Demain (Morocco)
Al-Diyar (Lebanon)
L'Etoile du Nord (Morocco, Tangiers)
Al-Hadath (Tunisia)
Al-Hawadith (Lebanon)
Al-Hurriyyah (Tunisia)
Al-'I'lam (Tunisia)
Al-Ittihad al-Ishtiraki (Morocco)
Jeune Afrique (Paris)
Jordan Times
Le Journal (Morocco)
Lettre d'Information du Ministère de la Communauté Marocaine à l'Etranger
Libération (Morocco)
Al-Liwa' (Lebanon)
Maghreb Resources Humaines
Al-Maghrib (Morocco)
Le Matin du Sahara (Morocco)
Al-Minbar
Al-Mun'atif (Morocco)
Al-Nahar (Lebanon)
L'Opinion (Morocco)
El País (Spain)
Parfum du Pays (Tunisia)
La Presse (Tunisia)

Al-Ra'y (Jordan)
Réalités (Tunisia)
Le Renouveau (Tunisia)
Rivages (Morocco)
Risalat al-Ummah (Morocco)
Al-Sabah (Tunisia)
Al-Safir (Lebanon)
Al-Sahara (Morocco)
Al-Sayyad (Lebanon)
Al-Shira' (Morocco)
Le Temps (Tunisia)
La Vie Economique (Morocco)
Al-Wahdah (Tunisia)
Al-Wasat (Lebanon)
http://www.Emigrants.gov.lb (the Website of the Lebanese Ministry of Emigrants)

UNPUBLISHED SOURCES

De Bel-Air, Françoise. "Expression, émigration, état rentier. Migration et politique en Jordanie depuis 1973." Paper presented at the Third Mediterranean Social and Political Research Meeting, Florence, 20–24 March 2002, Mediterranean Programme, Robert Schuman Centre for Advanced Studies, European University Institute.

Hamdan, Kamal. "Lebanon: Emigration Policies, Trends and Mechanisms" [Lubnan: Siyasat al-Hijrah wa-Tayyaratuha wa-Anthimatuha]. Paper presented at the ILO/UNDP Seminar on Migration Policies in the Arab Labor-Sending Countries, Cairo, 2–4 May 1992.

Hernandez, Juan, Omar de la Torre and Julie M. Weise. "Mexico's New Public Policies for its Citizens Abroad." Paper presented at the Metropolis Conference, Rotterdam, 28 November 2001.

Khasawneh, Saleh. "Labor Migration in Jordan: Policies, Flows, Organization." Paper presented at the ILO/UNDP Seminar on Migration Policies in the Arab Labor-Sending Countries, Cairo, 2–4 May 1992.

Michalak, Laurence. "A Comparison of Morocco and Tunisian Labor Migration Policies in the New Global Economy." Paper presented at the annual meeting of the Middle East Studies Association, Phoenix, Arizona, 19–22 November 1994.

Office des Tunisiens à l'Etranger. "Nadwah Wataniyyah l-il-Tunisiyyin f-il-Kharij, Waraqat 'Amal Lajnah: al-Ajyal al-Jadidah l-il-Hijrah bayna al-Muhafizah 'ala al-Hawiyyah w-al-Indimaj fi-Buldan al-Iqamah" (7 August 2002).

"Nadwah Wataniyyah l-il-Tunisiyyin f-il-Kharij, Waraqat 'Amal Lajnah: Ta'thirat Ahdath 11/9/2001 'ala Wad' al-Muhajirin bi-Buldan al-Iqamah" (7 August 2002).

"La politique d'encadrement des Tunisiens à l'étranger."

Raad, Milad Raad. "The Participation of Lebanese Emigrants in the Legislative Elections of Lebanon." Master's thesis, American University of Beirut, 1998.

Take, Khaled. "The Role of Lebanese Emigrants in the National Development of Lebanon." Master's thesis, American University of Beirut, 1998.

INTERVIEWS

'Abd al-Jabir, Taysir. Former Minister of Labor, Commissioner of the Jordan Securities Commission, Amman, 12 July 1999.

Abul-Hisn, Latif. Former Ambassador to Australia, Adjunct Professor, American University of Beirut, Beirut, 19 December 2002.

Abu-Odeh, 'Adnan. Former Minister of Information, Court Chamberlain and Advisor to King Husayn and King 'Abdallah II, Amman, 15 May 2003.

Ahaidar, Marzuk. Former MRE parliamentary representative, Tangier, 15 July 2002.

Amiyar, Jamal. Journalist and publisher of Les Nouvelles du Nord (Tangier), Tangier, 25 June 2000.

al-'Aql, Jihad. Section head for Emigrés and Emigration, Ministry of Foreign Affairs and Expatriates, Beirut, 28 October 2002.

Baouab, 'Abdelmajid. Director-General of Consular Affairs, Ministry of Foreign Affairs, Tunis, 10 August 2002.

Belguendouz, Abdelkrim. Professor, Faculty of Law, Mohammed V University, Rabat, 11 June 2002.

Ben Feguir, Khaled. Director-Adjoint, Tunisian National Radio, Tunis, 12 August 2002.

Bouzaidi, 'Abd al-'Aziz. Responsible for TREs, Rassemblement constitutionnel démocratique, Tunis, 9 August 2002.

Cassarino, Jean-Pierre. International Migration Organization representative with the Fondation Hassan II Observatoire project, Rabat, 28 May 2002.

al-Ghazi, 'Akka. Former MRE parliamentary representative, Rabat, 19 July 2002.

Ghurrah, Edward. Former Ambassador and former Director-General of the Mudiriyyat al-Mughtaribin in the Ministry of Foreign Affairs, Beirut, 20 November 2002.

Gueddara, 'Abd al-Moneim. Partenariat Pole, Fondation Hassan II, Rabat, June 2000.

Harfush, Nabil. Former Secretary-General of the World Lebanese Cultural Union, Beirut, 6 November 2002.

Hart, Laurence. Chargé de Programme, International Migration Organization, Tunis, 9 August 2002.

Isma'il, Fouad. Director of Marketing, Banque Populaire (al-Bank al-Chaabi), Tangiers, 28 June 2000.

El-Jema'i, Beshir. Director-General, Office des Tunisiens à l'Etranger, Tunis, 9 August 2002.

Jum'ah, Haytham. Director General, Ministry of Expatriates, Beirut, 21 October 2002.

Kala'i, Mondher. Director of Programs, Channel 7 (Tunisia's satellite channel), Tunis, 12 August 2002.

Khamlichi, Farideh. Ministry of Human Rights, Rabat, 13 June 2002.

Khiddar, Rachid. Head of Istiqlal Committee on MREs, Rabat, 3 July 2002.

Labaki, Butros. Emigration expert and Chairman, Lebanese Institute for Economic and Social Development, Beirut, 11 November 2002.

Lahlou, Rachid. Former Ambassador and MRE parliamentary representative, Rabat, 5 July 2002.

El-Mahdaoui, Kamel. Bureau of European Affairs, Ministry of Foreign Affairs, Rabat, 20 June 2002.

Messaouden, Djellal. Communications Pole, Fondation Hassan II, Rabat, 30 June 2000.

Rahahla, Naseem. National Competitiveness Team, Ministry of Planning, Amman, 23 June 1999 and 24 July 2000.

Snoussi, 'Adel. Agence Tunisienne pour la Coopération Technique, Tunis, 12 August 2002.

Tabbara, Riadh. Former Ambassador to the United States, demographer and migration expert, Economic and Social Commission for Western Asia (ESCWA), Beirut, 12 November 2002.

Tlili, Fathi. President, Union des Travailleurs Immigrés Tunisiens, Tunis, 14 August 2002.

Trabelsi, Mohammed. Assistant Secretary-General for International Relations and Immigration, Union Général des Travailleurs Tunisiens (UGTT), Tunis, 14 August 2002.

al-Turk, Fu'ad. Ambassador and former Secretary-General of the Ministry of Foreign Affairs and Expatriates, Beirut, 7 October 2002.

Yusuf, 'Ali. General-Director, Jordanian Businessmen's Association, Amman, 28 June 1999.

Zahi, Abderrahman. Director-General, Fondation Hassan II, Rabat, 21 June 2000.

Index

Cambridge Middle East Studies 23

CPSIA information can be obtained at www.ICGtesting.com
Printed in the USA
LVOW12s0021180713

343285LV00001B/57/P